The Fundamental Index

The Fundamental Index

A BETTER WAY TO INVEST

Robert D. Arnott

Jason C. Hsu

John M. West

WILEY

John Wiley & Sons, Inc.

Published by John Wiley & Sons, Inc., Hoboken, New Jersey.
Published simultaneously in Canada.

For general information on our other products and services or for technical support, please contact our
Customer Care Department within the United States at (800) 762-2974, outside the United States at (317)
572-3993 or fax (317) 572-4002.

Wiley also publishes its books in a variety of electronic formats. Some content that appears in print may
not be available in electronic books. For more information about Wiley products, visit our web site at www.
wiley.com.

Library of Congress Cataloging-in-Publication Data:
Arnott, Robert D.
    The Fundamental Index : a better way to invest / Robert D. Arnott, Jason C. Hsu, John M. West.
        p. cm.
    Includes bibliographical references and index.
    ISBN 978-0-470-27784-3 (cloth)
        1. Index mutual funds. 2. Stocks–Prices–Mathematical models. 3. Portfolio
management. I. Hsu, Jason C., 1974- II. West, John M. (John Michael), 1973- III. Title.
HG4530.A74   2008
332.6–dc22

                                                                        2007052404

Printed in the United States of America
10   9   8   7   6   5   4   3   2   1

For George Keane. None of this research would have taken place without his persistent insistence that "there has to be a better way." And there is.

Contents

Foreword

There is no free lunch.

—Milton Friedman

In *The Fundamental Index*, Rob Arnott and his colleagues essentially argue that a portfolio whose holdings are proportional to a suitable measure of the efficiency of a firm will outperform one whose holdings are proportional to the market value or capitalization of the firm. In other words, what I will refer to as an *efficiency-weighted portfolio* will outperform a capitalization-weighted portfolio.

The implications of efficiency-weighted index investing will be significant for investors and, thus, are worth the time of a short mathematical review of the logic. Over and above the dividends that corporations pay, and the long-run growth in their stock values, the holding and trading of securities is a zero-sum game. If some investors make more than others, then someone is consuming someone else's lunch. To analyze this argument, let us focus on the zero-sum value-added game that the market participants play, ignoring dividends and long-run growth.

Suppose we have four companies, each with $1 in reported earnings. Suppose two of these have ample future growth prospects that would justify a price 20 times the current profits, or $20, and the other two have less impressive prospects and fully deserve $10—10 times the current earnings. *But, no one can have a clear view of the future prospects of our companies, so the market merely guesses at these fair values.* Suppose the market does a pretty good job, but misjudges those prospects by 20 percent in each of the four cases, with one growth stock priced 20 percent too high and one 20 percent too low, and likewise for the value stocks. So, we have two stocks with a true value of $20 each, priced at $24 and $16, and two stocks with a true value of $10, priced at $12 and $8.

Suppose prices revert to fair value in the next year. The "cap-weighted" portfolio produces zero return; since the prices are symmetric around value, the errors cancel. If we could construct a fair-value-weighted portfolio, few would disagree that it should be better than capitalization weighting. It is. Half of our portfolio rises 25 percent in value, and half loses 16.7 percent, for an average of 4.2 percent return. Why? Because the fair value portfolio puts equal amounts in over- and undervalued stocks, while capitalization weighting put 60 percent of our money in the overvalued and 40 percent in the undervalued companies.

Since we have no idea what the fair value is for each company, and so there's no way for us to construct this fair-value-weighted portfolio, why should we care that fair value weighting beats capitalization weighting? What of the other construction methods? The portfolios weighted equally and by company profits (efficiency-weighted), which lead to the same weighting in this example, produce a return of 4.2 percent also, identically the same as the fair-value-weighted portfolio!

How can this be? It's at odds with classical finance theory, which says that we can't beat the cap-weighted portfolio. But classical finance theory is largely built on a foundation of efficient markets under doubtful CAPM assumptions, which implies that future prices are randomly distributed around current price. We are subtly changing this assumption. In fact, we are assuming the opposite: that current price is randomly distributed around fair value. As long as capitalization weighting has errors relative to fair value and prices revert toward fair value, capitalization weighting will suffer this drag relative to fair value weighting. And any portfolio that differs from fair value weighting in a fashion that is uncorrelated with the error in the price will match the return of the fair-value-weighted portfolio!

The reason I refer to this procedure as *efficiency weighting* is that, on average, the company that has greater profit per unit of market valuation is more efficient than the one with less profit per unit of market valuation. Perhaps there are extenuating circumstances in some instances. But this washes out on average. As a whole, the companies with greater profit per unit of market valuation are more efficient and are a more profitable investment.

The preceding example would seem not to be an equilibrium, since the cap-weighted investors gain nothing while the efficiency-weighted investors are getting richer. Asymptotically, the former disappear and the latter become the whole market. However, we have not said that the same players continue indefinitely. We may assume that some investors go out of the market and new ones come in.

In short, the answer to the question of how efficiency-weighted investors can continually take money from the cap-weighted investors is expressed in the saying attributed to P. T. Barnum:

There's a sucker born every minute.

—HARRY MARKOWITZ

Preface

Victory has a hundred fathers, and no one acknowledges a failure.
—1942 G. Ciano *Diary* 9 Sept. (1946) II. 196[1]

It is a rare joy to have an opportunity to explore an idea that offers both powerful practical applications and potentially important theoretical implications. Such is the case for the Fundamental Index[®2] concept—a simple idea which has the potential to "fundamentally" change the way we think about investing and markets. For 30 years, index funds, with next-to-nothing in trading costs and management fees, have proven to be formidable competitors to active managers who have had difficulty overcoming the corrosive effects of higher transaction costs and management fees.

Attractive as the index fund is as an investment concept, the capitalization-weighted implementation of the index fund concept is flawed. Because the size of our investment in any company is directly linked to stock prices, the capitalization-weighted portfolio overweights the overvalued stocks and underweights the undervalued stocks, leading to a performance drag on portfolio returns. The venerable index portfolio can be significantly upgraded by shifting our frame of reference from a market-centric to an economy-centric view of our investable universe, and the benefits to the investor are significant.

In the market-centric approach, we view our investment choices relative to those available in the stock market with companies weighted in accordance with their relative market capitalization. Finance theory supports this idea, subject to a few simplifying assumptions, notably that all prices are correct, that stock prices identically equal fair value, based on all available information. But these assumptions are not realistic. Most importantly for investors, if prices are wrong, we're going to wind up putting most of our money in overvalued stocks because the scale of our investment is explicitly linked to the stock's price, hence to the error in that price.

In the economy-centric approach, we view our investment choices relative to those available in the economy, with companies weighted in accordance with their relative economic scale. Because there are many measures of a company's economic scale—sales, profits, number of employees, dividends paid, net assets, and so forth—we can use any of these measures, or a combination of them, to gauge company size. If we do this, we still make mistakes—owning some companies that we wish we hadn't and underinvesting in the most stellar successes—but the size of our investment is no longer directly and irrevocably linked to the error in the price. As a result, pricing errors cancel and the performance drag is eliminated.

What causes this performance drag? The answer relates to the fact that structurally the market portfolio—the cap-weighted portfolio of all publicly traded stocks—will put most of our money in "growth companies," stocks that trade at premium multiples because they are expected to exhibit stronger future growth prospects than the broad market. What's wrong with that? In an efficient market, nothing at all. Their superior future growth will fully justify the premium prices that we pay. But are they superior *stocks*? Are they superior *investments*? In an efficient market, the answer to both questions is "no" because we're prepaying for their superior future growth *exactly enough* to result in the same risk-adjusted return as the value stocks.

This is the Achilles' heel of capitalization weighting: We invest much of our money in high-flying growth companies *because they're at premium multiples.* And if the market falters in its efficiency, pricing some stocks too high and some too low, capitalization weighting *assuredly* suffers a performance drag relative to its opportunity set. The indexing community and the academic community do not worry about this because they take the notion of market efficiency seriously. In academia, market efficiency is accepted with near-religious fervor—even though fair value can never be measured and so the thesis of market efficiency can never be proved!

The theoretical implications are potentially profound. If some stocks are above fair value, they are also above their fair value market capitalization. Because they will crowd out some companies that better deserve the high market capitalization, and because they will eventually underperform (after all, isn't that the ultimate definition of being overvalued?), this creates the much-studied "size effect." The overvalued stocks will also be above their fair valuation multiples (price-earnings, price-sales, price-book, and price-dividend ratios); as they eventually underperform, this creates the much-studied "value effect." Because most of the overvalued stocks will typically have reached that overvaluation by outperforming other stocks and will ultimately underperform, this creates the much studied long horizon mean-reversion effect.

Academia has developed many advances on the capital asset pricing model, including the arbitrage pricing theory, international CAPM, Fama-French-Carhart, and so forth. Some of these, notably Fama-French-Carhart, do a superb job of helping us to understand how one strategy may differ from another and why some strategies perform better than others. But the efforts to conform these models to an "efficient market" have been clumsy at best, with tortured explanations of "hidden risk factors" that attempt to explain performance differentials. If a strategy outperforms, they argue, it must have more risk, even if we can't see or measure it.

None of these complications is needed if we merely acknowledge that price and value may differ. If we allow that prices may equal fair value plus or minus a constantly changing error, the value effect is expected, as is the size effect, as is long horizon mean reversion. Three of the most examined "anomalies" in modern finance very nearly become *preordained* if we accept that price may be wrong!

This brings us almost all the way back to the single-factor Capital Asset Pricing Model (CAPM) of Sharpe, Lintner, Mossin, and Treynor. CAPM plus noise explains every bit as much of what we observe in the real world as the multifactor models, with their hidden risk factors, that have *almost* replaced CAPM. Isn't it more elegant to assume CAPM plus noise rather than to create convoluted explanations that can fit a "round" set of data into a "square" box of efficient markets?

The CAPM and the Efficient Market Hypothesis (EMH) are the reasons the Fundamental Index concept has stimulated such controversy in the academic community, with some of the top professors in finance, including Nobel laureates, squaring off on both sides of this debate.

The debate in the practitioner community is no less intense. Previous to the Fundamental Index idea, asset managers and advisors first made the determination of whether prices were *reasonably* efficient. Virtually none would subscribe to the notion that the market correctly values every stock at every moment of every day. Depending on where they came out on this market efficiency question, they would then choose whether to establish stock market exposure through active management or traditional index funds.

For those who believed, *indeed knew,* that price and value aren't identical, active management was the preferred choice. The amount of research in our industry would *seem* to suggest that such activities be rewarded. However, finding "good" active managers (and keeping them during the inevitable periods of underperformance) is a daunting task. Thirty years of performance data verify that the cumulative drag of management fees, trading expenses, and agency conflicts are large and that the indexes are tough to beat.

Still, even with its performance advantage, the index fund is no panacea. If prices drift from fair value, even if only from time to time, the traditional index fund, weighting stocks and sectors by their price, will pile ever-increasing amounts into the current favorites of the market. We call such episodes *bubbles,* and human history is littered with them. The tech meltdown at the turn of the century and the recent real estate downturn are just the latest in a long line of bubbles, subsequently bursting at massive expense to investors. Price weighting ensures investors have maximum exposure to a bubble's darlings right before they fall off a cliff.

The Fundamental Index concept preserves the many virtues of index funds while contra-trading against the market's greatest excesses, thereby letting mispricing accrue over time to the investor's benefit. By delinking price from the portfolio weight, the Fundamental Index method bypasses bubbles. As such, it is a powerful alternative for those disappointed by the hollow promise of active management and yet unsatisfied with the excess of traditional index funds.

In testing this very simple idea—moving from capitalization weighting to weighting companies in accordance with their economic scale— we find remarkable results. In U.S. large companies, we find that the idea adds over 200 basis points per year over a 46-year span relative to the cap-weighted market portfolio. In other countries, we find an average of almost 300 basis points added per year over a 24-year span. In small companies and in global applications, this margin of victory rises to the 300 to 400 basis points range, again over 20- to 30-year spans.

As we move into more speculative markets and markets for which fair value is nebulous indeed, the benefits escalate. In the speculative

Nasdaq stocks, the value add leaps to over 600 basis points over the past 33 years. In emerging markets, it soars to 1,000 basis points over an admittedly short 14-year span. Even in the fringes of the bond world, where fair value is less precise than in investment-grade bonds—high-yield and emerging markets bonds—we find 200 to 300 basis points value added. The data are overwhelming. One might well ask how much data a skeptic needs in order to be persuaded.

As many critics love to point out, past success doesn't presage future success. That's obviously true. But, based on this logic, we'd never learn a thing from history nor hire an experienced professional because neither the textbook or the resume offered any clues of the future. Still, a worthy question is: How might the Fundamental Index concept fail in the future? If the market makes no distinction between growth and value stocks, paying the same valuation multiples for all companies, then there is no difference between the Fundamental Index and cap-weighted portfolios; the return difference vanishes. But this would clearly leave much opportunity for the thoughtful investor to pay a penny extra for companies that have superior growth prospects.

There's a middle ground: If the market *under*pays relative to consensus expectations for expected future growth and *over*pays for companies that are struggling, then the performance drag of capitalization weighting will be *reversed* enough to offset the drag created by pricing errors. Such a world is possible, though perhaps implausible.

In this book, we explore the theoretical nuances of the Fundamental Index concept, its historical roots, and its many practical applications. We outline performance characteristics and implementation considerations in U.S. and global equities; small and large companies; niche categories like Real Estate Investment Trust (REITs) and the Nasdaq; and within economic sectors.

I have been blessed to work in the investment arena for over 30 years, with opportunities to explore ideas in global tactical asset allocation, multifactor risk and return models, the linkages between risk and return, and to test some of the core precepts of modern finance—often finding them far removed from reality. Ours is one of a handful of industries that offer so many unique challenges and, in my opinion, prospects to improve our understanding, practice, and, ultimately, our clients' well-being. But in order to do so, we have to be willing to challenge conventional thinking. I have dedicated my career to uncovering these opportunities for change and improvement, and to sharing my findings with investors through innovative investment products, published research articles, numerous conference presentations, and now a book. Despite all these experiences, this is the first time I have had the privilege of developing an idea that stirred so much controversy and comment, pro and con, from both practitioners and academics, so quickly.

As with so many powerful ideas, this one has many "fathers." It is built on the foundation of thousands of research papers identifying consistent market inefficiencies, the many theories that form the latticework for modern finance and investing, and the hard work of many, many people.

I'm grateful to my colleagues, most particularly Jason Hsu for carrying out the research that transformed a simple idea into reality. I'm grateful to our advisory panel and others—Keith Ambachtsheer, Peter Bernstein, Brett Hammond, Marty Leibowitz, Burt Malkiel, Harry Markowitz, Marc Rubenstein, and Jack Treynor, to name just a few—for serving as sounding boards as the idea took form.

I'm grateful to our Fundamental Index affiliates—PIMCO, Nomura Asset Management, FTSE (our partner on the FTSE-RAFI index series), IPM, PowerShares, Charles Schwab, Lyxor, XACT Fonder, Assetmark, Cidel Bank & Trust, Claymore, Columbia Management, Parametric, Pro-Financial, and Plexus Group to name a few—for embracing the idea and helping our work to gain traction in the marketplace.

I'm grateful to the people who explored fundamental—and valuation-indifferent—reweighting of the S&P 500 Index, setting a foundation for the acceptance of this idea. Bob Jones of Goldman Sachs Asset Management (GSAM) is the unsung pioneer in this domain, having developed a profits-weighted S&P 500 product in 1990. Sadly, this product never took off for GSAM and was overtaken by the firm's more conventional enhanced index products.

Subsequent efforts by David Morris and Paul Wood also helped to build the visibility of this line of research. I'm especially grateful to Paul Wood for his efforts—both in his 2003 *Journal of Indexes* article and in his conversations with us—to lay a foundation for the core principles of the Fundamental Index idea.

I appreciate Jeremy Siegel's efforts to popularize the concept. While he's suffered some "slings and arrows" for comparing this work with the efforts of Copernicus in the sixteenth century, his articulation of the "Noisy Market Hypothesis" in the *Wall Street Journal* is one of the most succinct descriptions of the theoretical foundations of the Fundamental Index concept that I've yet seen.

George Keane deserves special gratitude in our journey to develop this important idea. George relentlessly campaigned against the pitfalls of both capitalization weighting and the S&P 500 during the late 1990s. His conviction, persistence, and determination spurred us to take up his challenge to seek a better index solution.

I'm grateful to my coauthors, Jason Hsu and John West, for their respective efforts to assure the academic integrity and the easy flow of the book. I also thank Katy Sherrerd for spearheading the editorial process and marshalling the efforts of Jaynee Dudley, Kate Rouze, and Elizabeth Collins in their extensive editorial contributions, Dan Harkins for his compliance oversight, and Brett Myers and Bryce Little for analytical and research assistance. And I'm deeply grateful to a finance community that so values and encourages the exploration of new ideas.

Lastly, I'm especially grateful to my family for their patience with the lost weekends that are inevitable in the process of writing a book.

—ROB ARNOTT

CHAPTER 1

Efficient Indexing for an Inefficient Market

What could be more advantageous in an intellectual contest—
whether it be chess, bridge, or stock selection than to have opponents
who have been taught that thinking is a waste of energy?

—Warren Buffett
1985 Berkshire Hathaway Annual Report
Chairman's Letter

For 50 years, the finance community has been in the thrall of an idea known as the "efficient market hypothesis," a view that price identically equals fair value. The efficient market hypothesis is an idea of seductive simplicity, and it forms the foundation for much of modern finance theory and practice. It is a core principle for the multitrillion-dollar world of index fund management. Without the efficient market hypothesis, most of the theorems and proofs of modern finance come unglued.

In this worldview, the price equals the fair value for every asset, in every market, at every moment of every day. Not many academics, and even fewer investors, believe that this view is true. Those who hew to this notion tacitly—and often without realizing it— dismiss the concept of fair value as irrelevant. They define *fair value* as tautologically equal to the price: An asset is worth the price it will fetch in the market. But in so defining fair value, they strip the very concept of fair value of any meaning.

Buy low, sell high. This oft-heard aphorism is probably as old as the investment markets in which we operate. With efficient markets, however, the advice makes no sense because prices are always fair; there is no low, there is no high. In such a world, the best strategy is for us to own the market, weighting our holdings in direct proportion to the value of all of the companies we have at our disposal. But, as Warren Buffett has noted, if some investors assume that (or behave as if) markets are efficient when in fact they are not, the shrewd investor can benefit handily.

Evidence of Market Efficiency

Having a clear and informed belief regarding price efficiency is one of the most critical elements to formulating an investment strategy. Consider this: $500 billion lost in only 30 months. It is a staggering amount of money—more than 50 times the collective annual casino takings from Las Vegas tourists and two-and-a-half times the estimated losses domestic airlines and associated travel industries suffered after September 11, 2001. Shockingly, it's more than 100 times the losses incurred in the collapse of Long-Term Capital Management (the most spectacular hedge fund collapse in history) that many knowledgeable people—including former Federal Reserve Board chairman Alan Greenspan—thought could potentially bring down the entire global economy.

This massive wealth destruction wasn't the result of rogue traders with leveraged balance sheets. It occurred in the stock market—in the 30 months following the collapse of the technology bubble in March 2000. The $500 billion figure isn't even the total stock market loss over this dreadful stretch. This astronomical loss resulted from one stock: Cisco Systems, the largest stock in the world based on market capitalization at the peak of the tech bubble. This stock was valued at nearly $600 billion at a time when its sales were less than $20 billion, its trailing 12-month operating earnings were less than $3 billion, its cumulative profits since inception were well under $8 billion, and it had never paid a dividend. Additionally, Cisco's workforce numbered fewer than 30,000 people. Not only did investors collectively assign Cisco a price-earnings ratio (P/E) of nearly 200, they also assigned it a market value of $20 million per employee. Of that $600 billion, $500 billion was gone 30 months later.

Index fund investors as a group—people who believe in market efficiency and who do not believe in betting on single stocks—lost nearly $100 billion in Cisco. An average 401(k) participant with $100,000 invested in a Standard & Poor's (S&P) 500 Index fund lost more than $45,000 in those 30 bleak months, almost $4,000 of which was lost on Cisco alone. The damage was even worse for investors riding the growth stock revolution—a $100,000 investment in the Nasdaq 100 Index was worth less than $25,000 by the end of the tech bubble carnage. The wreckage experienced by only a few of the S&P 500 Index's largest holdings illustrates how the index investor ended up placing a surprisingly large chunk of money in companies trading at high—sometimes even astronomical—valuation multiples.

There have been countless historical episodes of speculative fever leading to unsustainable prices; inevitably, the fad of the day passes—at considerable cost to investors' psyches and pocketbooks. What is surprising is that *index fund* investors, who embrace diversification and shun the hubris of stock picking, suffered so drastically. Index funds are supposed to be the ultimate diversification choice—the "smart," risk-reducing vehicle for owning equities. MBA textbooks and the Chartered Financial Analyst (CFA) curriculum endorse index investing as the "optimal" method to eliminate unique stock risk.

Moreover, with dozens of industry groups having substantial representation in a market index, the risk reduction broadens beyond individual stocks to economic sectors. The pundit who first suggested "don't put all your eggs in one basket" would surely approve of index funds. But something went awry in the late 1990s. Cisco and the high-tech sector had become 4 percent and 33 percent of the market index, respectively, when they were less than 0.5 percent and 10 percent of the market a few years prior. Suddenly, the so-called passive indexes became heavily dominated by ultrahigh-P/E technology names.

You might ask, "So what? Bear markets happen from time to time." Whenever they do, the wealth destruction is immense, just as the wealth creation during bull markets can be breathtaking. But bubbles are different. They create ephemeral wealth that dissipates for those left holding the scraps of paper when the music stops.

One of the lesser-known twists associated with the tech bubble is that in the two years after the bubble burst, during which time Cisco lost $400 billion of its eventual $500 billion loss, *most stocks went up!* In the two-year period from March 2000 through March 2002, *the average U.S. listed stock returned more than 20 percent,* whereas the S&P 500 *lost more than 20 percent.*

Clearly, there was a vast disconnect between what the market index returned and what most of its component companies returned. What caused this divergence? The manner in which these market proxies are constructed. Standard market indexes are capitalization-weighted, which means the higher the price a share of stock becomes, the larger its weight becomes in the index. Because share prices are driven by both improved underlying fundamentals and shifting market expectations, the index weights reflect both fundamentals and popularity. In the late 1990s, Cisco and its tech buddies were winning the popularity contest by a landslide; content (fundamental measures of company sales and profits) simply did not carry much weight in this beauty pageant. As a consequence, the S&P 500 reflected a very narrow (if not narrow-minded) opinion and became a concentrated bet on the information superhighway's ability to collect a sufficient toll.

The bull market of the 1990s, for most companies, did not end until April 2002. While the S&P 500 lost 9 percent in 2000, the average stock on the New York Stock Exchange (NYSE) enjoyed a double-digit gain. When the S&P 500 lost another 12 percent in 2001, the average stock enjoyed another, albeit single-digit, gain. This drastic divergence is a stark reminder that the traditional market indexes can be dominated by a handful of extraordinary glamour stocks and therefore may bear little resemblance to the majority of the companies in the stock market. The bear market of 2000 through 2002 was a special period of index decline, one largely driven by a handful of overvalued stocks whose prices corrected sharply when growth fell short of expectations. In fact, many of these growth companies grew handily as their share prices cratered. But those prices had been predicated on even faster growth. It was the shortfall relative to *expectations* that spelled the demise of their share prices. This divergence between index performance and company performance is an alarming indictment of what is wrong with the traditional market indexes.

With cap-weighted index funds, if a company's P/E multiple doubles relative to the rest of the market because of an increasingly optimistic outlook on future growth, its market capitalization doubles *and its weight in the index doubles*. Is this because the stock is now twice as attractive after its P/E multiple has doubled? Of course not. The larger weight is merely a consequence of the doubling of valuation multiples, plain and simple. Similarly, if the P/E halves because of aggressive overselling, its weight in the index declines by half. By its very construction, the cap-weighted index puts more weight in stocks, which have become more expensive and reduces the weight of stocks that have become cheaper. Additionally, if a stock is trading at twice the market P/E, its share of the index weight will be twice as large as an average company with the same earnings. By construction, cap-weighted indexes put more of the investor's money in "growth" (or high-P/E stocks) and less money in "value" (or low-P/E stocks).

If the market prices growth and value stocks correctly—that is, if the market gets the relative prices exactly right—then growth and value stocks will offer the same *risk-adjusted* returns. In other words, a correctly functioning market will prepay for prospective future growth as if that expected growth were a *fait accompli*. But if the expected risk-adjusted returns for the growth companies and the value companies are the same, *why would we want to invest more of our money in growth and less in value?*

In the first two years after the tech bubble burst, the traditional indexes—and the index funds tracking them—were down, while the average stock was up, precisely *because* the indexes had loaded up on the pricey, high-flying growth companies. Many of the companies getting higher allocations were trading at multiples of earnings—or, for those with no earnings, multiples of sales—which were without precedent. At the peak of the bubble in March 2000, almost 30 percent of the Russell 2000 Index,[1] the popular small-cap market index, consisted of companies that had no earnings. Most of these companies had never had earnings in their entire history.

Broader and larger-cap indexes also had hefty doses of negative earners during this period. Why did these indexes have so much invested in companies at unprecedented valuation multiples? *Because* these companies were at unprecedented valuation multiples! Those multiples factored into the very market capitalization that determined the weights in the indexes. The stocks had not become more attractive. In fact, common sense suggests that these stocks had probably become less attractive. Index investors owned twice as much simply because the stock had doubled in price!

If a select few stocks rapidly soar in price, they will compose an increasing portion of the index. The resulting portfolio may then have less diversification than the broad economy, a peculiar scenario for a portfolio designed to reflect broad investment in that economy! It is almost akin to placing many of our eggs in the basket hanging from the highest—and windiest—branch of the investment tree.

The Case for Indexing

A multitrillion-dollar industry is now based on investing in or benchmarking to cap-weighted indexes.[2] As of year-end 2006, nearly $5 trillion in stock and bond assets were tied to cap-weighted indexes worldwide. Assets invested in index funds replicating the S&P 500 alone neared $1.3 trillion (*Pensions & Investments,* 2007). The Vanguard Group offers four S&P 500 mutual funds, with a combined $200 billion in assets, for various account minimums. The world's largest exchange-traded fund, S&P Depositary Receipts (SPDRs, or Spiders), managed by State Street Global Advisors, has another $50 billion.

For many investors who believe that the market is fairly efficient and that it is hard to identify mispricing in the market, investing passively through an index fund seems the natural way to access the equity markets. Certainly, this lesson is the one dispensed, without much question or inspection, in virtually all finance classrooms across the United States. Some of the industry's greatest leaders, including Jack Bogle, Burton Malkiel, Bill Sharpe, and Charley Ellis, endorse this path.

Even the father of security analysis (the antithesis of passive investing), Benjamin Graham, conceded late in his life that the index fund offered the best promise for the majority of investors. Graham (1976) uttered these words more than 30 years ago:

> I am no longer an advocate of elaborate techniques of security analysis in order to find superior value opportunities. This was a rewarding activity, say, 40 years ago, when our textbook *Graham and Dodd* was first published; but the situation has changed a great deal since then. In the old days any well-trained security analyst could do a good professional job of selecting undervalued issues through detailed studies; but in the light of the

enormous amount of research now being carried on, I doubt
whether in most cases such extensive efforts will generate sufficiently superior selections to justify their cost.

Right about that time, a group of pioneers took things a step
further by transforming this market proxy into an investment. In
1973, Dean LeBaron, while continuing to manage active strategies based on a contrarian, value-based approach, created the first
indexed portfolios for institutional investors at Batterymarch. Bill
Fouse set up not one but two of the largest managers of indexed
assets in the world at Wells Fargo Bank (in the division that is now
the cornerstone of Barclays Global Investors' worldwide investment
operations) and then at Mellon Capital Management. Jack Bogle
created the first index fund for individuals at the Vanguard Group
in 1976. And after publishing pioneering research on long-term
equity returns with Roger Ibbotson in 1976, Rex Sinquefield set
up Dimensional Fund Advisors, now the largest manager of small-
company indexed assets in the world.

These early advocates of the cap-weighted index fund touted the
idea as the ultimate investment vehicle that cannot be *reliably* beaten
after costs by most active managers, a view that they still espouse. *We
agree.* History has vindicated them, and common sense supports
their argument to this day. Their advocacy of indexing tends to rely
on two very different arguments. The first is the efficient market
hypothesis. *If prices perfectly match each company's fair value at all times,*
the cap-weighted index reigns supreme. Bill Sharpe, in his Nobel
Prize-winning development of the capital asset pricing model (often
described by its acronym CAPM, or "Cap-M"), proved the supremacy
of the cap-weighted index to be true, subject to an array of assumptions, including a world without pricing errors.

A second argument, far more powerful to those who don't accept
the efficient market hypothesis, is that the majority of active managers, with vast resources at their disposal, *must* underperform cap-
weighted indexes net of costs. Why? Because they collectively own
essentially that same portfolio. If we take the cap-weighted market
portfolio and take out the cap-weighted index funds, we're left with
the self-same portfolio for the collective ownership by the active managers. If well-informed, highly skilled, and well-resourced investment
professionals cannot outperform the standard indexes with any consistency and reliability, then index investing must be very efficient!

Evidence of Market Inefficiency

Intuitively, we know that perfect market efficiency isn't quite right. Almost no investment manager or adviser believes that price and fair value are identical at all times for all assets. Even most finance professors would say that price is only an approximation of fair value—though they would go on to say that it's a pretty good approximation and that the errors will largely cancel. Let's assume that price is the market's best *guess* at a company's intrinsic value. It's probably a pretty good guess most of the time, but it could be too high or too low. In fact, because the intrinsic value of a stock is the net present value, not of next quarter, not of next year, but of *decades of future cash flows*, the intrinsic value could actually be far removed from the price.

A few examples will demonstrate evidence of stock mispricing. In 1720, the South Sea Company—a narrowly limited monopoly for trade with South America and almost no profits—was being traded in London. What they lacked in financials, the company's directors more than made up for in the art of promotion. To "prove" the overwhelming promise of their monopoly, the company announced its intention to fund the entire sovereign debt of England. Politicians and insiders were influenced to pass the bill by the offering of stock options, which allowed the holder to "buy" the stock with no money and then "sell" it back to the company after the price had risen. With many of the country's elite among the ranks of stockholders and promises of South American gold, the stock price jumped to more than £1,000 per share. As word eventually leaked of directors selling their shares, the stock's meteoric rise reversed. The prospects of any future profits evaporated, along with the wealth of the investors in the "South Sea Bubble." Sir Isaac Newton, recognizing the company's price-linked dividend as a Ponzi scheme, shunned the idea of investing—until two weeks before the bubble burst. He then finally threw his lot in with the mob—and he lost most of his immense fortune. In the previous century, at the height of the "tulipmania" in Holland, one poor soul spent 3,000 florins (about 20 years' income for the average wage earner in Holland at the time) for a single Semper Augustus tulip bulb, only to see a sailor, thinking it was an onion, eating it.

If you think investors are different now, consider the late 1990s and the "Axis of Wealth Destruction" in the U.S. market—Cisco,

AOL, and Lucent Technologies—three of the top 10 stocks in the world by market capitalization at that time.[3] The rise of the Internet and the massive information technology (IT) expenditure aimed at fixing the Y2K problems of the legacy computing platforms proved to be a boon for technology infrastructure companies such as networking giant Cisco. From 1997 to 2000, Cisco's P/E rose from 30 to nearly 200 as investors' expectations rose even faster than Cisco's fast-growing operating results. At the height of the recent tech bubble, 3Com spun off its Palm division (maker of the Palm Pilot, a product that has since seen an array of competitors devour its market) for a price that was so high that Palm was briefly worth more than General Motors, whose quarterly dividend was many times Palm's annual sales! Meanwhile, 3Com remained Palm's largest shareholder and was trading at a price roughly half the value of its holdings in Palm stock. 3Com's remaining businesses were valued by the market at a very large negative value.

The same dynamic occurred in Canada, where another networking heavyweight, Nortel, saw its price skyrocket despite the company's posting net losses in 1998 and 1999, by which time this single company constituted 28 percent of the total value of the Canadian stock market. When Nortel sales tumbled, its share price fell by more than 99 percent—in the same 30 months that bludgeoned Cisco's stock.

The phenomenon took place even more dramatically in certain overseas markets, with telecommunications and cell phone giants Nokia and Ericsson both garnering P/E multiples nearing triple digits by early 2000. In fact, when Nortel, Ericsson, and Nokia became roughly one-third, one-half, and two-thirds of their respective national stock markets by value, the companies themselves composed a mere 1 percent to 4 percent of their nations' economies as measured by company sales as a percentage of gross domestic product (GDP). These exorbitant prices were based on future cash flows that were expected to grow annually at 25 percent to 50 percent for many years. Despite solid growth in two of the three companies (unlike the others, Nortel's business operations cratered), these high expectations weren't met. As Figure 1.1 shows, in the following 30 months, each of these stocks fell by 80 percent to 99 percent, leading to massive destruction in portfolio value for their investors, including the cap-weighted indexers.

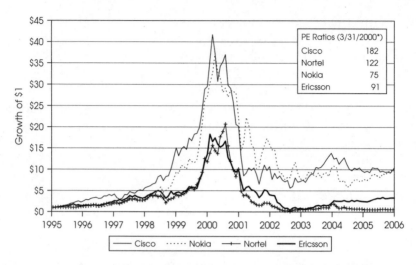

Figure 1.1   The Rise and Fall of Tech Stocks: 1995 through 2006
*Data from Bloomberg.
Source: Research Affiliates, LLC.

Another instructive example is the earlier biotechnology bubble. In 1991, major advancements in DNA research prompted a then-record 35 initial public offerings (IPOs) in the field. Meanwhile, the stock of established player Amgen surged 265 percent. Although biotech was still a relatively small industry on an economic scale, this massive mispricing significantly affected the cap-weighted indexes.

Examples of severely mispriced stocks are not limited to investors bidding up the latest technology or next big thing. Mispricing can occur in even the most low-tech and everyday industries, such as breakfast. The simple doughnut—a ball of dough deep fried, covered in a sugar glaze, and served with a cup of coffee—spawned a recent mini-bubble. After its April 2000 IPO, Krispy Kreme Doughnuts, a company founded in 1937 that serves a product invented in the 1800s, soared to a market capitalization of nearly $3 billion and a P/E of more than 150—pretty good for a company with $300 million in total sales and a profit margin of slightly less than 5 percent. Four years later, the stock had shed almost 90 percent of its value.

Conclusion

As Fischer Black, one of the most highly regarded theoreticians in the investment field, used to say on his move from the Massachusetts Institute of Technology to Goldman Sachs, "The markets seem far less efficient from the banks of the Hudson River than from the banks of the Charles River." We agree. The efficient market hypothesis has flunked most empirical tests to date, sometimes with remarkable statistical significance. Even if one accepts the tautological notion that price equals *current* fair value, no one makes the case that price will be precisely correct relative to the unknowable future cash flows.

Imagine an investor with a perfect crystal ball who is able to see every future cash distribution that will flow from an investment. These future cash distributions can be used to compute an after-the-fact intrinsic value for a stock. Bill Sharpe whimsically refers to this as the "clairvoyant value," a label that is both accurate and fun. Relative to a stock's "clairvoyant value," prices will usually be wrong, frequently by a large margin. The fact that these errors can be large does not justify linking the size of our investment to this error, merely because the error is unobservable until many years hence. In future chapters, we explore whether this particular "pricing error" allows for some reasonably powerful and reasonably reliable ways to outpace the cap-weighted indexes.

Origins of the Fundamental Index Concept

Trees do not grow into the sky.
— Johann Wolfgang von Goethe

Index funds provide assuredly average returns—tracking the market at next to nothing in fees, trading costs, or other expenses. They are a great idea for fund investors because most active managers deliver less performance than the market, but for higher fees. The problem occurs when the market does *not* get the price right. If stocks are routinely mispriced, we need to take a hard look at the way traditional capitalization-weighted indexes are constructed.

Errors in share prices lead to errors in stock weights for traditional cap-weighted indexes. Shares priced far above their eventual intrinsic value will have an erroneously high capitalization and, therefore, an erroneously high index weighting. An indexed portfolio weighted by the market capitalization of its constituent companies has a correspondingly high proportion invested in these stocks, each of which will eventually underperform as the market seeks out the intrinsic value (remember the Axis of Wealth Destruction). Similarly, stocks priced below their eventual intrinsic value will have erroneously low capitalization and, therefore, low index weights.

This latter description applies to *most* stocks in early 2000; they went on to two additional years of solid performance, even after the technology bubble burst and the cap-weighted indexes that tech dominated were well into a bear market. The result for the indexed portfolio is that *underpriced stocks constitute less of the portfolio than do overpriced stocks.*

In a world with pricing errors, a cap-weighted index will suffer a return drag by systematically overweighting overpriced securities and underweighting underpriced securities relative to their "eventual intrinsic value weights" (or, from Sharpe, their "clairvoyant value weights"). Jack Bogle, founder of the Vanguard Group and one of the strongest advocates of cap-weighted indexing, admits that cap-weighted indexes will allocate more money to the overpriced stocks and less to the underpriced. He concludes, however, that unless the investor can identify which is which ahead of time, there's no real value in this observation. He's right, of course. Because we cannot see the intrinsic value of any investment, we cannot know its intrinsic-value weight. We'll return to this nuance later.

Although this dynamic—overweighting the overvalued—occurs extensively throughout the constituents of all cap-weighted indexes, it is most vividly illustrated by an examination of the top 10 stocks in the S&P 500 Index (see Table 2.1). Some companies make this exclusive, *crème de la crème* list because they are *very* large companies whose

Table 2.1   Top 10 Stocks, January 1, 2000

The 10 Largest Companies[a]	The 10 Largest-Cap Stocks[b]
AT&T	AOL
Citigroup	Cisco Systems
Exxon Mobil	Citigroup
Federal National Mortgage	Exxon Mobil
Ford Motor Co.	General Electric
General Electric	Intel
General Motors	International Business Machines
International Business Machines	Lucent Technologies
MCI Worldcom	Microsoft
Philip Morris	Wal-Mart Stores

[a] Based on an average of four fundamental measures of company size.
[b] Based on float excluding closely held stock.
Source: Research Affiliates, LLC.

intrinsic values are accurately reflected in their stock prices. They deserve their top 10 ranking. Others make the list because they are smaller companies with lofty growth expectations, which are priced at high valuation multiples.[1] Of the latter group, some prove to be over-stated relative to the company's future business results (which were unknowable in earlier time periods). These stocks are overpriced and make the top 10 list only because they are overpriced. Recall AOL and Cisco leapfrogging Citigroup and Exxon Mobil as the two largest companies in the world in early 2000, despite having only a tiny fraction of the sales or profits of Citigroup and Exxon Mobil. As pricing errors are recognized and corrected by the market, the large-cap, overpriced stocks underperform the market and the cap-weighted index suffers a return drag.

The performance of the top 10 stocks in the S&P 500 illustrates the magnitude of the performance drag problem. As Table 2.2 shows, on average, only 3 of the top 10 companies in the S&P 500 outperformed the average result for all 500 companies in the index over the subsequent 10 years, while 7 of the top 10 underperformed. That's a darned lopsided coin toss, especially given 81 years and 800 coin tosses! Also, owning these top 10 names (equally) gave an investor an average of nearly 30 percent less wealth than owning the 500 stocks in the S&P 500 (equally) in just a 10-year span. This is a huge performance drag: With a cap-weighted index, investors have an average of 20 percent to 25 percent of their money tied up in these underperformers.[2]

Table 2.2 Performance of Top 10 Stocks by Capitalization

How often did the top 10 stocks in a cap-weighted portfolio outperform the average stock in the following period?

	1-Year	3-Year	5-Year	10-Year
1926–2006	44%	40%	37%	31%
1964–2006	38%	35%	30%	27%

By how much did the top 10 stocks underperform the average?

	1-Year	3-Year	5-Year	10-Year
1926–2006	–2.9%	–11.1%	–17.7%	–29.4%
1964–2006	–3.6%	–15.9%	–24.9%	–36.9%

Source: Research Affiliates, LLC.

Clearly, most of the top 10 companies lag the performance of the average stock in the S&P 500 most of the time. Why does this matter, and what does it mean? Maybe it's a time-specific phenomenon for many of these 10-year spans. To test this possible explanation, we evaluated how *often* a majority of the top 10 companies bucked the trend and beat the average stock in the S&P 500. The most startling aspect of this lopsided behavior for the top 10 list is its consistency. Over the past 81 years, how often did the majority of the top 10 companies in the S&P 500 outperform the average stock in the S&P 500? Zero. Zilch. Nada. It never happened.

How well does that conform to an efficient market that forms the foundation for most of modern finance? It doesn't. Practitioners and academics are full of examples of market inefficiency, but for many investors, this finding may be the most shocking indictment of the efficient market hypothesis (EMH). After all, very few investors— even among the most sophisticated institutional investors and in the academic world—are aware of this startling fact.

The interesting question, of course, is what causes this phenomenon. Could the cause be simply the small-cap effect—small companies paying investors a risk premium? Other examples of a stark small-cap bias abound. For example, equally weighting an existing index delivers excess returns, on average, over time, in almost all markets. Throwing darts at the stock tables in the *Wall Street Journal* usually outperforms the traditional cap-weighted index. Academic papers have studied both of these phenomena (equal-weighted portfolios and random portfolios[3]) in depth, and generally credited the excess returns to a small-cap effect and a value effect. These explanations provide some new insight over the initial EMH and capital asset pricing model (CAPM), but they are still based on the same basic economic model.

Let's consider an alternative view. Suppose price is merely the market's best guess of intrinsic value. Suppose the errors are more or less random and are uncorrelated with the fair value of a company. This view is intuitively appealing because a primary purpose of the capital markets is to provide a best guess at fair value for each asset in order to create liquid, continuous markets for all assets. If this is what's going on, then for equal weighting and for the dartboard portfolios, the pricing errors will be utterly random relative to portfolio weights. In simple, unsophisticated strategies, like random or equal-weighted portfolios, *the portfolios will be evenly split between overvalued and undervalued stocks.* As the errors cancel, their net impact will be zero.

The case is different for a cap-weighted index. It has a direct, structural, and irrevocable link between portfolio weight and pricing error. As a result, *more than half of the portfolio will be in the overvalued companies and less than half will be in the undervalued companies.* Why? Because the weight is explicitly linked to the price and, hence, to the pricing error. As the prices revert toward the unknowable "clairvoyant value," the net result is assuredly not zero; it is negative. Because time is needed for the market to discover the intrinsic value of a company—typically years and often decades—this drag won't be evident every quarter or every year, but it will be powerful over time.

Origins of the Research Affiliates Fundamental Index (RAFI)

The Fundamental Index concept can be traced to the tech bubble of the late 1990s and its aftermath. In early 2002, with the S&P 500 already down more than 20 percent from the peak of the tech bubble in March 2000, passive investors were suffering the devastating consequences of linking portfolio weights to market capitalization. One such investor, George Keane, challenged us to find a better way to index—one that didn't leave an investor overexposed to overvalued companies and underexposed to undervalued companies.[4] He believed—viscerally believed—that there had to be a better way. Keane proposed that our firm explore a new indexing approach that could finally solve this issue without the structural flaws of, for example, equal-weighting. We accepted the challenge.

The first step was to define the focus of our research. We started with the view that capitalization weighting is efficient *only if market prices are efficient.* We had already long believed that constructing and weighting an index by each company's scale of business would prove superior to weighting companies by their market capitalization in markets where pricing errors exist. Although Wall Street judges the size of a company by the price of its stock, most business owners quantify the economic scale of their organization by "Main Street" measures, such as annual sales, profits, net assets, or the number of employees. Moreover, when the popular press describes mergers, it rarely mentions the combined market capitalization.

Rather, it reports that the two companies have combined *sales* of "X," combined *profits* of "Y," or a combined number of *employees* of "Z." Conversations with Keane, Marty Leibowitz and Brett Hammond,[5] Peter Bernstein,[6] Jack Treynor,[7] Harry Markowitz,[8] and others, reinforced our notion that using a different measure of company size should be the starting point for our research.

Consistent with this notion, we decided to experiment with an index based on company sales. We turned to the Fortune 500 for a definitive list of the largest companies in the United States. The Fortune 500 rankings are determined by annual sales, not by market capitalization. So, if General Electric's sales composes 2 percent of the Fortune 500 companies as ranked and selected by sales, it receives a 2 percent weight in the sales index. We found that this sales-weighted approach outperformed the S&P 500 by more than 250 basis points annually over a span of more than 30 years. This was about three times the "alpha" we expected to see. This evidence powerfully supported our suspicion that capitalization weighting is efficient only if the market prices are efficient. We immediately realized that we were on to something important and well worth serious pursuit.

The next step was to extend the data to dig deeper and go back further. We created indexes in which each stock's weight was determined by its relative economic scale based on some particular metric of company size relative to the rest of the market. In addition to sales, we tested other measures of company size—revenues, reported earnings, cash flow, number of employees, dividends paid, and book value, to name a few—over a longer period of time. We went deeper—selecting, ranking, and weighting the 1,000 largest companies by each of these measures. We took the analysis back to 1962, the earliest year for which we could find a five-year history of financials on 1,000 companies. As Table 2.3 shows, *they all outperformed the S&P 500—significantly.*[9]

We were startled to note the relatively narrow dispersion in performance between the Fundamental Index constructs. Despite consisting of different stocks and the companies in them occasionally having sharply divergent weights, the indexes' long-term performance averages fell in a relatively tight band, none departing from the mean by even 50 basis points a year. This result held true even for Fundamental Index constructs that aren't listed in Table 2.3 (we tested quite an array of choices). *Capitalization weighting was the only outlier; it was fully 210 basis points off the pace.*

Table 2.3 Performance of Individual Fundamental Index Constructs: 1962 through 2007

Portfolio	Growth of $1	Annual Return	Annual Volatility	Sharpe Ratio	Excess Return
S&P 500	$90	10.3%	14.6%	0.37	0.0%
Cap 1000	$88	10.2%	14.8%	0.36	—
Book	$176	11.9%	14.6%	0.47	1.7%
Cash Flow	$214	12.4%	14.6%	0.50	2.1%
Sales	$248	12.7%	15.4%	0.50	2.5%
Gross Dividends	$174	11.9%	13.3%	0.50	1.6%
RAFI U.S. Large Composite	$207	12.3%	14.4%	0.50	2.1%

Source: Research Affiliates, LLC.

A Series of *Aha!* Moments

Our initial research led to a series of insights—*aha!* moments—that led to refinements in our thinking about the way to construct a better index. Our first *aha!* moment was when we realized that all of these Fundamental Index portfolios performed similarly—while capitalization weighting did not—because each one broke the link between portfolio weight and pricing error. If pricing noise pushes some stocks erroneously into the top ranks by market capitalization, by valuation multiples, and by price, then any weighting system that is price and valuation *indifferent* should avoid this push and outperform cap-weighted indexes.[10] Whether we are selecting and weighting stocks by their cash flow, by book value, or by other metrics, the Fundamental Index methodology does not automatically overallocate to the overpriced stocks and underallocate to the underpriced stocks, relative to the unknowable fair value weights. In a Fundamental Index portfolio, half of the portfolio is, on average, in overvalued stocks and half in undervalued stocks. The portfolios still have weighting errors—presumably no smaller than the errors in capitalization weighting—but the errors are random, so they cancel. *The return drag from capitalization weighting is gone, without one's having to guess which stocks are overvalued and which are undervalued.*

Our second *aha!* moment came when we realized that simply reweighting an existing cap-weighted index gets us only a fraction of the potential benefit provided by starting from scratch, and creating a wholly new Fundamental Index portfolio.[11] Overlap between the RAFI[12] indexes and cap-weighted indexes is considerable, typically 70 percent to 80 percent of the names, but some portions are not overlapping, as illustrated in Figure 2.1. As we move into the bottom range of a cap-weighted index such as the Russell 1000 Index, we begin to encounter companies that are small on an economic scale (cash flow, sales, etc.) but are trading at lofty enough multiples to make the top 1,000 by capitalization. When ranked based on the fundamental measures of size, these companies fall into the RAFI U.S. Small Company Index (RAFI U.S. Small). Similarly, near the top of the Russell 2000 Index, we encounter companies that have a large economic footprint trading at somewhat depressed multiples. In a fundamental framework, these companies move up to the RAFI U.S. Large Company Index (RAFI U.S. Large), shouldering aside the larger-cap small companies that don't belong in the top 1,000 based on fundamental measures of economic scale.

Much of the value added by the Fundamental Index concept is attributable to redefining the eligible universe of stocks on the basis of fundamental size rather than capitalization. Over the 45-year period, the small-cap/large-company stocks (members of the Russell 2000 and of the RAFI U.S. Large portfolios) outperform the large-cap/small-company stocks (members of the Russell 1000 and of the RAFI U.S. Small portfolios) by very nearly 1,000 basis points per year, compounded! Simply reweighting the Russell 1000—or any cap-weighted index for that matter—misses these wonderful opportunities.

Our third *aha!* moment came when we realized that multiple metrics of company size will result in a broader and more representative

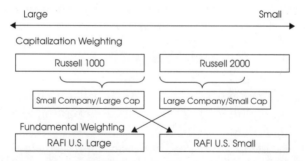

Figure 2.1   Index Stock Selection Differences: Cap vs. Fundamental Index Weights
Source: Research Affiliates, LLC.

investment portfolio than using any single metric. Each individual metric, we believed, has its own special vulnerabilities, making it suboptimal as a market index or a long-term core equity portfolio. For example, a dividend-weighted index will exclude more than half of all publicly traded companies in the United States, including many growth stocks and essentially all emerging growth companies. It will be a deep-value, high-yield index of mature value companies. And it will have profound sector biases—specifically, favoring financials, utilities, and consumer goods. It will sharply overweight so-called old-economy companies and underweight new-economy companies relative to their economic scale (not to mention their market capitalization). That being said, a dividend-weighted index *works very well.* Even though it's the worst performing of the single-metric Fundamental Index portfolios in average returns and in bull markets, it's also the best in bear markets.

Of course, a dividend-based Fundamental Index portfolio is not alone in exhibiting biases and peculiarities. A sales-weighted index clearly favors companies with vast sales at low margins over more profitable companies. A profit-weighted index clearly favors companies with cyclical earnings—especially at the cyclical peak in earnings. A book value–weighted index is overly reliant on companies with a history of aggressive accounting. An employment-weighted index values temps and McDonald's burger flippers as highly as Genentech biochemists. And so forth. A blended approach—using multiple measures—smoothes these rough edges, requires less trading, has better-than-average return at lower-than-average risk, and has the best risk-to-reward ratio of the lot.

Our fourth *aha!* moment came when we realized that we could cut the trading and turnover by smoothing the financial metrics over time. By using five-year smoothing, we are less exposed to the impact of peak or trough cash flows or sales. Further, we can include special dividends without distorting the dividend-weighted Fundamental Index portfolio, because the dividends are smoothed over time. To some, it seems like we're relying on old data to determine the weights for the companies in our indexes. In reality, we find that it's not terribly important to get the weights exactly right. The key source of value added from the Fundamental Index portfolios is that we sever the link between the weight in the index and the error in the price. As a result, it's somewhat surprising to find that five-year smoothed weights actually perform a little better than weights based on the most recent data—and with far lower trading and turnover!

Research Affiliates Fundamental Index

The Research Affiliates Fundamental Index (RAFI) is a price-indifferent index built on the intuitions of our research.[13] To mitigate the undesirable characteristics of the single-metric indexes, RAFI combines four individual Fundamental Index constructs into a multiple-metric index:

1. Sales
2. Cash flow
3. Book value
4. Dividends

We chose these four metrics because they represent the most objective measures from each of the major "categories" that people use to measure economic size. We think it's important that sales and cash flow involve less subjective accruals than revenues or earnings. If this Fundamental Index concept gains substantial traction, with hundreds of billions of dollars managed to these indexes, company management teams will have a financial incentive to "game" the indexes, by seeming larger and more successful than they really are. By using four metrics, spanning five years, and focusing on the metrics that are the most objective (with the least subjective wiggle room from accruals, pension assumptions, and goodwill), we create indexes that are very tough for company management to game. From the measures that we tested, the only category of metrics that we chose to exclude was the number of employees. Even though it worked fine in our research, it's a peculiar index: when it's used, McDonald's and Kelly Services reliably fall into our top 10 holdings. They're even "bigger" than capital-intensive powerhouses like Exxon Mobil!

Our research shows that the four-metric approach results in returns that are higher than the average of the single-metric approaches, risk that is less than the average of the individual metric approaches, tracking error against the cap-weighted indexes that rivals the lowest of the single-metric approaches, and a Sharpe ratio and information ratio that best *all* of the single-metric approaches.[14,15,16]

Table 2.4   Constructing a RAFI Index

	Trailing 5-Year Sales	Trailing 5-Year Cash Flow	Book Value (Last Quarter)	Trailing 5-Year Gross Dividends	RAFI Composite Weight[a]
Company A	$40	$6	$20	$1	
Company B	10	4	30	0	
Total index	1,000	200	1,000	50	
Company A weight	4.00%	3.00%	2.00%	2.00%	2.75%
Company B weight	1.00%	2.00%	3.00%	N/A	2.00%

[a] These RAFI weights are renormalized for final portfolio weights; renormalized weights are equal to these initial RAFI composite weights divided by the sum of RAFI composite weights. For Company B, the dividend weight is ignored because there are no dividends.

Source: Research Affiliates, LLC.

Fundamental Index portfolios are constructed by equally weighting the four individual Fundamental Index weights to create the RAFI weight for each company. The top 1,000 companies by RAFI weight are included in the RAFI U.S. Large. Companies that pay no dividends are weighted according to the average of the remaining three metrics and are not punished with a zero weight for the dividend component. The rationale for this adjustment centers on the changing nature of shareholder compensation. Stock buybacks have risen in importance, and investors increasingly view dividends as a negative for growth stocks. Table 2.4 illustrates the process for two hypothetical companies. This example also demonstrates the process for calculating a RAFI weight for a non-dividend-paying company. A portfolio of companies constructed using this approach will accurately represent today's economy with utter neutrality, favoring neither growth nor value companies, relative to their economic scale, and paying no regard to valuation multiples or price. This portfolio also has a host of other advantages, which will be outlined in subsequent chapters.

Fundamental Index Performance

The evidence is compelling that Fundamental Index portfolios outperform cap-weighted indexes. From 1962 through 2007, the RAFI U.S. Large produced annual excess returns of 210 basis points above the Cap 1000. The magic of compounding transforms this seemingly modest performance pickup into a truly staggering difference in wealth. As Figure 2.2 shows, a dollar invested in the RAFI U.S. Large portfolio in 1962 grew to more than $200 by the end of 2007, more than twice the $88 ending value of the Cap 1000. Importantly, the Fundamental Index portfolio managed to achieve these superior returns with less risk, as measured by annualized standard deviation, than the cap-weighted portfolio. Thus, when compared with U.S. Treasury bills (in a measure known as the Sharpe ratio), the risk-adjusted excess return was *nearly 40 percent greater for the Fundamental Index portfolio than for capitalization weighting.*

Recognizing that 46 years is a long time to wait for the benefits of compounding, consider the impact on an individual's retirement savings of an incremental return of 210 basis points per year. As Table 2.5 shows, an investor contributing $10,000 a year to her 401(k) plan would have an additional $20,000 in her portfolio after only 10 years from a Fundamental Index portfolio, assuming a 9.1 percent return versus a 7 percent return from a cap-weighted portfolio. After 20 and 30 years, the gap soars to $126,000 and $504,000.

Of course, the Fundamental Index strategy will not exceed the cap-weighted standard every month, every quarter, or every year.

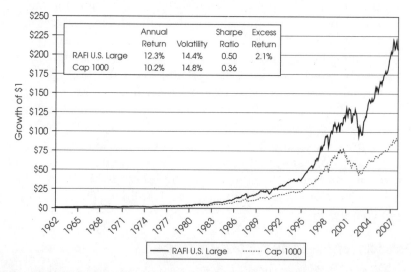

Figure 2.2   Growth of $1 Invested in RAFI U.S. Large and Cap 1000: 1962 through 2007

Source: Research Affiliates, LLC.

Table 2.5   Power of Compounding over Time

Year	Contribution	Ending Value @ 9.10%	Ending Value @ 7%
1	$10,000	$10,910	$10,700
2	$10,000	$22,813	$22,149
3	$10,000	$35,799	$34,399
4	$10,000	$49,966	$47,507
5	$10,000	$65,423	$61,533
10	$10,000	$166,548	$147,836
15	$10,000	$322,856	$268,881
20	$10,000	$564,460	$438,652
25	$10,000	$937,906	$676,765
30	$10,000	$1,515,140	$1,010,730

Source: Research Affiliates, LLC.

To provide investors a fuller understanding of the concept and properly manage expectations, it helps to break the results down into different environments. Table 2.6 presents the performance of the RAFI U.S. Large in bull and bear markets, economic expansions, and recessions. The Fundamental Index strategy has outperformed most powerfully when excess returns are needed most—when assets are tumbling, when the economy is struggling, and portfolio "top-ups" are the least affordable. That is, in bear markets, the RAFI U.S. Large beat the S&P 500 by more than 500 basis points annually. In a recession, it historically added 340 basis points a year. Similar results can be obtained with any defensive strategy, but most defensive strategies give away those relative gains

Table 2.6   Fundamental Index Performance in Good Times and Bad: 1962 through 2007

Portfolio	Bull Markets	Bear Markets	Expansions	Recessions
RAFI U.S. Large	20.3%	−18.1%	13.4%	6.4%
S&P 500	19.6%	−23.9%	11.6%	3.0%
RAFI U.S. Large excess return over S&P 500	0.7%	5.8%	1.8%	3.4%

Source: Research Affiliates, LLC.

during the good times. Note that the Fundamental Index concept continues to add value during most economic expansions and bull markets at an average of 180 basis points a year and 80 basis points a year, respectively.

Nominal-return environments are also instructive. What happens to the Fundamental Index advantage in *extended* periods of high and low returns? Figure 2.3 provides a scatterplot with the RAFI U.S. Large return versus the Cap 1000 return for rolling five-year periods. Dots above the solid 45-degree line indicate that the Fundamental Index strategy outperformed during that five-year period; dots below the 45-degree line indicate that the cap-weighted index outperformed the Fundamental Index portfolio. The dashed line is a "line of best fit," which shows us how the *average* RAFI advantage varies as we move from bleak to extraordinarily strong five-year spans.

As Figure 2.3 shows, in the big bull markets (cap-weighted returns of 20 percent to 30 percent annually for a rolling five-year span), the RAFI U.S. Large maintained a batting average of not quite 50 percent—it outperformed almost half the time, and it underperformed just over half the time. As returns move into the moderate bull stage, where equities average returns of 10 percent to 20 percent a year, the RAFI U.S. Large begins to consistently outperform—to the tune of 97 percent of the periods, with an average excess return of 1.79 percentage points. In disappointing markets, single-digit equity returns or worse,

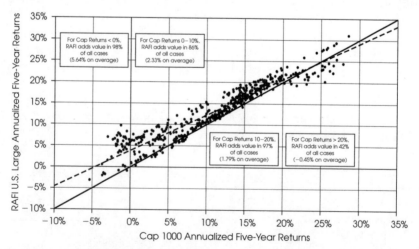

Figure 2.3 RAFI U.S. Large versus Cap 1000: Annualized Five-Year Returns, 1962 through 2007

Source: Research Affiliates, LLC.

the Fundamental Index concept maintains this high win rate and the average margin becomes very significant indeed.

In short, we find that the Fundamental Index advantage is modest when we least need its benefits and is frequently at its very best when we most desperately need good results.

Concluding Thoughts: A Better Way to Invest

The Fundamental Index strategy is a better way to index the large-company U.S. market, at least in extensive historical tests. In upcoming chapters, we will report similar results in a variety of equity markets—international, small company, emerging, the Nasdaq—all confirming the superiority of long-term Fundamental Index performance. This result shouldn't come as a surprise because capitalization weighting overweights the overvalued and underweights the undervalued *regardless of where it is applied.* As the overvalued companies, which comprise the bulk of our portfolio, eventually underperform, the investments in undervalued companies are too small to erase the damage. This creates a performance *drag.* An index constructed using fundamental measures of company size will arguably eliminate this tendency and the associated performance drag.

One of our critics dismisses the Fundamental Index idea as simply another form of value investing but also likens it to gravity, which, of course, *works everywhere!* Although we disagree that the Fundamental Index idea is merely another form of value investing (more on that point later), we *do* agree that the idea works everywhere. As a matter of fact, in less efficient markets, such as small-company stocks and emerging markets, the Fundamental Index advantage actually widens even as the value bias diminishes. These markets receive little coverage by Wall Street and institutional managers, which leads to a greater likelihood of pricing errors. And as the frequency and magnitude of mispricings proliferate, cap-weighted indexes suffer a greater return drag—as even more money is allocated to the overvalued and even less is allocated to the undervalued stocks. The Fundamental Index advantage turns the whole notion of passive investing upside down: No longer is the index fund an inferior choice in inefficient markets where the potential returns from active management are greatest. Its benefits are greatest where the opportunities to add value are greatest!

Managing money is an endeavor in trust. The vast majority of assets that managers oversee—pensions, foundations, individual retirement accounts (IRAs), 401(k) accounts, college tuition funds—are intended to enrich the lives of our clients and our communities. With $10 trillion and more in assets serving socially important goals, this is serious money indeed. Those we serve expect diligence and a steadfast desire to seek the most efficient manner in which to achieve their investment goals. With the Fundamental Index strategy, investors no longer have to allocate to an index fund that overweights every overvalued security and underweights every undervalued security. The return drag from capitalization weighting is no longer a necessary evil for investors seeking low-cost stock market exposure. There is now a choice for investors seeking an efficient index fund in an inefficient market. There is a better way.

Investors' Greatest Errors

. . . [I]n the short term, the stock market behaves like a voting machine, but in the long term it acts like a weighing machine.
—Benjamin Graham & David Dodd
Security Analysis, 1934

As long-term investors, we are confronted with a large shortfall between likely future portfolio returns and what we might hope to achieve. With the stellar stock market returns of the 1980s and 1990s—clearly evident in our rear view mirror—most investors now plan on at least 10 percent returns going forward. Given the current market environment, it will be difficult for most investors to achieve these lofty return goals. Rather than ratchet down expectations and endure the associated belt tightening, investors increasingly turn to *alpha* (value added from investor skill) as the elixir to cure their long-term problems.

Meander through just about any investment publication and you cannot avoid the cascade of references to all things alpha—the quest for alpha, bids to increase alpha, alpha overlays, currency alpha, loosening constraints for alpha, and the list goes on. The concept is pervasive in today's investment landscape and contributes to the surge of interest in "alpha-friendly" asset classes such as private equity, real estate, and, most especially, hedge funds. There seems to be a tacit assumption that all efforts to find alpha will be successful that all alpha is positive. The very word *alpha,* like *chocolate* or *love,* seems to stimulate pheromones and trigger warm, happy thoughts. It is almost as if manager skill is a harvestable commodity. But it's not. Alpha is a two-edged sword. Positive alpha is wonderful; negative alpha is, most assuredly, not. There is an often-ignored symbiosis: The one cannot exist without the other.

Talking about alpha and pursuing alpha do not imply that it will be found. The quest for alpha is a zero-sum game—less costs—regardless of whether it is sought in a traditional or alternative structure, like a hedge fund. The quest for alpha incurs costs, which means that most alpha, net of those costs, is negative. While the herd is turning over every rock in search of positive alpha, we know with absolute certainty that *the majority of them won't find it.*

In investing, what is comfortable is rarely profitable. So, if the crowd is bent on unearthing positive alpha, our contrarian inclination points us in a different direction—identifying and eliminating *negative alpha.* Few of today's market participants are focusing aggressively on eliminating negative alpha. S*eeking out, identifying, and eliminating negative alpha is every bit as profitable as seeking out, identifying, and employing sources of positive alpha.*

Negative Alpha

We define *negative alpha* as the slippage investors incur unnecessarily in the ongoing management of their portfolios. A fancier term is *implementation shortfall.* Eliminating these various mistakes is not only profitable, it is also much easier than competing with the crowd of alpha chasers. Four major sources of negative alpha are worth noting. They are (1) overreliance on equity returns, (2) ignoring rebalancing opportunities, (3) chasing winners, and (4) capitalization weighting equity portfolios. Countless more—such as overpaying for investment products, which is discussed in subsequent chapters—also deserve consideration, but the four discussed here require considerably more effort than simply lining up expense ratios.

Overreliance on Equity Returns

"Equities for the long run" is a nearly universal mantra among investment advisers, but many other markets—such as commodities, emerging-market bonds, real estate, timberland, and private equity—also appear to offer a "risk premium." To be sure, finance theory tells us that these investments can't offer a risk premium for any "diversifiable" risk, but that's an ivory tower world, not the real world. An overreliance on equity allocations limits one's ability to reduce portfolio risk through diversification across these other asset classes.

One of the best-kept secrets in investing is the minuscule diversification achieved in the classic 60 percent equity/40 percent bonds balanced portfolio. Because of the stock market's significantly higher volatility, sizable equity moves will overwhelm bonds in this supposedly "balanced" portfolio. For this reason, the 60/40 mix has a 98 percent to 99 percent correlation with the S&P 500 Index! If one uses other "risky" markets opportunistically when they offer premium yields, and on a scale large enough to matter, one can earn equity-like returns at far lower risk than the 60/40 balanced portfolio.

Few investors have fond memories of the bear market of 2000 through 2002. Profit opportunities were hard to come by and losses plentiful. The bull market from late 2002 until mid-2007 barely recovered the equity market losses incurred from 2000 through 2002. But as Table 3.1 illustrates, for those who are not invested in an equity-dominated portfolio, especially those willing to stray outside of both mainstream stocks and mainstream bonds, many asset classes have delivered lofty returns. Nearly every category produced meaningful positive returns—except stocks and money market accounts. It was a bear market only for those wedded to an equity-centric "normal" portfolio. The problem with 2000 through 2002 was not a lack of return opportunities, but rather that almost everyone was wedded to an equity-centric portfolio, relying for risk reduction on supposed diversification benefits from small allocations to bonds and trivial allocations to other assets. Indeed, most people would be surprised to learn that the average return in this list of markets was essentially the same: 9.3 percent a year from 1995 to 2000 and 8.7 percent in the subsequent six years!

Overreliance on equities leads to "negative alpha" for investors. Comparing the traditional 60/40 stock/bond portfolio with an equally weighted portfolio of a wide array of dissimilar markets—real estate investment trusts (REITs), commodities, emerging-market bonds, and U.S. Treasury Inflation-Protected Securities (TIPS), for

Table 3.1   Return Opportunities from 1995 through 2006

	6-Year Returns (cumulative)		12-Year Characteristics	
Asset Class	2001–2006	1995–2000	Standard Deviation	Correlation with 60/40
Emerging-market stocks	*222%*	**−23%**	**23%**	68%
Real estate investment trusts (REITs)	*218*	82	14	32
Emerging-market bonds	*100*	*121*	13	59
Commodities + Treasury Inflation-Protected Securities (TIPS)	85	46	**16**	7
High-yield bonds	71	47	7	52
S&P 500 Equal Weight Index (SP EWI)	68	*179*	16	90
TIPS	52	**45**	6	*2*
Unhedged foreign bonds	52	49	5	*−6*
Convertible bonds	46	82	12	**75**
Long-term government bonds	45	86	8	*2*
Lehman Aggregate	38	62	*4*	10
Government National Mortgage Association (GNMA) bonds	36	64	*3*	15
S&P 500	**19**	*219*	**15**	**99**
Money markets	**18**	**38**	*1*	8
Hedged EAFE (Europe, Australasia, and the Far East)	**13**	61	**15**	70

Excluding SP EWI, **bold** = worst three; *italic* = best three.
Source: Research Affiliates, LLC.

example—we find this "All Assets" portfolio exceeds the 60/40 portfolio by more than 1 percentage point annually over the past decade, with about 20 percent less risk. Because the S&P 500 had scarcely any advantage over bonds in this span, our All Assets portfolio beats the S&P 500 by a similar margin, with half the risk. Figure 3.1 illustrates these results in a traditional risk-and-return chart. Adjusting both portfolios for risk, the Sharpe ratio for the All Assets portfolio of 0.58 trounces the Sharpe ratio for the 60/40 portfolio of 0.29. The return is higher and the risk is lower. That's true diversification.

Reducing this negative alpha comes with two caveats. First, not all investors can adopt the All Assets approach. Most of these alternative and niche asset categories cannot absorb massive new investments. The equity market is much larger than the market for emerging-market bonds and REITs. If tens of billions move into these markets, no problem. If the amount is measured in hundreds of billions, big problem! Second, if equities rise substantially, leaving other asset classes in the dust for a year or two, this portfolio will trail badly relative to equity-focused peers. So, moving toward this approach may lower the risk of huge portfolio swings but can incur significantly greater career or maverick risk. Nonetheless, in widening the opportunity set to include meaningful allocations to alternative strategies, we can avoid the negative alpha due to an

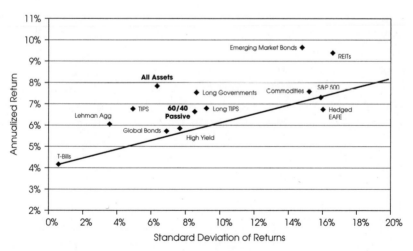

Figure 3.1   The Benefits of True Diversification from August 1996 through July 2007

Source: Research Affiliates, LLC.

overreliance on equities, lower our risk, and likely earn meaningful excess returns.

Ignoring Rebalancing Opportunities

Buying low and selling high—through rebalancing—is an ages-old adage for investors. But it's also a perennially underrated and underutilized investment strategy. Why? Because selling our most profitable investments runs contrary to human nature. And buying the bleakest underperformers is even more offensive to our natural instincts! Neglecting this simple exercise is an almost universal source of negative alpha, especially when risk is taken into account. The strong tendency of the capital markets to mean-revert—in so many ways—translates to incremental profits for those willing to sell their long-term winners and buy their long-term losers.

Rebalancing, however, is not an easy discipline to embrace. Let's consider Table 3.1 again. Imagine the courage required to sell the S&P 500 and buy emerging markets at the start of this decade, after six years in which U.S. stocks had risen 219 percent and emerging-market stocks had lost one-fourth of their value.

A disciplined rebalancing policy adds about 0.5 percentage point to risk-adjusted returns for a well-diversified portfolio.[1] Suppose you started in 1995 with $100 in each of the 15 asset classes listed in Table 3.1. By the end of the 12 years, your $1,500 would have grown to $4,412. If you rebalanced *only once* halfway through the 12 years, reallocating so that each market had one-fifteenth (6.7 percent) of the portfolio, you would have boosted your final wealth by $165, or 11 percent of the starting portfolio value! Remarkably, this result required one set of trades totaling merely 12 percent of the portfolio, which is effectively an average of 1 percent turnover per year. At least in this case, 1 percent increase in turnover average delivers a whopping 1 percentage point increase in annualized returns.

Of course, these excess returns accrued solely to those willing to look uncertainty in the eye and to follow through on selling the comfortable winners in order to buy more of the disasters! Eliminating the slippage is far easier said than done. The more comfortable course—"waiting for things to settle down"—allows the asset mix to drift with the whims of the capital markets, squanders rebalancing opportunities, and suffers the associated "negative alpha."

Chasing Winners

Chasing the latest investment craze is our path of least resistance because investors are bombarded with success stories at every turn—the neighbor who got in on the hot initial public offering, your brother-in-law with his 30 percent hedge fund return last year, and the mutual fund companies' advertising campaigns proclaiming their latest star performers (isn't it odd that they never seem to list their worst-performing funds?!). These siren songs lure us to chase the latest winners—whether asset classes, managed portfolios, or individual stocks. If we own a poorly performing fund, we will often then sell it at the bottom of its performance cycle after it's become a "proven" loser. Inevitably, it is replaced with a "good manager" who has experienced strong results recently. Of course, the performance of the replacement manager is all too often near his high and begins to recede not long after he is hired.

This practice is equivalent to selling low and buying high; its damage to investor wealth is devastating. Russel Kinnel (2005) of Morningstar quantified the negative alpha associated with chasing winners in a study of equity mutual funds. Kinnel found that over 10-year periods, the return earned by investors trailed the return on the *fund* for all 17 categories tested (see Table 3.2). The average slippage amounted to 2.8 percentage points annually—a damning indictment of investors' tendency to chase recent performance.

The mathematics behind this shortfall is simple. Consider a small fund with $100 million of assets and an excellent three-year return of 20 percent per year. Investors take note and, consistent with observed behavior, move money into this hot new portfolio so that over the next three years, the fund's asset base swells to $1 billion. Meanwhile, the strong performance evaporates and the fund finishes with a 0 percent return in the next three years. On a time-weighted basis, the fund delivered an average of just under 10 percent per year, compounded. But on a dollar-weighted basis, which is what the individual investor experiences, the fund earned less than 2 percent, indicating a slippage of nearly 8 percentage points per year.

Professional investors are as likely to succumb to this behavior as individual investors. Imagine a pension officer in 2000 or 2001 recommending an investment in a new asset class, emerging-market value stocks, with the following message: "Emerging market stocks have performed particularly badly over the past seven years, losing

Table 3.2   Chasing Winners: Dollar-Weighted versus Time-Weighted Returns

	Dollar-Weighted 10-Year Return	Official 10-Year Return	Gap
Large value	9.60%	10.02%	–0.40%
Large blend	7.46%	9.05%	–1.59%
Large growth	4.35%	7.76%	–3.41%
Mid value	10.43%	12.16%	–1.73%
Mid blend	10.59%	11.41%	–0.82%
Mid growth	6.32%	8.84%	–2.53%
Small value	11.64%	13.63%	–2.00%
Small blend	8.95%	11.32%	–2.37%
Small growth	5.35%	8.41%	–3.06%
Conservative allocation	7.21%	7.46%	–0.25%
Moderate allocation	7.27%	8.43%	–1.16%
Communications	3.00%	8.37%	–5.37%
Financials	12.81%	14.36%	–1.55%
Health	8.54%	12.49%	–3.95%
Natural resources	10.31%	12.37%	–2.06%
Real estate	13.43%	15.40%	–1.97%
Technology	–5.67%	7.68%	–13.35%

Data through April 30, 2005.

Source: Russel Kinnel (2005). Morningstar, Inc. All Rights Reserved. Reprinted by permission of Morningstar.

a fourth of their value in the face of a global bull market of historic proportions. Valuations in this category are at historical lows, especially relative to those here in the United States, where we have our largest investments. I thus propose initiating a 10 percent allocation to emerging markets. I've also identified the manager to handle this new assignment. Practicing a deep value orientation, they have underperformed the emerging market index by nearly 10 percent annually over the past five years. So I think there is a good chance that the next five years could be particularly profitable for their discipline."

At the time, search activity was still buzzing for U.S. growth managers, with impressive three- and five-year annualized gains. Accordingly, the pension officer was more likely to face termination, with such a "reckless" recommendation, than have his idea adopted. Yet, emerging-market value stocks went on to post a cumulative gain of 500 percent over the next five years versus an essentially flat return for developed-market equities.

The urge to act on recent successes and abandon yesterday's laggards is so powerful that most investors, individual and institutional alike, lose the requisite patience and miss a large part of the equity market's return.

Capitalization Weighting Equity Portfolios

The last source of negative alpha happens to occur in the asset class where most investors have most of their money—equities. The shortfall from traditional active management in stocks is well known: Over long periods of time, the combined handicaps of management fees and trading costs cause the average equity fund to underperform the S&P 500 by 0.5 percentage point to 2 percentage points per year. Kinnel finds that most investors lose *another* 2 percentage points to 3 percentage points trading into and out of these funds. These facts have driven more and more investors toward index funds.

But equity index funds also incur a stealth form of slippage. It's hidden because these funds are measured against their own indexes! Capitalization-weighted index funds chase performance, allocating more of our money to recent winners and less to recent losers. A stock that doubles in price gets double the weight solely because it has doubled in price. To be sure, we're not *buying* more as a stock soars, but we most assuredly are *owning* more. How did Cisco Systems' weight in the S&P 500 increase from 0.4 percent to 4.0 percent in the last three years of the bubble? Its weight rose 10-fold because its price had risen 10-fold relative to the rest of the market. Ironically, as its price then cratered, it eventually delivered growth in profits, sales, and book value well ahead of the broad economy— but not enough to justify its astronomical multiples at its peak.

Virtually all traditional indexes and their associated index funds and exchange-traded funds use market capitalization, the total value that Wall Street assigns to the enterprise, to determine the weight of each security. Those shares that are priced above their eventual intrinsic value (think AOL, Cisco, or Lucent Technologies in early 2000) will have an erroneously high capitalization and, therefore, a large index weighting. An indexed portfolio weighted by capitalization will inherently invest most of our money in stocks that are trading above their intrinsic values, each of which will eventually underperform as the market seeks out that intrinsic value. This happens even though we cannot know which companies compose this troublesome list. Stocks priced below eventual intrinsic value will have an erroneously low capitalization, hence index weighting, and will offer a performance boost. But they carry a weight in the portfolio that is correspondingly too small. The relative losses of the overpriced stocks overwhelm the relative gains of the underpriced stocks *because the underpriced stocks constitute less of the portfolio.*

Because alpha is usually measured relative to "the market"— which is cap-weighted—a cap-weighted index cannot have a positive (or negative) alpha. But capitalization weighting—because it links portfolio weight to security price so that more than half of a cap-weighted portfolio will be in overpriced stocks—introduces a return drag and a negative alpha *relative to its opportunity set.*

The Fundamental Index methodology avoids this structural return drag. By weighting securities on such fundamental metrics of company size as sales or earnings, we sever the link between allocation to a stock and its over- or undervaluation. Using a valuation-indifferent weighting scheme should leave the resulting portfolio with roughly equal parts of overpriced and underpriced securities, *even without our knowing which ones are which!* As these pricing errors are corrected, the relative gains and losses cancel each other out.

John Maynard Keynes was not only one of the most important economists, he was also a legendary investor. He liked to say that he chose not to invest in speculations and expectations; he preferred to invest in what companies own and produce. What better reflects the market's constantly shifting consensus for "speculations and expectations" than market-cap weighting? What better reflects what companies own, produce, *and deliver to their shareholders* than weighting by companies' sales, profits, net assets (book value), and dividends?

Practicing What We Preach

Most wealth advisers have seen their clients drawn into the first three errors, the first three sources of negative alpha. Strong returns in equities, or any investment category for that matter, tempt clients to forgo proper diversification. The stellar results of recent winners can make them irresistible, luring investors to chase performance—a nasty habit in this mean-reverting world.

Rebalancing often implies adding assets to the worst performers, what some refer to as "watering the weeds." Of course, as any gardener knows, weeds can grow like crazy!

Explicit investment policies are necessary to mitigate these three costly temptations—to overweight equities, to chase recent returns, and to forgo rebalancing. The resulting stable asset allocation structures, automatic rebalancing procedures, and long-term performance evaluation criteria are time tested and theoretically sound. Indeed, one of the main contributions the best wealth advisers make to their clients' success is to introduce these policies and, in so doing, help their clients avoid simple and costly errors. The policies can help us and our clients to exhibit patience, discipline, and commitment—three traits vital to investment success.

The return drag associated with capitalization weighting, however, is a relatively new idea, largely because we don't notice this drag if we're measuring ourselves by the selfsame indexes! The notion that capitalization weighting imposes a drag on our results—relative to our opportunity set—has stirred considerable controversy in the practitioner and academic communities. The very idea challenges some of the most beloved core precepts of modern finance and calls into question the merits of some of the most respected (and largest) products in the investment world. But much of the advantage of the Fundamental Index strategy is attributable to the fact that traditional indexes ignore the simple Investing 101 tactics we just reviewed.

The tendency to allocate more to recent darlings—and to bypass rebalancing—can also lead to a relatively less diversified equity portfolio in times of bubbles and fads. As a few favorite economic sectors surge in price, a natural side effect is a more heavily concentrated cap-weighted index portfolio, directly reflecting a more concentrated market. In extreme instances, such as the technology bubble, the outstanding diversification of our traditional index funds is compromised. In the past half century, no market sector that exceeded 25 percent of the S&P 500 ever delivered enough future success to justify that immense allocation. Nor has any market sector that exceeded twice its *economic* scale ever produced market-beating returns over the subsequent decade. Technology in 2000 was only the latest victim of this pattern.

Why should advisers emphasize the time-tested methods of diversification, rebalancing, and not chasing winners in their clients' overall asset allocation, then turn around and invest in an index fund that largely ignores those methods within the stock market itself?

Conclusion

The Fundamental Index concept, in contrast to capitalization weighting, does not chase recent returns. It practices disciplined rebalancing back to the economic scale of each enterprise, and it achieves reliable diversification. Stocks that double in price aren't automatically given twice the weight—unless their economic footprint in the economy has also doubled. The annual rebalance ensures discipline and avoids the return-chasing behavior inherent in traditional cap-weighted indexes. Outperformers are rebalanced back to their economic size, with the proceeds invested in shares that have recently fared poorly relative to their operating results. Because most enterprises' share prices loosely follow their economic scale, annual turnover is low—almost as low as with capitalization weighting. Most importantly, weighting by fundamental metrics bypasses the pricing bubbles—whether small, medium, or large—that so regularly plague the stock market.

The Virtues of Index Funds

Most investors, both institutional and individual, will find that the best way to own common stocks is through an index fund that charges minimal fees.

—Warren Buffett
1996 Berkshire Hathaway Annual Report
Chairman's Letter

With more than $5 trillion indexed globally by the end of 2006, growing by at least a half trillion a year, it is safe to say that indexing has caught on all over the world. And for many compelling reasons. In this chapter, we present the many merits of index funds and show why this simple investment strategy has become such a valuable tool for investors. To properly frame its many benefits, we compare the index fund with its primary competition—the legions of actively managed funds.

Some of our critics think that we're attacking the legacy of the pioneers of modern finance and of the indexing world. We disagree. We think we're building on the solid foundations they put into place. By recognizing that simple pricing error—noise—is a part of the real world, we sow seeds that may move us back toward Bill Sharpe's capital asset pricing model (CAPM) and its single-factor risk model. Multiple risk factors, which have been identified as an Achilles' heel for CAPM, may just be a manifestation of pricing errors. By recognizing that many of the best active strategies are built on a foundation of value, of rebalancing, and of contra-trading against the market's most extreme bets, we help to bring these expensive active strategies under Jack Bogle's umbrella of low-cost, low-turnover indexing *without* sacrificing their potential for superior performance.

Traditional indexing in its current form has a host of advantages well worth preserving. By respecting and building on such a strong foundation, we think we create an even better equity index solution. In short, we see the Fundamental Index concept as a sensible evolution in equity indexing.

Appeal of Equity Investing

Stocks are arguably the main engine that allows investment managers—and their clients—to reach their investment goals. Equity investors participate in the rewards and the risks associated with entrepreneurial capitalism. This economic participation has paid off handsomely for many, many years. Since 1926, the stock market, as measured by the S&P 500 Index, has produced an average return of more than 10 percent per year, compounded—more than twice the return for a portfolio of long-term U.S. government bonds.

Of course, this reward wasn't free: Equities are inherently riskier than bonds. Remember that when a company falters, the bond-holders are higher in the bankruptcy food chain and are to be paid first. The equity shareholders are entitled to whatever is left over after the bondholders are paid. In addition, equities typically have a lower yield than bonds (although this has not always been true!), so equity investors are heavily reliant on future growth to make up the yield difference.

Most advisers use the statistical measure "standard deviation" to quantify the level of risk embedded in an investment. Standard deviation measures how much the returns fluctuate around the mean. A higher standard deviation indicates a wider band and thus greater probability of a loss (on the negative side of the band) or a gain (on the positive side of the band). Of course, lofty returns rarely elicit risk concerns, even though they should. For the vast majority of investors, protecting against downside risk is the critical element of portfolio planning. But no investor in the stock market should ever forget that risk can cut both ways. Investors may, indeed *should,* earn a premium for equity ownership *because they are willing to bear that downside risk.*

Equities periodically incur nasty performance downturns, with the tempests occasionally lasting years. Yet with proper diversification, the long-term investor can weather these inevitable storms and still earn outsized returns. The S&P 500, with an annual standard deviation of 15 percent in the 60 years since the end of World War II, has delivered an average return of 11.5 percent per year, compounded, and experienced 12 years of negative total returns and only scant 2 years in which losses exceeded 20 percent.

Of course, part of the reason for this superb history is that share prices have risen relative to the growth of earnings and dividends. At the start of the 1950s, stocks yielded just under 8 percent on average, which means that investors wanted their money back in the form of dividend distributions in just 13 years. Today, stocks yield 1.9 percent, which means that investors are content to see return of their investment capital in 52 years! That quadrupling of the amount that we're willing to pay for each dollar of dividend income contributes a good chunk of the index's lofty historical return.

The incremental return difference between stocks and government bonds (or cash) is called the "equity risk premium." Although the risk premium can and does vary widely over time, it has averaged 300 to 600 basis points per year over the past 25, 50, 100, and even 200 years. The consistency of that premium over long periods of time leads to a widely held view that stock market investors are *entitled* to an extra 500 basis points per year for bearing equity market risk. But keep in mind that risk is symmetrical. In the nineteenth century—a 100-year span—stocks beat bonds by *less than 100 basis points a year;* indeed, they offered the *same* return for the 70 years ended in 1872. Drilling deeper, we find that the 70-year period from 1802 to 1872 consists of a 55-year secular bear market in which stocks lagged bonds relentlessly and a recovery that finally repaired the damage over the remaining 15 years. So, when people speak confidently of "stocks for the long run," they must be referring to a multigenerational long run in order to have real confidence in their ultimate success!

Even so, for those with a sufficiently long investment horizon, compound interest—which Albert Einstein called "man's greatest invention"—translates any "risk premium" for stocks into exponential differences in ending wealth. An initial investment of $100 in

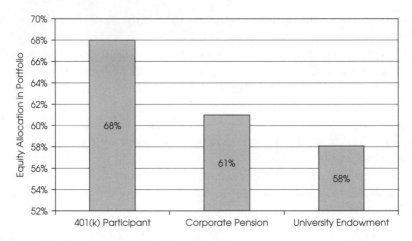

Figure 4.1 Average Equity Allocation

Notes: 2006 EBRI/ICI database for 401(k), 2007 Milliman Pension Funding Study for Corporate Pension, and 2006 NACUBO Endowment Study for University Endowment.
Source: Research Affiliates, LLC.

1802 compounded at the historical return for the broad U.S. stock market would have grown to very nearly *$1 billion* by mid-2007. That same money invested in 10-year U.S. government bonds would have produced a balance of $2.3 million. The bond return is impressive, but the differential is 400-fold in a little more than 200 years. Because most of us expect the future to resemble this long-term history, stocks constitute the lion's share of our portfolios, as shown in Figure 4.1.

Equity Investing Choices

Investors wishing to take advantage of this tremendous wealth creation machine can choose two distinct paths: active management or passive management. Of course, there is a whole array of gradations in between (enhanced index, conservative or aggressive active strategies, long-short or 130/30 strategies, etc.). For our purposes in this chapter, we will focus on these two primary paths.

Theory says that prices are the market's best estimate of a company's fair value, which should be the properly discounted present value of its expected future cash flows to its investors. Investors who believe prices do not always reflect intrinsic value—*and that they can identify the winners*—will tend to prefer active investment strategies.

Those who believe that prices are reasonable approximations of intrinsic value, or who lack the time or resources to identify mispricing, should prefer to own the aggregate market through passive investment strategies.

Volumes have been written about the superiority of one approach over the other. We aren't so audacious as to attempt to settle this colossal debate once and for all. Suffice it to say that each approach has potential merit as part of client portfolios, although active management faces two daunting hurdles. First, active managers cannot collectively outpace the indexes. Relative performance is a zero-sum game: any winners must have losers on the other side of their trades. Indeed, the higher costs for active management make this a negative sum game. Second, our ability to win with active management hinges on identifying the superior managers *in advance.* That being said, a brief discussion of active and passive investing will help us identify the advantages of each we wish to preserve in any new indexing approach.

Active Management

Active managers start with the premise that one can outperform "the market" by actively allocating to stocks that are underpriced relative to their "fair values." To find these opportunities, they typically engage in research to identify stocks that are poised for higher appreciation than the market.[1] If the insights derived from this research are sound, the manager's portfolio will outperform a representative index, such as the S&P 500 or the Russell 1000 Index.

The approaches used in the quest for these undervalued stock market opportunities are almost as varied as the managers themselves. Value managers hunt for temporarily distressed and underpriced shares; momentum players seek to ride the recent winners; and growth managers seek to identify companies with growth prospects that exceed consensus expectations. Some managers engage in technical analysis—relying on charts, trend lines, moving averages, and trading ranges. Others use bottom-up security analysis, with a platoon of analysts scrubbing balance sheets and footnotes, calling suppliers and customers, and interviewing company management teams. Top-down managers focus first on the global economy to determine the current stage of the business cycle and, from there, allocate to the sectors and industries that are expected to outperform in their worldview. Many managers develop broad secular themes, such as the aging of the Baby Boomers or the globalization of world trade, in positioning their portfolios. Quantitative firms develop complex computer models using vast amounts of security data that, in their determination, should reveal mispricing opportunities.

These research activities are then packaged into a wide variety of investment products with various degrees of expected outperformance. Concentrated managers invest in a small group of securities (often fewer than 30 stocks). They are seeking large excess returns at the expense of wide swings (high tracking error) when measured against the market indexes. In contrast, enhanced indexes, with a multitude of tiny active bets and hundreds of individual stock holdings, intend to closely track the market averages in the hopes of achieving smaller, but more reliable, value added. Falling somewhere in the middle is the traditional active portfolio, with perhaps 40 to 80 securities diversified by security and sector bets.

Passive Management

Passive investing is based on the premise that stock prices are reasonably accurate representations of intrinsic value—or at least that the consensus expectations of the market are more accurate than the assessments of any single investment manager. Accordingly, passive investing assumes that outperforming the market through active stock selection is very difficult, especially net of costs. Passive investing involves "owning the market" without a view on the prices of the individual stocks. Typically, people invest passively through funds that closely match a published market index—that is, they buy *index funds*.

Index funds do not require analysts to research companies or the economy or traders to monitor the daily price fluctuations for entry and exit points. They are designed to reflect the broad market or a specific segment of the market, such as small companies or growth stocks. To achieve their ends, index funds first define the *market*—for the S&P 500, the market is defined as "the leading 500 companies in leading industries of the U.S. economy," for the Russell 1000, the definition is "the largest 1,000 companies by float-adjusted stock market capitalization," and for the Wilshire 5000 Index, the definition is "the largest 5,000 stocks by capitalization." The individual constituents are then weighted by either their stock market capitalization or their available float.[2] For example, if the S&P 500 has a total capitalization of about $15 trillion and Exxon Mobil Corporation has a market capitalization of $450 billion, Exxon Mobil's weight in the S&P 500 will be approximately 3 percent. This arithmetic doesn't require a raft of PhD-level analysts; a clerk with a calculator can do the job just fine!

The One Guarantee in Investments—Cost Matters

Jack Bogle, who popularized indexing for the masses beginning in the 1970s, is fond of referring to the CMH, the "cost matters hypothesis" that he describes as more important than the EMH, the efficient market hypothesis. He's absolutely right! From the perspective of the individual investor contemplating his or her eventual wealth, it is hard to argue with Bogle's thesis. After all, the returns the investor gets to keep are the returns after asset management fees and expenses (and, for that matter, taxes and inflation). As investors, we cannot know what those returns will be. But we can know that higher fees require higher returns if we want to break even on the decision to use a high-fee fund. And, as many studies have shown, high fees do not go hand-in-hand with higher returns.

Index funds are an efficient, low-cost way of gaining broad market exposure. By design, index funds are much cheaper to run than active strategies, and the savings are passed on to investors in the form of lower fees. The goal is to achieve the return of the market. No research is necessary to determine which stocks are likely to outperform. Free of overhead such as analyst salaries and data services, which are associated with active management research, the index fund can charge next to nothing in management fees.

But the cost advantage doesn't stop there. One of the beauties of capitalization weighting is that trading and the resulting brokerage costs are virtually eliminated. With companies' weights based on capitalization, the portfolio self-adjusts to reflect price movements, so the manager has no need to turn over the portfolio in any meaningful way. Aside from adjustments related to corporate actions (mergers, bankruptcies, new share issuance or buybacks, etc.), the only time the index fund manager is required to rebalance the portfolio is at the time of index reconstitution, when a batch of newly eligible stocks replaces those that no longer meet the index's criteria.[3]

Table 4.1   Passive Beats Active in U.S. Markets

	10 Years	15 Years
S&P 500	8.21%	10.88%
Average equity fund[a]	7.80%	10.22%
Index advantage	0.41%	0.66%

[a]Consists of Morningstar Large Blend category.
Note: Time periods ending March 31, 2007.
Source: Morningstar.

In an ultra-competitive market such as investment management, these cost advantages make the index fund a formidable competitor when compared with actively managed funds over long time periods. Indeed, most active managers fail to deliver on their promise of beating the market, despite their massive research budgets. Table 4.1 shows that over the recent 15-year period, the average equity mutual fund trailed the S&P 500 by 70 basis points. *And that's for the survivors!* A 2000 study by Arnott, Berkin, and Ye shows that when the failed funds (those that did not survive) are included, the shortfall is 200 to 400 basis points.

Net of taxes, the gap widens. Indexes don't need to sell their winners because they don't do any rebalancing! This means that we don't realize gains—and incur the resulting capital gains tax obligations—on stocks that have soared to lofty heights. Active managers sell stocks that hit their price targets or stocks the managers think are no longer priced attractively relative to other new opportunities. As a result, most of the return earned on actively managed portfolios is fully taxable, whereas most of the return on index funds is tax deferred.

The disappointing after-fee performance of active managers isn't restricted to the United States. Table 4.2 illustrates a similar

Table 4.2   Passive Beats Active in International Markets

	10 Years	15 Years
MSCI World ex U.S.	7.97%	9.56%
Average International Equity Fund[a]	7.15%	9.31%
Index Advantage	0.82%	0.25%

[a]Consists of Morningstar Foreign Large Blend category.
Note: Time periods ending May 31, 2007.
Source: Morningstar.

failure of international managers' returns to measure up to their benchmarks, again ignoring the presumably dreadful results of the funds that failed.

Index Fund Advantages

The index fund's long-term return advantage is impressive, even overwhelming. The problem is not that active managers lack talent. The superiority of the index is *structural*: the advent of the mutual fund and the growth in the professional asset management industry has led this hard-working group of investment professionals to, for all intents and purposes, *become the market*. The total market is capitalization-weighted, as are the indexers. Take away the index funds, and what's left is essentially the same portfolio. The aggregate portfolio that active managers collectively own—give or take a little wiggle room—is that selfsame index! So the average active manager—dollar weighted—should have the same returns as the index funds before costs. But active managers' costs and fees are higher, so their average net returns to investors must be lower.

The fact that the average active manager can't seem to beat the market does not mean that no active manager can beat the market. It just means that the quest for alpha—for outperformance relative to the market—is a zero-sum game, minus costs, and that you can't win unless there's a loser on the other side of your trades. In much the same way, the average winning percentage for all of the teams in professional baseball can't be anything but .500. This simple fact doesn't mean that the players on the last-place team are lousy players; nor does it prevent the best teams from winning. In asset management, half are going to win and half are going to lose *before costs*. After fees and expenses, the coin-flip proposition of active management becomes negative, leading to the stark comparisons we've already explored.[4] The human tendency to chase the hot managers, funds, and strategies just exacerbates the problem (Kinnel, 2005).

Certainly, some managers have outperformed the market averages over long periods of time. Ironically, the fact that *everyone* seems to cite Warren Buffett as an example shows how very rare this talent is! Finding these managers with hindsight is easy, but it's very difficult to determine who those managers will be in advance. To find these managers, an investor needs to gauge whether a manager's strong track record is the result of above-average skill or just being on the lucky side of a random coin toss. The investor also needs to gauge whether the historically successful manager is still driven to win.

Ideally, the investor should not limit the search for skill to those managers with a strong historical track record. There are bound to be managers who have above-average skill among those with disappointing results—they just happened to be on the wrong side of a random coin toss. Consider a manager who has exceptional skill—skill sufficient to deliver an average annual excess return of 2 percentage points above that of the stock market, with variability of just 4 percent in that impressive relative performance, for an "information ratio" of 0.5 (2 percent excess return divided by 4 percent tracking error). This manager will beat the market roughly 7 years out of 10. But this manager—despite skill that has never disappeared—will also lag the market in roughly 1 *full decade* out of 10. It will take an average of 16 years to determine with 95 percent confidence, based on the manager's track record, whether the manager is skilled.

Adding to the difficulty of finding active managers who will be able to outperform in the future is a second problem: Is this manager, after 16 years of success, so wealthy that he or she coasts on that past record, spending more time on the yacht than in the office? Does the manager lack the drive that fueled the 16 years of success? It is mighty hard to determine the answer to these questions in time to make the appropriate investment decision.

So, how long would it take to determine whether a "typical" manager has skill? For a manager with an information ratio of 0.3—the median for surviving large-cap equity investors in the eVestment Alliance institutional database over the 10 years ending June 30, 2007—it would take roughly 44 years of performance data! No wonder so many people give up on the task of picking winning active managers, opting instead for dull, reliable index funds!

Clearly, the *average* equity investor is likely to do better in low-cost index funds than by trying to pick the best active managers. A number of additional advantages also accrue to index investors. These stealth benefits aren't as obvious as the cost comparison but nonetheless contribute to the overall attractiveness of the index fund. They include the following:

- Liquidity and immense investment capacity.
- Diversification and representation of the broad market.
- Low turnover and low taxes on realized gains.
- Ease of implementation and monitoring.

Liquidity and Capacity

Because most index funds are cap-weighted and broadly diversified, the vast majority of index fund assets are in the largest-cap stocks, which makes them very liquid. The mega-caps have the largest daily trading volume and suffer the lowest price impact from large flows. As a result, index funds can easily meet redemption requests or absorb vast sums on any given day with a minimal impact on pricing.

In addition, because index funds own the entire market (more or less), they are scalable to immense capacity. Trillions of dollars are invested in cap-weighted indexes. They do not disrupt the markets—except in the relative value of stocks in the index and stocks that are left out—because they mirror the markets. The market looks like the cap-weighted index. By the end of 2006, $5 trillion was indexed worldwide. Doubling that sum would cause little disruption, at least in the large-company arena. Because funds would be moved from active managers to passive indexes, and because active managers collectively own very nearly the same portfolio as the indexes, few companies would see large *net* trades.

Contrast this situation with that of active managers. Even the active managers who concentrate on large-cap portfolios run into liquidity and capacity issues because their portfolios, individually, look so different from the market (as well they should, given their mission of beating the market!). Their research is designed to identify the most undervalued securities, so they hold fewer names. Common sense dictates that having fewer holdings translates to less capacity. Furthermore, when a manager takes a large position in a small-cap stock, liquidity is directly affected. These intertwined issues make historical active manager performance difficult to judge. Was the manager's strong record built on a smaller asset base? Can the manager continue to perform with 10 times the assets? Both are valid questions for active managers but rarely need to be asked of the index fund because of its liquidity, capacity, and infrequent trading.

Built-in Diversification

Indexes were originally designed to be barometers of market performance. As such, they deliberately span the full market. With the advent of performance measurement in the early 1970s, they also became benchmarks for actively managed portfolios. Both purposes require the index to be representative of the broad market, essentially the investor's opportunity set. Because the broad market is cap-weighted, so too are the indexes. Because they span the full market, the benchmark indexes, such as the S&P 500 and Russell 1000, have broad exposure to all major economic sectors, scores of industries, and many hundreds of individual holdings. They are far more diversified on this measure than active managers.

Although the best indexes mirror the broad market with near-perfect neutrality, they do *not* mirror the broad economy—or even the publicly traded portion of the economy. Companies trade at different valuation multiples, reflecting different consensus expectations for future growth. Quite simply, companies with strong growth prospects tend to have larger market capitalization—relative to the size of the company—than like-sized companies with weaker growth prospects. As a result, the cap-weighted indexes favor the growth companies—or, more accurately, the companies that investors collectively believe will grow faster. As a result, the indexes mirror the consensus expectations for the look of the *future* economy. As we examine later, this means that the cap-weighted indexes probably are disproportionately invested in the best companies—but not necessarily the best stocks or investments!

Low Turnover, Low Taxes

The low turnover of index portfolios has two direct benefits: lower implementation costs and lower taxes (for taxable portfolios). Remember, the only time a stock is sold in a cap-weighted portfolio is when it is dropped from the index because its market capitalization has fallen below the cutoff, or through merger, acquisition, or bankruptcy. Because these dropped stocks have typically fallen in price—apart from mergers and acquisitions, which must be sold—the realized gain, if one exists, is tiny.

The situation is quite the opposite for active managers. When an active manager has successfully identified underpriced stocks

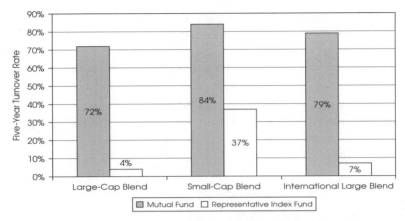

Figure 4.2   Average Turnover Rates for Morningstar Categories versus Representative Index Funds, 2002 through 2006
Notes: Based on Morningstar data. Turnover is average of five calendar years ending 2006. Representative index funds include Schwab S&P 500 Index Investor Class for Large Blend, Schwab Small Cap Index for Small Blend, and Vanguard Developed Markets Index for International Large Blend.
Source: Research Affiliates, LLC.

that subsequently increase to their "fair value," these stocks are sold, often for a sizable, realizable gain. New stocks are purchased to replace the sales, resulting in much higher turnover than the indexers have. This fact is evident from a quick comparison of annual turnover rates of different mutual fund categories versus representative index funds in Figure 4.2.

The gap between index funds and active managers only widens when taxes are taken into consideration. A 2000 study by Arnott, Berkin, and Ye found that only 14 percent of actively managed equity mutual funds managed to outperform the Vanguard 500 Index Fund after capital gains and dividend taxes over a 20-year period were taken into account.[5] And these were the survivors! It's a fair bet that most of the failed funds underperformed. The tax man *loves* investors who rely on actively managed funds.

Ease of Use

Perhaps the most overlooked benefit of the cap-weighted index fund is its ease of implementation and monitoring. Picking and following an index fund manager, whether based on the S&P 500, the Russell 1000, or any other conventional index, is a straightforward proposition.[6] They are all investing in the same portfolios! The difference between superb and sloppy implementation is relatively modest, so the index fund track records are much the same. With identical stocks and weights, fees are often the only criterion on which investors can make a decision. If there's one guarantee in the investment world, it is this: All things being equal (and with an index fund, they pretty much are), the lowest-cost provider wins. So, investors can simply line up the annual expenses and pick the cheapest option, which typically is the fund with the most assets.[7] The same does not apply for active managers, enhanced indexes, and specialty indexes.

Evaluating index fund performance is relatively easy because the standard is fixed, published, and transparent. After costs, the main relevant question is how well the index fund tracked the intended index (tracking error). There need be no performance attribution and no discussion of individual portfolio laggards. Style drift is a nonissue; style is defined by the index being benchmarked. While that benchmark may have plenty of "style drift" relative to the composition of the economy as it tracks the shifting preferences and expectations of the broad market, this style drift is invisible because the fund and its benchmark are the same thing! The Russell 1000 Value Index becomes the definition of large-cap value because a fund based on such an index will never suddenly drift to growth *relative to that index*.[8]

Monitoring is made easy also because investors in indexed funds don't have to worry that their managers or the management processes have suddenly "lost their touch." Issues such as portfolio manager departures are not stressful because the list of stocks and the rationale for owning them remain unchanged. Ownership changes at the firm level aren't a cause for concern. Neither is the possibility of a fund that has grown beyond its capacity suddenly going into "closet indexing" mode by tying its holdings, sector weights, and thus returns to the benchmark. With an index fund, we're already there. And because portfolio managers have little to no discretion, conflict-of-interest and other agency issues are largely nonexistent. This advantage saves precious investment committee or client time for more value-adding pursuits, such as asset allocation, goal setting, or golf!

Avoiding the Performance Game

One of the biggest costs to investors over time is losing at the "performance game." Consider Figure 4.3, from a published piece by Vanguard founder Jack Bogle, that shows the returns of the Vanguard Index Fund, the average active equity mutual *fund,* and the average equity mutual fund *investor* over a 20-year period. The investment industry is obsessed with performance measurement, with each component of client portfolios run through a battery of analytics, typically quarterly. The resulting analysis paints a vivid picture of the active managers' scorecard:

> Last quarter, Mutual Fund A placed in the 75th percentile of similarly managed funds, and it trailed its primary style benchmark by 250 basis points and its secondary benchmark by 150 basis points. Furthermore, we find 85 percent of the relative shortfall is due to poor stock selection, ironically the manager's professed area of strength.

These objective cut-and-dried figures tell us nothing about whether the shortfall was bad luck or a lack of skill. In reality, it is nothing more than data, indeed noisy data, describing a short span

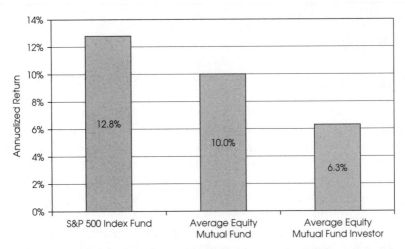

Figure 4.3   Costs to Playing the Performance Game, 1983 through 2003
Source: Bogle (2005).

of mostly meaningless results. Nearly all investment strategies have experienced a certain cyclicality, with periods of good performance and bad performance. All too often, investors—armed with their seemingly irrefutable performance reports—terminate a fund at the bottom of its cycle, after its relative returns have been lagging.

This shouldn't come as a surprise. Mutual fund companies heavily advertise *their most recent winners.* The financial media also tout the latest outperformers in such terms as "the five best funds to pick up laggard portfolios."[9] Mutual fund rating companies contribute to the performance game: Nearly every 401(k) sponsor is seeking to offer Five-Star funds. Collectively, these influences lure investors like the sirens' song to switch from the poor performers in their portfolios, even though, all too often, the investor is better off staying put.

Passive investors can easily avoid the performance game. Passive strategies replicate the market, and the market cannot collectively underperform itself. By construction, index funds virtually never show up in the bottom decile of peer-group rankings over long periods. As a result, index funds rarely find themselves on a performance "watch" list, and investors committed to passive strategies are less likely to replace their index funds with (currently) top-performing active funds.

The performance game is played not only by individual investors. The large pension plans, even with their savvy investment staffs and consultants, often make the same mistake. A recent study (Goyal and Wahal, 2005) found that in the three years after transition, fired managers outperform the corresponding hired managers by 1.6 annually on average.

Concluding Point

In a sense, a commitment to active management is a lot like a day spent fishing. Each day is unique: The tides, water clarity, currents, cloud cover, temperature, and a host of other factors cause a large degree of unpredictability from one day to the next. The fish may have been jumping in the boat yesterday but are elusive today. With constantly changing conditions, catching fish (or finding excess returns) isn't assured each time out. If the fishing was best in the northwest corner of the bay yesterday, that tells us little about where the fish will be biting tomorrow. This unpredictability doesn't mean that the fish (or investment manager skill) have vanished. But patience and time are required to hook both. Like the can of tuna on the grocery market shelf, the index fund is always there—not as exciting as fishing, but cheap, utterly reliable, and good for you.

Human nature conditions people to shun disappointment and seek out success. In investing, the urge to act on underperformance (and for many managers, outside pressure from clients) is so powerful that most investors, individual and institutional alike, lose the requisite patience and squander a large part of the equity market's return. By and large, however, it is much easier for the index fund investor to steer clear of the performance game.

The deeper we delve into the advantages of indexing, the more the superiority of the index fund becomes apparent. Improving it is a daunting task. To merit serious consideration, any "new" index, no matter how compelling its advantages, needs to preserve the many benefits of the "old" indexes.

CHAPTER 5

The Index Fund's Achilles' Heel

Most of the time common stocks are subject to irrational and excessive price fluctuations in both directions as the consequence of the ingrained tendency of most people to speculate or gamble . . . to give way to hope, fear and greed.

—Benjamin Graham

Today's capitalization-weighted index funds are built on the foundation of theories developed in the 1950s and 1960s—theories and insights that led to Nobel Prizes and important innovations in how wealth is managed. The first significant work in this area was Harry Markowitz's seminal paper "Portfolio Selection," published in 1952, which elegantly formalized the concept of diversification. Markowitz's mean-variance framework shows investors and managers that portfolio volatility can be reduced through the addition of assets—even risky assets—that have low correlations with those already in the portfolio. Diversification means that holding a large basket of securities makes sense even if the investor possesses no special information about the stocks in the basket.

Merton Miller and Franco Modigliani later built on the work of Markowitz, demonstrating that, in the equilibrium world that they had constructed, capital structure (e.g., dividend policy and debt/equity decisions) does not matter. Subsequently, in 1963 through 1966, Bill Sharpe, Jan Mossin, John Lintner, and Jack Treynor independently developed the CAPM by extending Markowitz's portfolio choice mathematics into an equilibrium model. One of the predictions of the CAPM is that a broad-based cap-weighted portfolio will be mean-variance optimal: You can't beat the market without taking on more risk. This series of insights—and the mathematical tools that they spawned—led the Nobel committee to award the Nobel Prize (the first ever Nobel Prize in economics awarded to a finance professor) to Sharpe, Markowitz, and Miller. In a sense, the CAPM told the investment management community that in promoting the use of capitalization weighting for broad market indexes (which had begun only a few years earlier with the launch of the S&P 500 Index), the industry had inadvertently stumbled on the true and correct answer. We need explore no other metrics for index construction. Additionally, because the CAPM proves that the cap-weighted broad market portfolio is optimally diversified, a concentrated portfolio of *undervalued* stocks—even if we could reliably identify them in advance—might still underperform the S&P 500 because of a lack of diversification!

Considering these new insights, one need not be an efficient market fanatic to believe that indexing to the S&P 500 or the Russell 1000 Index might be the simplest—and best—investment solution in the equity space. Managers and investors who understood the mathematics of the CAPM soon realized that outperforming the S&P 500 might be harder than previously thought. This insight set in motion the indexing revolution.

Market Efficiency: Two Interpretations

The concept of efficient markets is central to much of modern finance. Analogous to a carpenter's hammer, it is a tool so critical to academia that many would be unable to perform without it. But the form of the concept is by no means uniformly accepted.

The drawing "My Wife and My Mother-in-Law" in Figure 5.1 illustrates, depending on the interpretation of the viewer, either a portrait of a young woman with pristine features or a portrait of an old woman with a long face (the chin of the former is the nose of the latter).[1] In the same manner, market efficiency can be viewed from two different angles depending on the frame of reference.

Figure 5.1   "My Wife and My Mother-in-Law"

One group of investors believes that markets are not efficient, that prices deviate from fair value, and that they can beat the market through stock selection. These investors actively manage their portfolios in an effort to add value.

The second group of investors believes that markets are efficient, that stock prices closely reflect intrinsic value, and that investors cannot beat the market through stock selection, so it is better to own the market. These investors passively manage their portfolios by buying and holding a diversified portfolio of assets reflecting the market, typically through owning index funds. Table 5.1 outlines these views.

At first glance, the evidence is strongly in favor of the indexers' view of the world. The data from the performance measurement and mutual fund tracking firms do not paint a picture favorable to active investing. On average, active managers collectively trail the S&P 500 after fees over the long term by 50 to 200

Table 5.1   Core Beliefs of Active Managers and Passive Indexers

Active Manager	Indexer
Prices deviate from intrinsic value.	Prices closely reflect intrinsic value.
Active managers can beat the market.	Active managers cannot beat the market.

Source: Research Affiliates, LLC.

basis points (or more!) annually. Does this suggest that the market is efficient? No! If the markets are cap-weighted and the indexes are cap-weighted, then what's left is much the same portfolio. Therefore, it is a tautology that active managers must *collectively* approximately match the market and the indexes, before costs. This means that they will *collectively* underperform net of fees. The fact that the average active manager cannot win says nothing *for or against* the notion that skilled active managers can win. The data merely suggest that indexing makes sense if we can't pick good active managers.

But what about the first core principle of active and passive investors—the existence, or not, of mispricing? Thus far, we have given some anecdotal examples of overpricing of individual securities—Cisco Systems, Nortel, Krispy Kreme Doughnuts, Amgen, Palm, and others—that appeared, after the fact, to have suffered significant errors in pricing (in fact, in some of these more flagrant cases, we might argue that the mispricings were also evident at the time). Of course, mispricings can also work in the opposite way—by undervaluing a distressed company whose long-term prospects remain sound. The market's evident tendency to overreact applies to negative events as well as positive news. The same psychology that led to a Cisco and a Krispy Kreme can lead to undervaluation of out-of-favor companies.

Academic studies have presented strong evidence of mispricing in the market for a variety of "anomalies." Behavioral biases may contribute to this mispricing. For example, investors may underreact or overreact to information. Or herding behavior might bias prices away from rational values. As has been noted by many practitioners and respected academics, prices may also differ from rational values because of trading by investors without information (noise traders). Or liquidity-driven selling could produce temporary

Table 5.2   Core Beliefs of the Fundamental Indexer

Active Manager	Indexer
Prices deviate from intrinsic value. ~~Active managers can beat the market.~~	~~Prices closely reflect intrinsic value.~~ Active managers cannot beat the market.[a]

[a]Not *collectively!*
Source: Research Affiliates, LLC.

mispricing, as could mean reversion in stock pricing (which has been observed by financial econometricians).

John Maynard Keynes suggested that prices are often influenced by the "animal spirits" of the market and are often unrelated to actual underlying economic activities. Keynes, however, predated, and so didn't benefit from, the perceived wisdom of "efficient markets." By comparing the evidence with the tenets of active and passive management shown in Table 5.1, we have arrived at the paradox illustrated in Table 5.2: *We agree with both the indexers and the active managers.* We believe pricing errors exist but that active managers cannot *collectively* exploit them reliably for above-benchmark returns.

Investors on both sides of the active-passive debate should be frustrated by this contradiction. Some investors, *certain* that mispriced stocks exist, seek out well-managed mutual funds to identify underpriced companies, and all too often, their hopes are dashed when the funds fail to meet expectations. Seeing these failures, the indexers eschew the performance game and invest in cap-weighted market proxies. Their confidence shrinks when, over time, they realize that their reliable index has reliably loaded up on shares of companies that are later proven to be overpriced, even into bubble territory. Until recently, no intellectually satisfying and commercially available solution seemed to exist to address these frustrations.

Constructing a Well-Functioning Index

The prospects of success for investors from active managers—taken collectively—cannot all will not improve unless the managers (and their brokers) can be convinced to work for free. Even then, the negative expected value added only becomes a zero expected value added. The alternative, then, is to improve the index itself.

To make this change for the better, we need to critically examine current index construction and expose its flaws.

Taking a pragmatic approach, we start with what makes a proper index or passive portfolio. We believe an index should have four key attributes:

- An index should be **representative** of our investment opportunity set. Clearly, an index of only 20 stocks wouldn't qualify as a broad market index: It would be poorly diversified and would not mirror the overall performance of the market it was attempting to measure. The Dow Jones Industrial Average (DJIA), in the late 1800s, contained just 12 stocks. Add up the prices, divide by 12, and there's your index—ostensibly for the overall U.S. stock market!
- An index should be **replicable** because the portfolio manager needs to be able to purchase the stocks in the prescribed weights. An index of illiquid or privately held securities would prove difficult to manage on a day-to-day basis.
- An index should be **transparent and rules-based** so that it is *historically* replicable. A subjective or closely guarded approach to index construction may lead to inconsistencies in the adding and removing of index constituents, making historical comparisons and comparative analysis difficult. The rules alone should determine which companies are included and at what portfolio weights. A transparent selection process also allows the portfolio manager to know likely index changes ahead of time and to prepare for their inclusion or deletion in a cost-effective fashion.
- Finally, an index designed for passive investing should have **low turnover**. Why bother to index if much of the cost advantage will be eaten away by transaction costs?

Note that none of these "ideal" characteristics imply capitalization weighting, which matters only in a pristine efficient market.

Violating these characteristics of the "ideal" index can lead to flaws in the index. Even so, most index providers violate one or another of these attractive features in our pragmatic definition of an index. The Russell indexes are largely formulaic, but they maintain enough secret sauce in the definition of *available float* to keep them from being entirely transparent at reconstitution time. The

Morgan Stanley Capital International (MSCI) indexes have elements of subjectivity and also of secret sauce. And the old standby,
the Dow Jones Industrial Average (DJIA), which even its publishers
cheerfully acknowledge is a bit of an anachronism, flunks most of
these tests.

Consider the Standard & Poor's methodology. The S&P 500 has
a stated goal to accurately reflect the U.S. equity market by having
exposure to "leading companies in leading industries." To make
the list, companies must *generally* meet established criteria, such as
financial viability, minimum capitalization, liquidity, and sector representation (Standard & Poor's, 2007). The process is *subjective*—not
entirely rules based and certainly not formulaic. There are many
who argue that the S&P 500 isn't an index at all: It's an actively
managed portfolio selected by a committee—whose very membership is a closely guarded secret!—and has shown a stark growth bias
throughout its recent history of additions and deletions.

From these criteria, we can see that additions will be stocks that
have done well in the recent past—in both operating results and
stock performance—not necessarily ones that are going to do well
in the future. The result is that Standard & Poor's is predisposed to
add "popular" stocks and those that have performed well recently,
rather than those with potential to improve on recent poor results.

The late 1990s provides a great example of the potential dangers
of such an approach. From 1995 to 2000, the S&P 500 experienced
235 changes—each involving an addition and a deletion (see Blume
and Edelen, 2003). One of the S&P rules is that if two S&P 500 members merge, the new entity takes one spot in the index and a new
company is added to the index. Therefore, in periods of intense
merger and acquisition activity, the number of new entities entering
the index will increase rapidly. So, in the 1995 through 2000 period,
"new economy" companies joined the S&P 500.

In 1995, the Nasdaq, laden with technology and emerging growth stocks, contributed only 4 of the 33 additions to the
S&P 500. In 2000—right at the top of the technology bubble—24
of the 58 companies added to the S&P 500 were Nasdaq issues.
Furthermore, apparently, in keeping with the times, the committee
even bent its own rules: It bypassed the stated requirement of positive earnings in order to include AOL, a company that had shown
only negative earnings and was internally forecasting losses for the
foreseeable future (Keane, 2003). The performance impact of this

Table 5.3   Additions to the S&P 500 in 1995 and 2000

	Nasdaq Additions to S&P 500	Total Additions to S&P 500	Percent of S&P 500 Additions from Nasdaq	Subsequent 5-Year Performance of Nasdaq
1995	4	33	12%	436%
2000	24	58	41%	−45%

Source: Research Affiliates, LLC.

approach can be seen in Table 5.3, which illustrates the percentage of additions to the S&P 500 from the Nasdaq and the subsequent five-year returns of the Nasdaq in 1995 and 2000. Clearly, the S&P committee's timing was uninspired.

A subjective process may also lead to a style bias in the index. Standard & Poor's process, for example, will lead to a higher proportion of growth stocks in the S&P 500 because growth stocks are more likely to have the kind of operating results and higher price-earnings ratios (P/Es) that imply a "leading company." How many times has a beaten-down stock been added to the S&P 500? Meanwhile, traditional value stocks, which are often associated with a host of problems—operating losses, accounting restatements, management scandals, and berths in slow-growth industries—are prime candidates for index removal—*not that the newly added growth stocks don't subsequently fall prey to many of these same problems!*

We might parenthetically note that this trend chasing can also take place in a rules-based, cap-weighted construct. Presumably, strong operating results and rapid growth could generate excitement-induced high P/Es, pushing many smaller enterprises into the larger cap indexes. Meanwhile, distressed stocks trading at depressed multiples with cyclically low sales or profits would be pushed out, by either a committee or periodic rebalancing based on capitalization.

The Achilles' Heel of Cap Weighting

The selection of past winners for an index is an important vulnerability, but the most serious flaw—indeed the Achilles' heel of the cap-weighted fund—is the return drag from linking portfolio weights to price. This flaw is particularly severe for the stocks that trade massively above or below their eventual intrinsic value. With the blessing of hindsight, investors can look back and ask why anyone would ever invest much in a company like Pets.com at the peak of the technology bubble. This was a company with no profits *ever contemplated* in its business plan. Its ultimate means of value realization was the intended sale of the business. One might ask: Sale to whom? Any price paid was too much because its true value was zero. Yet, Pets.com was in the broader index portfolios. *Every one of these "ex post" overvalued stocks was overweighted in the cap-weighted indexes.*

Conversely, the blessings of hindsight tell us that Microsoft was undervalued 20 years ago (relative to its eventual intrinsic value). Investors might not have been able to see the future that led to Microsoft's relentless successes in the 1990s, but they can now see that it was more valuable than its share price at that time. *Every one of such undervalued stocks was underweighted relative to its eventual intrinsic value^2 weight at that time in the cap-weighted indexes.*

At first blush, trying to fix the mispricing problem seems pointless: No one knows which stocks are overvalued and which are undervalued today. Microsoft's P/E was very high 20 years ago. Few self-respecting value investors saw any opportunity there. Fundamental Index advocates aren't any smarter or more perceptive than the investment managers and analysts trying to make such determinations. However, we don't need this foresight. The issue can be solved with relative ease by assigning portfolio weights on *some measure other than price*. This is done by severing the link between portfolio weight and any error in the price, which means severing the link between portfolio weight and the price itself.

Probably the easiest way to remove the link between portfolio weight and price is to select stocks randomly. If we throw enough darts at the *Wall Street Journal,* we wind up with an equally weighted portfolio. Many academic papers in the 1960s and 1970s examined the tendency for random portfolios or equal-weighted portfolios to outpace the market indexes. Standard & Poor's began publishing an equal-weighted version of the S&P 500 by the end of 1989. In the S&P 500 Equal Weight Index (SP EWI), each stock receives a 0.2 percent ($\frac{1}{500}$) portfolio weight regardless of its market capitalization, and the stocks are rebalanced back every quarter. Because price no longer dictates a company's position, half of the portfolio is likely to be in overvalued stocks and the other half in undervalued stocks. Apart from the selection of the names that go into the

Table 5.4   Return and Standard Deviation of S&P 500 and SP EWI, 1990 through December 2007

	Return	Standard Deviation
S&P 500	10.5%	13.7%
SP EWI	12.0%	14.8%

Source: eVestment Alliance.

portfolio, the index is free from the burden of overweighting the overvalued stocks and underweighting the undervalued stocks.

Eliminating this encumbrance is valuable. As Table 5.4 shows, the SP EWI outperformed the S&P 500 by 1.5 percentage points annually from 1990 through December 2007. These results assume, of course, no fees or trading costs. When allowed to compound over several years, this difference is significant. Say an investor placed $10,000 in a fund tracking the equal-weighted approach at the beginning of 1990. At the end of December 2007, the investor's equal-weighted portfolio would have grown to $76,900 versus growth of the same amount invested in the S&P 500 to $60,328— a $16,500 difference in ending wealth.[3] This is a pretty hefty premium, and all one had to do was divide by 500 and rebalance.

Examining the performance a little more deeply, however, we find that the outperformance of the equal-weighted portfolio came with a little extra risk. The annual standard deviation of returns (the volatility) of the S&P 500, of 13.7 percent over this span, increases to 14.8 percent with equal weighting. The risk data are a bit misleading, however, because much of the extra volatility of the SP EWI came in up markets when making *more money* is hardly a concern. If the performance is sliced into up and down markets, we find that the monthly "upside capture" of the SP EWI is 104 percent, whereas the "downside capture" is 91 percent, which implies that equal weighting produces modestly larger gains in the good times while also helping to cushion losses in rough quarters.[4]

The Problems with Equal Weighting

Attractive as an equal-weighted index strategy is from a return standpoint, it is not a viable solution for the indexing industry. On the surface, the most obvious shortcoming of the equal-weighted approach is portfolio turnover. In an equal-weighting strategy, price changes require that each stock be rebalanced periodically back to its 0.20 percent target weight. Compared with the cap-weighted strategy, which does not require rebalancing as a result of price movements, the SP EWI will have higher turnover and higher trading costs. If the rebalancing is done quarterly, turnover can rapidly escalate, with a lot of those trades in thinly traded, illiquid stocks. Increased trading invariably translates into higher brokerage costs. The least liquid stocks in the portfolio are more expensive to trade, particularly in large blocks. In addition, increased trading usually translates to increased realized capital gains, so the equal-weighted portfolio can also be expected to generate a larger tax bill.

Another serious shortcoming of the equal-weighted approach to index construction is that it fails to reflect the broad economy. The amount allocated to each sector, for example, depends solely on the number of companies in that sector, not the economic scope of the sector in the economy. For example, as Table 5.5 shows, the energy sector constitutes almost 11 percent of the S&P 500 but it accounts for only 6 percent of the SP EWI. Energy is dominated by a few very large companies—such as Exxon Mobil Corporation, Chevron Corporation, ConocoPhillips. These three alone represent about 6 percent of the S&P 500, but they represent only 0.60 percent (0.20 percent each) in the SP EWI. Similarly, sectors containing many small companies will be overrepresented.

Table 5.5 Comparative Sector Weights: S&P 500 vs. SP EWI, June 2007

Industry	S&P 500	SP EWI
Consumer discretionary	10.2%	17.8%
Consumer staples	9.3%	7.9%
Energy	10.8%	6.3%
Financials	20.6%	17.7%
Health care	11.6%	10.6%
Industrials	11.4%	10.7%
Information technology	15.5%	15.2%
Materials	3.1%	5.6%
Telecommunication services	3.8%	1.8%
Other	3.8%	6.3%

Source: Standard & Poor's.

In the consumer discretionary sector, which includes media and retailers, nearly 90 stocks translate to an 18 percent weighting in the SP EWI versus only 10 percent in the S&P 500. The number of different stores in the mall dwarfs the number of gas station choices. To have a representative portfolio, investors need to know how much of their paychecks go to each. So, equal weighting fails to adequately reflect the economy.

Clearly, at the company level, the equal-weighting approach disconnects the value of an individual company in the economy from its weight in the portfolio. In the SP EWI, the largest company (Exxon Mobil, the largest company in the world by sales and profits) gets the same weight as the smallest (Circuit City Stores, a niche retailer) as if they made an equal contribution to the economy. And the 501st stock, 502nd stock, and so on, receive no allocation whatsoever.

The biggest problem with equal weighting as an approach to index construction is the lack of scalability—an equally weighted index simply cannot be run on a very large scale. Therefore, it is really not an option for large institutional portfolios. The small company stocks do not provide enough capacity to handle much volume. As a rough approximation, consider the $1.3 trillion invested in cap-weighted index funds that track the S&P 500. Suppose 20 percent of these investors decided tomorrow that capitalization weighting is inefficient and shift their $260 billion to follow the SP EWI, investing just over a half billion dollars in each company, regardless of its size. This tremendous shift in wealth would have a dramatic impact on the smallest companies in the cap-weighted S&P 500. Circuit City, stock number 500 with a market capitalization of $1.5 billion as of September 2007, would suddenly have a half billion dollars of buy tickets. Clearly, a small stock like Circuit City could not immediately absorb such an immense flow of capital from a liquidity standpoint, to say nothing of the influence of additional new investments and quarterly rebalancing.

Finally, we have to recognize that we're not equally weighting a random list of companies. It's a list selected by the S&P committee, which has shown a pronounced growth bias over the years, adding companies when they're hot and dropping them when they're not. This means that we're still subject to a problem of selection bias. If this 500-stock index includes 100 companies that are popular today with valuation multiples that reflect that popularity, and excludes 100 large but unpopular companies, that fact can impose a drag on the S&P 500 *and* on the SP EWI.

In short, equal weighting fixes the main return drag of our cap-weighted indexes while introducing an array of other problems. One of the primary leaks in the traditional cap-weighted boat is now patched. But investing in an equally weighted index in the real world causes a variety of new holes to break out. The investor who assumes smooth sailing ahead may be bailing as hard as ever, because many of the original benefits of indexing are now lost to trading costs and higher volatility.

Concluding Thoughts

The question of whether markets are efficient has been debated for years, and it's not clear that an ultimate answer is any closer today. Stock pickers, active managers, and the $6.5 trillion equity mutual fund industry—all answer the question of whether the market is efficient with an emphatic "no!" Most indexers, academics, and a handful of advisers have a different view—that the markets are *largely efficient* and thus provide few opportunities to add value through skill or through insights that diverge from the market consensus.

For our purposes, the important issue is *how the question is framed.* Does the aggregate failure of mutual funds and institutional investment managers to outpace market averages confirm market efficiency? We've already demonstrated that the one does not prove the other. If the market is cap-weighted and our indexes are cap-weighted, what's left after the indexes are removed? That same index, give or take some minor differences at the margin. This is what active managers and private investors collectively hold. Because their costs are higher, active managers collectively provide market returns, give or take some minor differences, less their incremental costs. A fact that is tautologically true proves nothing else.

Does the market accurately price thousands of stocks every day? We believe not. Even the grand statesman among efficient market proponents, Burton Malkiel, wrote in his timeless classic *A Random Walk Down Wall Street* (2007):

> I have emphasized that market valuations rest on both logical and psychological factors. The theory of valuation depends on the projection of a long-term stream of dividends whose growth rate is extraordinarily difficult to estimate. Thus, fundamental value is never a definite number. It is a fuzzy band

of possible values, and prices can move sharply within this band whenever there is increased uncertainty or confusion. Moreover, the appropriate risk premiums for common equities are changeable and far from obvious either to investors or to financial economists. Thus, there is room for the hopes, fears, and favorite fashions of market participants to play a role in the valuation process. Indeed, I emphasized in early chapters how history provides extraordinary examples of markets in which psychology seemed to dominate the pricing process, as in the tulip-bulb mania in seventeenth century Holland and the Internet bubble at the turn of the twenty-first century. I therefore harbor some doubts that we should consider that the current array of market prices always represents the best estimate available of appropriate discounted value (pp. 271–272).

If *Random Walk,* the gospel on efficient markets, openly proclaims the existence of often significant pricing errors, shouldn't we? The fact that active managers haven't been able to exploit pricing errors for above-benchmark performance does not provide any evidence that those errors are small, because the average results of the average active manager are a foregone conclusion. Indeed, it is self-evident that, relative to "clairvoyant value," the mispricings are large and recurring; this truism is supported by the various large and small market bubbles. It's a mistake to assume that pricing errors don't matter because of the failure of active managers as a group to exploit them.

If prices are inefficient, traditional cap-weighted indexes are likely to be decidedly suboptimal. More efficient index construction requires building a broad portfolio of stocks by using indexing metrics that are *independent of price.* Empirically, this chapter shows a significant and large advantage of equal weighting over capitalization weighting. This evidence supports the hypothesis that prices are inefficient and, therefore, capitalization weighting is suboptimal. Equal weighting is instructive in illustrating the point that capitalization weighting creates a significant return drag, relative to our opportunity set. Although equal weighting fails, by several important criteria, to be a compelling index construction method it hints at a surprising and elegant way of constructing an efficient index for an inefficient market.

CHAPTER 6

A Fundamental(ly) Better Index

By the end of the 20th century, even casual investors have become comfortable with the idea of index funds. The idea of a better index fund, however, is mind-boggling.

—Jack Treynor[1]

Aristotle and Ptolemy saw the earth as the center of the universe, with the sun, moon, planets, and stars revolving around it. For this system to be consistent with observations of the movements of the sun, moon, and planets, complicated movements, with circles on circles, were needed. Copernicus moved the sun to the center, and with a later assist from Sir Isaac Newton's theory of gravity, the complex movements were no longer required. A complicated framework for the structure of the universe became far simpler.

In a *Wall Street Journal* op-ed piece, Jeremy Siegel (2006) likened the Fundamental Index idea to the Copernican revolution. In the article, he points out that modern finance has price—always and forever equal to fair value—at the center of the finance universe; the eventual realized value of a company, then, randomly distributes around that price. There is no point to examining the company's fair value by examining the underlying fundamentals of the company and economics of the environment. Fair value, quite simply, is exactly reflected by the company's market price.

This simplifying assumption lies at the heart of much of modern finance theory. But it comes at the expense of requiring an unsatisfying explanation for stock price behavior that is anything but random. Siegel points out that the Fundamental Index concept restores the importance of fundamental metrics of a company's scale and success. The concept essentially puts the fundamentals at the center of the finance universe again. The market's quest for the company's intrinsic value then leads to price hunting for that fair value. This assumption allows for a much richer set of possibilities for understanding asset prices and the equity risk premium than did the old system.

Siegel's Copernicus analogy is a bit over the top. Copernicus upended 1,500 years of scientific orthodoxy, risked burning at the stake (despite dedicating his treatise to the pope), and was not absolved for his heresies by the Roman Catholic Church for more than 300 years. In contrast, the Fundamental Index concept points the way out of some problems that have bedeviled finance theory for 50 years, hints at some possible directions for future research, and doesn't expose us, we hope, to any likelihood of being burned at the stake. Accordingly, although we are disinclined to wrap ourselves in Copernicus's cape, we do think these ideas are important.

With companies' fundamentals—not price—situated in the center of the valuation universe, and market price seen as an imprecise estimate of the fair value, using prices to create index portfolio weights leads to inferior portfolios. We will show in this chapter that if one ignores prices in building a passive portfolio—by using a dartboard, equal weights, or fundamental measures of company size—the resulting non-price-based portfolio will trump traditional capitalization-weighted index funds on average over time.

Intuitively, a non-price-based approach avoids the return drag that comes from the propensity of capitalization weighting to overweight the overpriced and underweight the underpriced. But previous approaches to avoiding that structural flaw introduced new problems for the investor. For example, while equal weighting eliminates the performance drag of capitalization weighting, it leads to a host of other problems. Equal weighting only vaguely resembles either the market or the economy, has limited capacity because of the number of tiny companies in the index, and requires high turnover in many relatively illiquid stocks. It's neither intellectually satisfying nor scaleable nor particularly practical as a solution to the problems of capitalization weighting.

Building the Fundamental Index

Knowing the problems with both capitalization weighting and equal weighting, the focus of our work beginning in 2002 was to explore alternative measures of size. We note here that indexing to non-capitalization-based measures of company size offers a stable index that does mirror—with utter neutrality—the composition of the economy, enjoys vast capacity, and has very low turnover, mostly concentrated in large, liquid stocks. These non-price-based measures do not capture *any* forward-looking information about stock attractiveness. The non-price-based size measures *do* largely eliminate the inevitable correlation between pricing errors and portfolio weight that is inherent in capitalization weighting. These features create a structural portfolio advantage of non-price-based size measures over traditional index construction.

Building on our definition of an index from Chapter 5, the first step in creating a Fundamental Index portfolio is to pick a set of simple and widely available non-price-based measures of company size that we can use to create a broadly representative, high-liquidity, high-capacity, low-turnover index. Virtually any measure will work,[2] but the underlying data for the metric have to be accessible and reliable. The square footage of a company's combined facilities or the number of nonexecutive staffers working for the company may be interesting measures of a company's economic scale, but they are potentially worthless if we can't readily locate such information.

Many valid measures of size are available. The financial measures of size seem to fall into four broad categories: They are all in some fashion measures of sales, profits, net assets, and distributions to shareholders.[3] To be sure, one could choose financial measures that are not in one of these four categories (e.g., aggregate indebtedness), but those measures wouldn't typically be seen as measures of a company's *economic footprint.*

Ultimately, for the Research Affiliates Fundamental Index (RAFI) methodology, we selected a composite approach that uses equally weighted measures of four size factors—sales, cash flow, book value, and dividends paid. This composite approach represents a better and more robust construction than any single metric to construct an index portfolio. Using this approach, then, a company's size is determined by averaging the weights of the four size metrics. Table 6.1 illustrates the approach for the five largest companies in the United States measured by their economic footprint.

For example, the composite weight for Exxon Mobil Corporation's *current* economic footprint is (3.79 percent + 4.29 percent + 3.26 percent + 2.46 percent) / 4, or 3.45 percent. But we then average across five years because cyclicality in any business can lead to distortions. By using five years for Exxon Mobil, for example, we avoid the risk of overrelying on the recent surge in oil prices. This process leads to an adjusted weight of 2.8 percent for Exxon Mobil.

We perform this series of calculations for all publicly traded companies. In this manner, the Fundamental Index methodology can be narrowed to any subset of the market or expanded domestically and overseas. In the United States, the RAFI U.S. Large Company Index (RAFI U.S. Large) is composed of the 1,000 largest U.S. publicly traded companies, selected and weighted by the companies' economic footprints in the U.S. economy as measured by our four metrics of company size. Small-company stocks are captured in the RAFI U.S. Small Company Index, defined as the next 2,000 stocks (1,001st largest to 3,000th largest) by fundamental size.

The RAFI approach is intuitive, transparent, and rules-based. It can be tested historically across almost any market worldwide. It is straightforward, objective, and easy to explain to clients and investment committees. Even investing tyros can readily grasp the concept.

Adjustments for Non-Dividend-Paying Companies

Dividends are the primary way companies repay their shareholders for providing investment capital, but not all companies pay dividends. The degree to which companies choose to return capital in the form of dividends has changed over the past 20 years. As Figure 6.1 shows, from 1960 through 1998 the dividend payout ratio for the S&P 500 Index—the ratio of annual dividends paid as a percentage of the annual reported earnings—averaged 50 percent (Bernstein, 2005b) and never fell below 39 percent. Half of Corporate America's profits were paid to shareholders in the form of dividends.

Table 6.1   The Five Largest Companies Based on Fundamentals, June 30, 2007

Company	Sales			Cash Flow		
	$ Billion	Weight	Rank	$ Billion	Weight	Rank
Exxon Mobil Corp.	335	3.79%	2	68	4.29%	1
General Electric Co.	161	1.82%	6	33	2.09%	6
Citigroup Inc.	147	1.66%	8	39	2.45%	4
Bank of America Corp.	116	1.32%	9	41	2.55%	3
Wal-Mart Stores Inc.	349	3.95%	1	26	1.63%	10
Top 1,000 Total	8,831			1,595		

Company	Dividend			Book Value		
	$ Billion	Weight	Rank	$ Billion	Weight	Rank
Exxon Mobil Corp.	8	3.26%	4	114	2.46%	5
General Electric Co.	11	4.60%	1	112	2.43%	6
Citigroup Inc.	10	4.21%	2	119	2.57%	2
Bank of America Corp.	10	4.16%	3	132	2.86%	1
Wal-Mart Stores Inc.	3	1.21%	18	62	1.33%	13
Top 1,000 Total	232			4,626		

Note: Using most recently available trailing 12-month financial data.
Source: Research Affiliates, LLC.

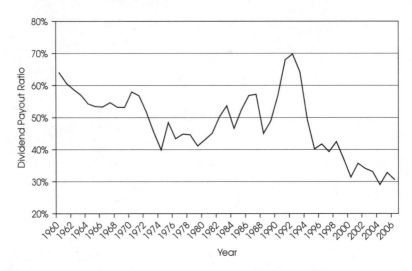

Figure 6.1   Dividend Payout Ratio for the S&P 500, 1960 through 2006

Source: Research Affiliates, based on data from Aswath Damodaran (http://pages.stern.nyu .edu/~adamodar/).

Throughout the 1990s, however, payout ratios plunged to eventually settle near 30 percent at the peak of the technology bubble, where they remain today. With the growing role of stock options in management compensation, which began in the early 1990s when Congress capped tax deductibility of management salaries at $1 million,[4] it's unsurprising that stock buybacks are becoming more popular than dividends. The former may help share prices, hence the value of manager's stock options, while dividends result in a price drop equivalent to the dividend, which doesn't help the manager's stock options.

The payout ratio settled near 30 percent at the peak of the bubble in 2000 and again since late 2006. In both cases, bull markets propelled stock returns well into the double digits. In such an environment, what's the appeal of an extra couple of percent from dividends? Accordingly, investors didn't value their quarterly checks and, in keeping with the law of supply and demand, companies increasingly decided to retain their earnings or buy back stock.

Contrary to popular belief, this downward trend in payout ratios has been largely unaffected by the Job and Growth Act of 2003 that lowered the taxes on dividends from ordinary income rates (which had reached 38.6 percent in the 1990s) to a more reasonable 15 percent. Remarkably, payout ratios have *fallen* since the legislation was passed. While dividends have soared since 2003, reported profits have soared even more. It is also possible that the low payout ratios reflect some caution by corporate management, given that the lofty reported earnings may, in part, reflect aggressive accounting. By the end of 2006, the aggregate payout for the S&P 500 stood at an all-time low of 28 percent, and only three industry sectors—telecommunications, consumer staples, and utilities—had payout ratios above 50 percent (Bary, 2006).

It is worth further exploring how share repurchases are becoming a more accepted way to compensate stockholders. Once considered a fraction of shareholder compensation, share repurchases have grown by leaps and bounds. Share repurchases increase the corporation's flexibility and potentially afford the investor tax advantages. According to Morgan Stanley, net stock buybacks (total share repurchases less new share issuances) among S&P 500 companies in 2006 amounted to $371 billion—versus the $233 billion S&P 500 companies paid out in cash dividends (McVey, McNellis, and Lim, 2007). We can't know how sustainable this surge in stock buybacks may be, but these figures make it clear that dividends are not the only measure of shareholder compensation.

Rapidly expanding enterprises, preferring to reinvest profits for future growth, often pay no dividends at all. Today, fast growers are indeed *expected* to pay no dividends; dividend distributions can be perceived as an admission that internal growth prospects are slowing. This situation also bucks historical trends. In the 1950s, growth stalwart IBM was increasing earnings at more than 20 percent per year, but still managed to keep its dividend payout ratio in the 20 percent range (Bernstein, 2005b).

As the examples suggest, companies that do not pay dividends are often concentrated in certain sectors and/or growth phases. If we exclude those companies from the indexes, we leave out meaningful segments of the economy, deemphasize the role of growth companies, and exclude almost all emerging growth companies, all of which will alter the character of the index. We wind up with a heavy concentration in some of the most mature segments of the economy, such as financial services, utilities, and consumer goods companies.

For these reasons, the four-metric variant of the Fundamental Index methodology makes a special provision for zero-yield companies: We rely on a three-metric average for companies that have paid no dividends in the past five years and equally weight the other three metrics—sales, cash flow, and book value.[5]

Why Multiple Measures of Company Size?

Although using one metric to construct a Fundamental Index portfolio would have an element of simplicity, each measure has its own shortcomings in adequately defining a company's economic footprint. To understand this point, think about your last time at the beach. A footprint in the sand can be measured a variety of ways—length, width, depth, and so on. Alone, each metric tells us only a little about the size of the individual; combining multiple measures provides a more complete picture. The same is true for publicly traded companies. Reliance on a single measure of size leaves an index vulnerable to over- or underexposure to certain segments of the economy. It's worth exploring a few of these exposures.

Dividends

An index based on dividend payments alone will overweight sectors of the economy that pay large dividends, such as utility companies and financial services companies, and exclude segments that do not pay cash dividends, such as technology and growth companies. Recall from Table 6.1 that General Electric pays the largest dividends in the U.S. economy, but it ranks sixth in sales, cash flow, and book value. As Figure 6.2 shows, non-dividend payers compose a substantial share of several market segments.

In the S&P 500, 24 percent of the companies did not pay dividends in 2006, versus only 6 percent in 1980 (Bary, 2006). Although these excluded stocks compose far less than 24 percent of the market by capitalization, they are by no means a random cross-section of the market. In growth sectors, the problem is acute—67 percent of S&P Information Technology Index stocks do not pay dividends. And, not surprisingly, moving down the size spectrum, we find that more than 60 percent of the companies in the small-company Russell 2000 Index are nonpayers.[6]

Consider the sector composition, for example, of the Dow Jones Select Dividend Index, an exchange-traded fund (ETF) that

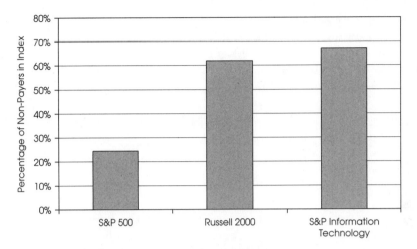

Figure 6.2   Non-Dividend Payers Are Significant
Source: Research Affiliates, based on data from Kittsley (2006).

reweights the S&P 900 Index.[7] Its weight in financials and utility companies, which are the primary companies that take the place of the non-dividend-paying stocks, approaches 60 percent of the index—more than double the 25 percent allocation to such stocks in the S&P 500.

In short, dividend weighting produces long-term returns well in excess of those produced by capitalization weighting, but it fails as a *broad market index*. Because a dividend-based index will concentrate our money in high-yield, mature, deep-value companies, this approach tends to perform well in bear markets and to underperform in most bull markets. Excessive exposure to banks and utility companies in a dividend-based index adds a degree of uncertainty to the returns because of its exposure to the risks affecting only these sectors.

Sales

A sales-based metric overweights stocks that have high sales and low margins, such as trading companies, companies whose profit margins have deteriorated, or companies that deliberately seek to buy market share by keeping profit margins thin and focusing on volume (the "Wal-Mart Syndrome"; in Table 6.1, we can see that Wal-Mart has the largest sales of any U.S. company, but the best ranking it can muster on any of the other metrics of size is 10th). Airlines and automobile manufacturers, which have recently had large dollar volumes of sales but suffer from negative profits, are examples of companies that could get a larger index allocation on the basis of sales weighting than on another metric of company size.

In contrast to the dividend-based index, a sales-based index concentrates on companies that have thinner margins and higher volatility. So, it tends to struggle in bear markets while performing better than most Fundamental Index strategies in bull markets. It offers the highest risk of any of the Fundamental Index constructs.

Profits (Cash Flow)

Profit metrics may lead to over- or underexposure to companies with highly cyclical incomes because profits are linked to the economic cycle experienced by a company.[8] Distressed companies may receive little to no weight at all in a profits-based index, even if their economic scale is large by another metric and even if they are positioned to enjoy large *future* profits in a cyclical upturn.

Similarly, using only cash flow as a measure of profits may give too much weight to mature and slow growing companies or cash cows while underweighting young, fast growing companies. Sole reliance on cash flow may also expose us to companies whose lofty profit margins draw aggressive competition or unwelcome scrutiny from regulators: In Table 6.1, we can see that Exxon Mobil sits with this sword of Damocles hanging over it, one which posturing political pundits playing the populist card are always threatening to drop. Most companies experience a certain amount of mean reversion in profits, so this metric alone may also increase exposure to the cyclical companies at precisely the wrong times in their economic cycles.

Book Value

A book value metric may lead to overexposure to companies with aggressive accounting practices or underexposure to companies with conservative accounting practices. It may also rely too much on older companies with legacy assets on the balance sheet or acquisitive companies with large "goodwill" balances that have no cash value. When a book value weighting approach is used, companies that are capital intensive with large book assets may be overweighted in relation to companies that are more reliant on human capital or intellectual capital. For example, banks and heavy industrial companies receive much higher weights than, say, a similarly sized (in sales or profits) software company. This is why Bank of America and Citigroup land the first and second spots in the rankings for a book value measure of company size.

Other Measures

So far, we have examined only the four measures that we combined into our composite measure of company size. But these four are by no means all we considered. For example, we could use revenues instead of sales or we could adjust the sales metric for debt-to-equity ratios to remove the impact of leverage from this metric of company size. Instead of cash flow, we could use reported earnings; operating earnings; earnings before interest, taxes, depreciation, and amortization (EBITDA); or some other measure of profitability. Instead of book value, we could use gross assets, liquid assets, operating assets, or even gross indebtedness. Instead of dividends, we could use stock buybacks or the sum of the two.

We could even use nonfinancial measures of company size, such as geographical scale (how many offices, in how many countries or states) or employment (number of employees, full-time employees, total salaries paid). Each has its drawbacks. *But they all work. They all outperform relevant cap-weighted indexes in most markets and in most years.*

We do not rely on nonfinancial measures for the simple reason that, even though they offer long-term performance roughly in line with the financial measures, they are peculiar in regard to reflecting (or not reflecting) a company's role in the economy. A case in point is number of employees. A McDonald's burger-flipper would count the same as a Genentech biochemist. In our original research, the index based on number of employees generated performance comparable with the performance of the financial measures, but it was less scalable, less liquid, and a bit peculiar (it would result in Kelly Services being one of the 10 largest holdings) than the financially based measures.[9] And, for investors, only the financial measures really matter.

Advantages of a Composite Measure

As we've discussed, using any single measure of company size can expose investors to a biased sample of companies and result in a portfolio that fails to adequately reflect the composition of the economy in a comfortable, well-balanced fashion. Even though it would be difficult to eliminate all such biases, their impact can be mitigated by using multiple measures of company size. Is Exxon Mobil, General Electric, Bank of America, or Wal-Mart the largest company in the United States? There are four correct answers to this question! By relying on multiple metrics, we find that Exxon Mobil has the largest overall "footprint in the sand" because it ranks in the top five on each of the four metrics of size. But, unlike capitalization weighting, there is no single right answer to this question.[10]

Our goal for the Fundamental Index construct is to use a reasonable combination of financial variables, each of which captures a different aspect of company size. In so doing, we create a multidimensional measure of company size that will be more robust than any single measure. If one were to poll investment professionals to list how one might measure company size, apart from market capitalization or float, most lists would include variations on the categories *profits, book value, sales, dividends,* and number of *employees.* Because each category provides a different perspective on company size, a composite of several measures will provide that multidimensional view of company size.

For the RAFI indexes, we choose one from each category (except number of employees). We select the one that is either the most widely accepted (e.g., book value) or is most objective and least susceptible to gaming by company management (e.g., cash flow rather than reported earnings). The relative accessibility of data is also a factor. All four measures can be quickly retrieved from the various financial data platforms for any of *70,000* publicly traded companies worldwide! Another criterion is that the metrics be reasonably comparable in countries around the world, allowing the Fundamental Index methodology to be applied globally.

As the investment world has been reminded in recent years, some companies do manage, manipulate, and even cheat on their financials. Some companies use less aggressive accounting practices than their peers; some use more aggressive accounting—for example, the companies with biannual write-offs of so-called extraordinary items. An index built on fundamental measures of company size will not eliminate our exposure to these games, but a composite approach—focused on the more objective measures averaged over several years—can sharply reduce our vulnerability to accounting differences.

The use of multiple size metrics also reduces the impact of occasional data errors in the widely used stock databases.[11] For example, if sales are incorrectly coded, and if the error is too small to be caught by simple quality control screens, the remaining three metrics will minimize the impact of this potential error.

An Index of the Broad Economy

Using this combination of four financial measures of company size, the resulting RAFI indexes are neutral reflections of the publicly traded parts of the broad economy. The cap-weighted indexes are neutral relative to the market, but veer far from neutrality relative to the economy. Cap-weighted indexes favor the segments of the economy that are *expected* to enjoy the greatest future growth. In a very real sense, the cap-weighted indexes reflect the market's expectations for the look of the broad economy in the distant future! Reciprocally, while Fundamental Index portfolios are studiously neutral relative to the composition of the current economy, they are not at all neutral relative to the market.

Because the market, which is cap-weighted, favors companies with above-average growth expectations and shuns companies with below-average growth expectations, the market has a clear growth tilt *relative to the economy*. Fundamental Index portfolios do not. Reciprocally, an index weighted on fundamental measures of company size will have a clear value tilt *relative to the market*. The critics who suggest that the Fundamental Index concept is a value index are correct in the sense of a value tilt relative to the cap-weighted market.

RAFI indexes do have a special kind of value tilt. It is dynamic, changing its magnitude as a direct mirror image of the constantly changing premium that the market is willing to pay for growth. Basically, Fundamental Index portfolios will contra-trade against whatever the market is making its most extreme bets on.

The distinction between owning the market versus owning the economy is worth exploring further. Does capitalization weighting lead to a larger commitment to the "best" companies? Are these growth companies, which are accorded higher valuation multiples, likely to grow faster than the economy? If the markets have any skill in gauging differing economic prospects, the answer to both questions is "yes." Does capitalization weighting invest more in these companies than their economic scale would support because they are better stocks or better investments? If the markets are functioning properly, the answer is an emphatic "no!" In a correctly functioning, efficient market, the growth stocks are bid up and the value stocks are sold off to precisely the right extent to *equalize their risk-adjusted returns.*

If the forward-looking returns for growth and value are the same, why should index investors always have more invested in growth companies than in value companies? If the markets overrely on growth expectations—and there's ample historical evidence that they do—this bias in favor of the growth companies will be expensive. If the markets are pricing these assets correctly relative to one another, will RAFI investors harm themselves by holding these same companies on the basis of their economic footprint rather than their market footprint? No! In an efficient market, the cost of the modest "active bet" that a Fundamental Index portfolio makes relative to the cap-weighted market weights is negligible.

An important attribute of an index is that it widely reflect the investor's opportunity set. Cap-weighted indexes are alleged to be superior to other kinds of indexes because they represent the full market. But the "market" differs in many ways from the economy. A Fundamental Index portfolio will never reflect market weights. Rather, it will reflect the *economic* opportunity set available to the investor. The reciprocal is equally true. A cap-weighted portfolio will never reflect the composition of the economy. It reflects the composition, the biases, and the constantly shifting expectations of *the market* as to the future look of the economy, and hence of the market opportunity set.

The difference between market representation and economic representation can be illustrated by comparing the top holdings of the two types of indexes. Table 6.2 shows the top 20 stocks in the RAFI U.S. Large compared with the 20 largest stocks in the top 1,000 by market capitalization (Cap 1000). The two lists are very similar. Both the RAFI U.S. Large and Cap 1000 lists comprise leading companies with household names—companies whose products we use daily in our business and personal lives. Indeed, the overlap is striking, with 17 shared stocks on both top 20 lists and almost 800 names held in common by the two indexes. In contrast, an equal-weighted index—or a niche dividend strategy or, indeed, any single-metric Fundamental Index portfolio—will show clear differences with both the RAFI and the cap-weighted indexes.

Table 6.2 Top 20 Holdings, June 30, 2007

	RAFI U.S. Large		Cap 1000	
No.	Security Description	Weight	Security Description	Weight
1	Exxon Mobil Corp.	2.8%	Exxon Mobil Corp.	3.1%
2	General Electric Co.	2.7%	General Electric Co.	2.5%
3	Citigroup Inc.	2.1%	Microsoft Corp.	1.8%
4	Microsoft Corp.	1.7%	Citigroup Inc.	1.6%
5	Bank of America Corp.	1.7%	Bank of America Corp.	1.4%
6	Wal-Mart Stores Inc.	1.6%	Wal-Mart Stores Inc.	1.3%
7	Verizon Communications Inc.	1.5%	Altria Group Inc.	1.3%
8	Chevron Corp.	1.4%	Proctor & Gamble Co.	1.2%
9	Altria Group Inc.	1.4%	Pfizer Inc.	1.2%
10	Pfizer Inc.	1.3%	Chevron Corp.	1.2%
11	JPMorgan Chase & Co.	1.3%	American International Group	1.1%
12	General Motors Corp.	1.2%	Johnson & Johnson	1.1%
13	AT&T Inc.	1.2%	JPMorgan Chase & Co.	1.1%
14	Berkshire Hathaway	1.1%	Cisco Systems Inc.	1.1%
15	Ford Motor Co.	1.1%	AT&T Inc.	1.0%
16	American International Group	1.1%	IBM	1.0%
17	Proctor & Gamble Co.	1.0%	Intel Corp.	0.9%
18	Johnson & Johnson	0.9%	ConocoPhilips	0.8%
19	ConocoPhilips	0.9%	Coca-Cola Co.	0.8%
20	IBM	0.8%	Berkshire Hathaway	0.8%
Total of Top 20		28.8%		26.2%

Source: Research Affiliates, LLC.

A broad market index should have sizable exposure to the largest economic groups. Table 6.3 displays the sector allocations of the RAFI U.S. Large and the Cap 1000. Again, one can see similar portfolios that would be difficult for many investors to differentiate if the index names were hidden. Indeed, 5 of the 10 sector allocations are within 1.5 percentage points of one another. This shouldn't come as a major surprise—one portfolio is built on economic weights, and the other is based on market weights linked to the same economy's expected composition some years into the future. The composition of an economy doesn't change overnight. It took decades for the United States to transform from a

Table 6.3   RAFI U.S. Large and Cap 1000 Sector Weights, June 2007

Industry	RAFI U.S. Large Weight	Cap 1000 Weight
Consumer discretionary	13.4%	11.0%
Consumer staples	11.5%	9.0%
Energy	9.7%	11.1%
Financials	21.2%	20.6%
Health care	8.2%	11.7%
Industrials	11.0%	10.8%
Information technology	9.6%	15.4%
Materials	3.8%	3.7%
Telecommunication services	4.1%	3.0%
Other	7.5%	3.6%

Source: Research Affiliates, LLC.

manufacturing to a service-based economy. The largest sector for both a fundamentals-weighted and a cap-weighted index is finance with weights of 21.2 percent and 20.6 percent, respectively, while materials and telecommunications are the two smallest in both portfolios.

Capacity and Liquidity

By reflecting the economic weights of companies in the economy, Fundamental Index portfolios are able to absorb vast sums of money, just like portfolios based on a cap-weighted index. Recall that this attribute was perhaps the most critical flaw of the equal-weighted approach. By design, the Fundamental Index composition is size weighted, so it places most of our money in the largest companies and generally, therefore, the largest, and most liquid stocks. In most instances, the composition parallels that of the cap-weighted portfolio reasonably closely. Indeed, reflecting back on Table 6.2, we see that the concentration in the top 20 names is much the same for both lists. But one shows the concentration of the U.S. economy in its 20 largest companies, while the other shows the concentration of the market's bets as to the 20 companies deemed most important in our future economy.

The nonoverlap names are as important as the overlap names. The 20 largest companies based on fundamental measures of the companies' economic footprint include Verizon Communications,

General Motors (GM), and Ford. The market doesn't credit these companies as top-20 players in the future economy. By the same token, the cap-weighted list includes Cisco, Intel, and Coca-Cola, none of which makes the top-20 list in today's economy. Will these companies collectively grow faster than Verizon, GM, and Ford? We wouldn't bet against it! But the market is suggesting that each of these companies is a bigger player in tomorrow's economy than Verizon, GM, or Ford. That's an aggressive statement. The real question is whether we're paying too much for that superior prospective growth. If the market is doing its job right, they're all priced to give us the same future return, so we won't be hurt by betting away from the cap-weighted market.

The degree of scalability can be gauged by looking at some practical measures of liquidity and capacity. Capacity can be esti-mated by comparing the relative size, defined in terms of capitaliza-tion, of the average company in the RAFI U.S. Large portfolio with the relative size of the average company in the Russell 1000 Index. As Table 6.4 shows, the RAFI U.S. Large figure of $83.5 billion is actually just *larger* than the Russell 1000 figure. The $83.5 billion implies nothing in the way of a small-cap bias and, consequently, reflects a good deal of capacity. The aggregate amount that can be invested in the RAFI U.S. Large is thus presumably about the same as for the Russell 1000. Because the turnover is a bit higher, it might have slightly less capacity, but we're not looking at a capac-ity constraint that would prove remotely worrisome for many years. Not surprisingly, this "cap ratio" is much worse for the S&P Equal Weight Index (SP EWI) because it places the same amount in the smallest stocks as the largest.

Of course, the relative capitalization of a RAFI index versus a representative cap-weighted index will shift over time. When large-cap stocks are priced at higher valuation multiples than small-cap

Table 6.4   Size Comparison, June 2007

Index	Weighted Average Market Cap ($ Billions)
RAFI U.S. Large	$ 83.5
Russell 1000	$ 83.4
S&P 500	$ 100.5
SP EWI	$ 26.7

Source: Research Affiliates, LLC.

stocks, as they were in the late 1990s, cap-weighted indexes will over-weight the large-cap stocks, whereas fundamentals-based indexes, blissfully ignorant of these valuation multiples, will not. The result is that in late 1999, the RAFI U.S. Large had approximately half of the average capitalization of the Russell 1000, still with a hefty enough dose of large-cap companies to make it scalable. By the end of 2006, small-cap stocks were trading at a premium. The RAFI U.S. Large rescaled these stocks *down* to their economic scale, leading to an average market capitalization slightly higher than the Russell 1000—in effect, the RAFI U.S. Large sometimes will exhibit a large-cap tilt! We'll come back to the myth of the small-company bias of the Fundamental Index portfolios in Chapter 10.

In addition, the concentration in the largest holdings provides an excellent indication of portfolio capacity and liquidity. In Table 6.5, we outline the fraction of total index capitalization belonging to the top 100 stocks in each index. Both portfolios are relatively concentrated: The RAFI U.S. Large has 56.5 percent of its portfolio in the top 100 names and the Cap 1000 is virtually identical, at 56.1 percent. Because of the large number of companies that pay no dividends and the modest number that pay the largest dividends, concentration in the dividend index is far higher—another example of the problem of single-metric approaches. In comparison, the concentration ratio of the SP EWI is, by construction, exactly 20 percent.

The liquidity of a Fundamental Index portfolio is comparable to that of a similar cap-weighted portfolio. Table 6.6 compares the RAFI U.S. Large and the Cap 1000 by two standard measures of liquidity—the weighted average trading volume and the number

Table 6.5   Concentration Ratio: RAFI U.S. Large versus Cap 1000 as of 2006

Portfolio/Index	Concentration Ratio
Cap 1000	56.1%
Book	57.2%
Income	58.8%
Sales	56.2%
Dividends	68.3%
RAFI U.S. Large	56.5%
SP EWI	20.0%

Source: Research Affiliates, LLC.

Table 6.6   Liquidity Comparison: RAFI U.S. Large versus Cap 1000, 1993 through 2003

Portfolio/Index	Weighted Average Dollar Trading Volume (millions)	Weighted Trading Days
Cap 1000	$191	0.9
Book	$134	1.5
Income	$126	1.3
Sales	$ 99	1.7
Dividends	$110	1.6
Composite (RAFI U.S. Large)	$102	1.5

Source: Research Affiliates, based on data from Arnott, Hsu, and Moore (2005).

of days required to trade a billion-dollar portfolio—for the 1993 through 2003 period. With an average trading volume of $191 million on the Cap 1000, it takes slightly less than a day to trade $1 billion based on the Cap 1000. For the RAFI U.S. Large, with its average volume of $102 million, it takes slightly longer—a day and a half. Of course, it's worth noting that market volume has risen significantly since the 1993 through 2003 period covered in this study, so the liquidity comparison is even more favorable today.

Clearly, plenty of capacity exists to implement the RAFI U.S. Large strategy on a wide scale. The portfolio is similar enough to the cap-weighted market that it probably has a collective capacity of $1 trillion or more. At that magnitude, the RAFI U.S. Large strategy would be roughly 5 percent of total U.S. stock market capitalization and would own 20 percent or more of the available float in only 20 of the top 1,000 U.S. companies. Most of these companies are near the bottom of the list so that less than 1 percent of the portfolio would face constraints for available float, *even at a scale of $1 trillion!*

Reconstituting the Fundamental Index: Keeping Turnover Low

Turnover is a major transgression in the eyes of diehard indexers, because high turnover leads to return-eroding trading costs. The average mutual fund realizes trading costs of 1.44 percent per year (Edelen, Evans, and Kadlec, 2007) that no doubt contributes to the significant shortfall in performance of these active funds, relative to the indexes over long periods. Higher turnover is also one of the major drawbacks of the equal-weighted SP EWI portfolio.

Remember that in a cap-weighted construct, the only required trading outside of corporate actions such as mergers and stock buybacks is the portfolio reconstitution. In the case of the Russell 1000,[12] reconstitution takes place annually at mid-year. Figure 6.3 displays the annual turnover for the RAFI U.S. Large and the Cap 1000, both reconstituted annually.[13] The turnover of the Cap 1000 was 6.3 percent annually over the 42-year evaluation period; this is modest, but it's more than most people think. The RAFI U.S. Large was close behind with a still small 10.6 percent per year. Turnover in both has been even lower in the three years since this study was published.

There is an interesting difference in the character of the trading when we compare cap-weighted indexes with Fundamental Index portfolios. Neither index can avoid corporate actions. If a company goes bankrupt, merges, or is acquired by another company, it *will* come out of both portfolios and *will* trigger the purchase of another company to complete the roster of the portfolio.

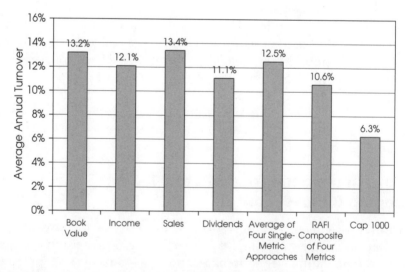

Figure 6.3   Turnover Comparison, 1962 through 2004
Source: Research Affiliates, based on data from Arnott, Hsu, and Moore (2005).

All other trading is *discretionary* trading. That is, we could trade or we could just let the portfolio drift with the whims of the markets.

The vast majority of the *discretionary* trading in a cap-weighted portfolio is swapping stocks that have fallen off for new stocks that have climbed into the index. While the companies falling off of the list may have done so because of corporate actions—takeovers, mergers, bankruptcies, and so forth—the ones that come off the list on a discretionary basis will typically be out-of-favor companies trading at deep discount multiples. The companies that are added, whether they are replacing companies dropped for discretionary reasons or for corporate actions, are usually hot new growth companies that are often too small to make the top 1,000 of the Fundamental Index portfolio but are trading at a sufficiently lofty valuation multiple to make it onto the cap-weighted list.

For both the discretionary removals and almost all new additions to the index, the cap-weighted index will tend to experience most of its turnover near the bottom—in smaller companies with their higher transaction costs. One of the indexing world's dirty secrets is that their trading costs are a disaster, only alleviated by the very low annual turnover. If indexing is 20 percent of the U.S. stock market, then any new addition to the index faces turnover of 20 percent of the shares outstanding, all on the same day, with the indexers all trading in the same direction, as soon as it's added to the cap-weighted index.

In contrast, only about 2.7 percent of the annual turnover of the RAFI U.S. Large relates to index deletions and additions. Changes in fundamentals are much less volatile than changes in stock price. Moreover, the remaining turnover, about 8 percent, relates to reweighting, contra-trading against companies that have seen share prices rise or fall relative to the changes in company fundamental weights. This 8 percent turnover occurs across the whole size range and tends to be proportioned to company size. In other words, if 50 percent of the portfolio is in the 100 largest companies, 50 percent of our reweighting—4 percent turnover on the overall portfolio—happens in the largest and most liquid 100 names in the market.

The Fundamental Index approach involves less disruptive turnover than the cap-weighting approach. The approach inherently involves selling high (the stock whose share price has lofted well ahead of its financial success in the economy) and buying low (the stock whose share price has lagged its financial success), the hallmark of sound investment management. In contrast, trading in the cap-weighted indexes involves adding new stocks to the indexes after big run-ups or dropping existing stocks after bleak results.

Of course, cap-weighted indexes are only one comparison for assessing the relative turnover of the RAFI U.S. Large. The reader can develop a greater understanding by seeing how the RAFI U.S. Large stacks up against other equity portfolio choices—from an equal-weighted index to an actively managed portfolio. According to Lipper and eVestment Alliance, for the year ending March 31, 2007, the Rydex SP EWI ETF experienced turnover of 16 percent. This amount pales in comparison with the turnover of the average (actively managed) large-cap blend mutual fund, which, according to Morningstar, has seen its annual turnover vary from 64 percent to a whopping 111 percent (for the average fund!) from 1996 through 2006.

Two attributes of the Fundamental Index approach help keep its turnover relatively low. First, three of the four fundamental measures of company size—sales, cash flow, and dividends—are averaged over the preceding five years.[14] Portfolio weightings are thus less susceptible to large, often cyclical, surges in operating results or sudden reversals in dividend policy. Second, the multimetric approach mitigates portfolio turnover. Changes in the size of a company on one fundamental measure may be offset by changes in another size metric. For example, U.S. automakers recently experienced a large increase in sales accompanied by a reduction in cash flow. This netting effect in the RAFI indexes can leave the overall fundamental size of the company and the need to rebalance unaltered.

These two aspects of the RAFI methodology contribute to lower turnover than can be had in more simplistic Fundamental Index approaches. Referring back to Figure 6.3, note that the average turnover of the four single-metric fundamental index constructs is almost 2 percentage points higher per year than the turnover of the RAFI composite. Further, the annual turnover of the RAFI composite is lower than the lowest of the single-metric approaches.

Some critics suggest that the Fundamental Index approach has high turnover. By the standards of the cap-weighted index, perhaps it does, with turnover of 10 percent against 6 percent for the most comparable cap-weighted index. Also, for those who rely on quarterly rebalancing, especially without the fundamental size metrics smoothed over time, the turnover can easily leap to 25 percent to 50 percent or even higher. Still, by the standards of enhanced indexes or active managers, the turnover of the Fundamental Index portfolios is very low.

Concluding Comments

Perhaps it's time for us—practitioners and academics alike—to recognize that share prices are derivatives of—and are linked to—the fundamentals of a company. It will be provocative to view stocks as derivatives. But just as options derive their fair value largely from company share prices, stocks derive their fair value largely from present and future financials for the underlying company. Viewed from this perspective, the cap-weighted indexes are downright peculiar. These indexes recognize that share prices contain a wealth of information about the market's consensus expectations for the future prospects of a company. But they then ignore the fact that those expectations are fully discounted in the price of the company's stock. So most indexed money goes into companies with rosy expectations, companies that are priced to deliver merely average returns *only* if those rosy expectations come true.

Suppose, 50 years ago, Standard & Poor's had launched a "Capitalization 500" and a "Fundamental 500." The former would today be a quaint anachronism, used mainly for measuring the success of both active and passive strategies, with few (if any) passive strategies tied to the Capitalization 500 Index.

What would this have meant for finance theory? Modern Portfolio Theory, in formalizing the importance of diversification, the capital asset pricing model, in defining the link between equilibrium pricing and the market clearing portfolio (still capitalization weighted, of course!), and many other pioneering theoretical advances would still have been developed, and would still be viewed with well-earned respect. Markowitz, Sharpe, Miller, and others would still have won their Nobel Prizes, which are amply deserved whether markets are efficient or not. But, perhaps, we might not have wandered in the "efficient market hypothesis" desert for 40 years. Perhaps, we might have been less dismissive of data that contradict our most elegant finance theories and might have been more ready to see these theories as *approximations* of the real world. Perhaps, we might not have strained to identify "hidden risk factors" to explain "so-called anomalies" of the markets, such as the value effect, the size effect, and long-horizon mean reversion, if a simple acknowledgement of "pricing error" can explain all three.

What would these differences have meant for investment practice? The dominance of the "Fundamental 500" over the "Capitalization 500" might have served to hasten the adoption of indexing strategies. That earlier—and larger—adoption might have served to rein in some of the more spectacular bubbles of the past 40 years and might have led to more sensible capital allocation in the economy. Finally, these effects might collectively have served to diminish the gap between the performance of the stock market (cap-weighted) and the performance of the average (fundamentals-weighted) stock, because of the flow of capital into the Fundamental Index portfolios.

All of this is speculation, of course. What is clear is that there is now a credible, scalable alternative to capitalization weighting. It's equally clear that this idea will be helping the practitioner and academic communities revisit their core assumptions for some time to come.

Fundamental Index Performance in U.S. Stocks

A wise man, therefore, proportions his belief to the evidence.
—David Hume, 1777

One of the main roles of the stock market is to help determine fair values for companies and so to facilitate the allocation of capital to its best uses. This "fair value" discovery process, from active managers assisted by all of their research, should produce prices that are noisy approximations of company fair values. Academics will argue that value will be randomly distributed symmetrically around price. Common sense, and most practitioners, will argue that pricing error can just as easily be symmetrical around value. Under this second assumption, the capitalization-weighted portfolio will invest most of our money in companies that are trading above fair value. If so, then any alternative weighting scheme that breaks the link between a stock's pricing error and its weight in the portfolio, as the Fundamental Index construction should do, will produce additional performance against traditional cap-weighted indexes.

As long as value drives price, and not the other way around, we can show that capitalization weighting will underperform fundamental weighting. The mathematics and the historical evidence are compelling. Our research, confirmed more recently by the performance of live portfolios, shows that Fundamental Index portfolios outperform cap-weighted alternatives over long spans of time in the vast majority of markets. This finding is consistent with our core hypothesis: excess return can be achieved by breaking the link between the price of a stock and its weight in the portfolio, thereby eliminating the return drag of price or capitalization weighting. In this chapter, we provide more detail on the performance of the Fundamental Index concept.

RAFI U.S. Large Company Performance

We begin our review of the Fundamental Index portfolio with large U.S. companies. As illustrated in Chapter 2, the RAFI U.S. Large Company Index (RAFI U.S. Large) averaged annual returns that exceeded the Cap 1000 Index and the S&P 500 Index by 2 percentage points per year over the 46-year period from 1962 through 2007. Furthermore, as Table 7.1 shows, the RAFI U.S. Large achieved this outperformance with slightly lower risk than cap-weighted alternatives. By putting much of an investor's money into the companies that carry the highest valuation multiples, which are often *more* volatile (or riskier) than companies at lower valuation multiples, capitalization weighting frequently ends up with more risk, even as it delivers less return, than valuation-indifferent indexes like the RAFI portfolios.

If Fundamental Index portfolios can outpace a broad cap-weighted index by 200 basis points or more per year with less risk, the result should be a higher risk-to-reward ratio, or Sharpe ratio.

Table 7.1   Fundamental Index Performance Statistics, 1962 through 2007

Portfolio	Ending Value	Annual Return	Annual Volatility	Sharpe Ratio	Excess Return	Tracking Error	t-statistic
S&P 500	90	10.3%	14.6%	0.37	0.0%	1.7%	0.19
Cap 1000	88	10.2%	14.8%	0.36	—	—	—
RAFI U.S. Large	207	12.3%	14.4%	0.50	2.1%	4.0%	3.47

Source: Research Affiliates, LLC.

Because most investors think of short-term U.S. Treasury bills as the classic so-called risk-free investment, the Sharpe ratio is usually calculated by how much return an investment delivers above the T-bill return divided by the risk of the investment.[1] In this case, the Sharpe ratio on the Fundamental Index portfolio is 0.50 compared with the Sharpe ratio of 0.36 for the Cap 1000 portfolio—roughly a 40 percent improvement in the reward-to-risk ratio. This performance boost is substantial in dollar terms and significant in statistical terms.

If an active manager claims to add 200 basis points return per year over long spans of time with less risk than the broad cap-weighted markets and so delivers 40 percent more return per unit of risk (Sharpe ratio) than the broad market, an investor's initial reaction ought to be skepticism. But this "manager" is neither a brilliant stock picker nor a sophisticated "black box" quantitative model for ranking different companies. The manager simply has a different frame of reference for constructing a broad market index. The index is based on the footprint each company has in the broad economy, measured by fundamental metrics of company size, rather than its footprint in the stock market as measured by its market capitalization.

This improved performance translates into significant wealth for investors. Over the past 46 years, cap-weighted broad market indexes have offered impressive returns, sufficient to turn every $1 invested at the end of 1961 into approximately $90 by year-end 2007. That's remarkable. But an equally simple idea—weighting stocks by economic footprint instead of market value—could have delivered more than $200 of end-point wealth! This vast difference is visible in Figure 7.1, where the results are shown in two ways—a linear scale and a log scale. The linear scale shows a gain from $10 to $20, the same as a gain from $110 to $120. The log scale shows a gain from $10 to $20, the same as a gain from $100 to $200. The linear scale shows the cumulative gain in wealth quite vividly, but it makes the early gains look tiny because the scale itself is so small in the early years. The log scale makes the cumulative gain seem modest, but it shows that the early gains were proportionally similar to the later gains. Both graphs are correct. Together, they provide a more complete picture than either alone.

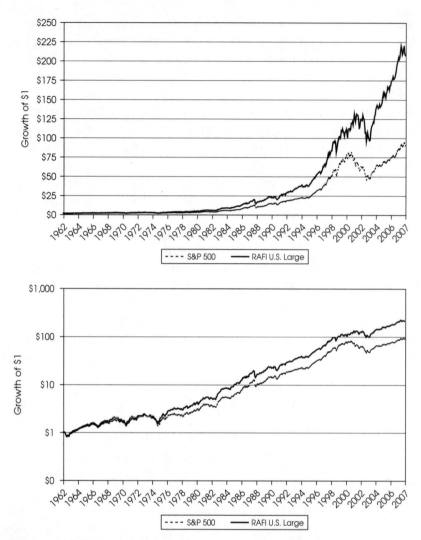

Figure 7.1   Growth of $1, RAFI U.S. Large versus S&P 500, 1962 through 2007
Source: Research Affiliates, LLC.

Digging Deeper across Market Cycles

Clearly, the Fundamental Index portfolio adds value over long periods of time. But can it add value when investors most need it? If a strategy boosts returns and reduces risk, common sense says that it will work better than other strategies when the market is performing

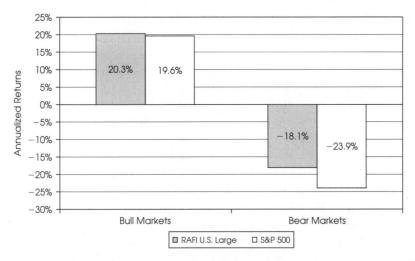

Figure 7.2   RAFI U.S. Large and S&P 500 in Bull and Bear Markets, 1962 through 2007
Source: Research Affiliates, LLC.

badly. Such a strategy will be applauded by most investors. After all, that's when they most *need* stronger investment results.

The lower risk profile of the Fundamental Index portfolio is most evident in bear markets. As Figure 7.2 shows, in falling markets, the RAFI U.S. Large outperforms cap-weighted portfolios by a far wider margin than its overall record. In the 1973 through 1974 bear market, for example, the RAFI U.S. Large outperformed the S&P 500 by more than 370 basis points annually. During the aftermath of the tech bubble, in 2000 through 2002, the margin was even wider. Similar results were obtained throughout our study horizon: On average, the RAFI U.S. Large outpaced the cap-weighted alternative by 5.8 percentage points annually in bear markets. Meanwhile, unlike most defensive portfolios, a Fundamental Index portfolio can achieve modest excess returns in the good times as well, as evidenced by its 70-basis-point excess return in bull markets.

Digging Deeper into Different Time Periods

Adding value *consistently* over time is as important as ending wealth potential. It may be even more critical in light of investors' tendency to abandon even the most proven of long-term strategies in

times of short-term disappointment. Long-term, cumulative annualized performance can hide a lot of short-term sins. A fantastic
calendar year can transform a consistent laggard's longer-term
numbers into the top quartile. Accordingly, savvy advisors want
strategies that have a high probability of achieving excess returns
over intermediate stretches, such as the five-year periods typically
used as the measurement horizon for institutional guidelines and
mutual fund ratings.

As Figure 7.3 shows, the Fundamental Index advantage is
remarkably reliable across decades of equity returns and various
economic environments. In the 1960s, when growth stocks and low
inflation were the order of the day, the Fundamental Index strategy
outperformed in the 0 to 200 basis point range. The Fundamental
Index advantage steepened considerably, briefly touching the 600
basis point mark, in the high-inflation period of the 1970s, a time
when equities failed to keep pace with consumer prices. Even after
Business Week (1979) ran its now famous cover story, "The Death of
Equities," the value added by the Fundamental Index strategy continued in the 1980s, a period of tremendous equity market performance. And its superior performance continued in the first and

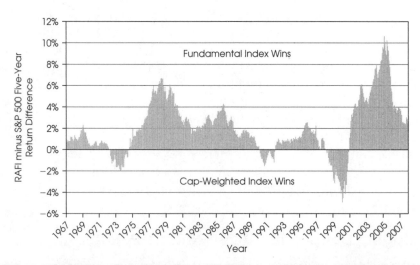

**Figure 7.3 Rolling Five-Year Annualized Excess Returns: Fundamental
Index Portfolio versus Cap-Weighted Index, 1962 through 2007**
Source: Research Affiliates, LLC.

middle parts of the 1990s, when the Fundamental Index advantage was modest but generally sound.

Of course, Figure 7.3 also reveals times when the Fundamental Index strategy failed to add value. There have been three such periods since the early 1960s—the Nifty Fifty period of the early 1970s, the biotechnology run-up of the early 1990s, and the technology bubble of the late 1990s. Needless to say, similarities extend across each of these instances. They were all growth-dominated markets, in which the price premium accorded to the growth stocks was ramping up. So, an index with a growth tilt would have an advantage over an index with a value tilt. Because a Fundamental Index portfolio has a value tilt relative to the cap-weighted market, a growth market will help the cap-weighted market relative to a Fundamental Index portfolio. Also, these three instances are all considered, with the blessings of hindsight, to be *price bubbles*, during which investors paid ever-higher premiums for growth expectations that failed to materialize, and gave ever-lower credence to the fundamental measures of a company's current business scale.

Through a combination of euphoria and greed, whenever the market experiences a dramatic—and subsequently unjustified—run-up in certain segments of the market, a cap-weighted index benefits handily as overpriced stocks become increasingly overpriced. A stock that doubles in price doubles its weight in the index, so when it doubles again, the cap-weighted portfolio enjoys the rewards of the price appreciation and doubles its weight again—until the bubble deflates and the good times end.

This discussion is anathema to those in academia and in practice who embrace the efficient market hypothesis. To them, bubbles don't exist; nor does over- and undervaluation. Price is value, and value is price. Facts change, fully and precisely justifying whatever changes occur in the price of any asset, and that price is always equal to fair value.

But if just one assumption is relaxed—that price and fair value are always equal—our entire discussion becomes intuitive and sensible. Indeed, we think it is useful to change the frame of reference from price-centric to value-centric. Our view is close to that implied in Jeremy Siegel's Copernicus analogy with one important difference: Value isn't the sun in our universe, attracting price toward it; it's a black hole. We don't mean that price collapses into the black hole or that price and value converge. We mean that prices revert toward an unknown and unknowable fair value. Value's gravitational pull is powerful, and it draws price toward it, but, as with the black hole, we can't see it!

Because a Fundamental Index strategy derives much of its advantage from the *correction of mispricings*—overpriced stocks reverting toward their true values and underpriced stocks appreciating toward theirs—the strategy will not help investors when the opposite occurs. In most cases, when growth beats value by a wide margin, a growing dispersion in valuation multiples also occurs. Typically, this should happen in a world in which pricing errors are increasing. At these times, returns from a Fundamental Index strategy will typically fall behind those of capitalization weighting. But because the Fundamental Index strategy's value bet grows bigger and bigger as the markets pay ever more for growth, it quickly recaptures the lost ground when circumstances reverse and value again wins. When bubbles burst, the gains of Fundamental Index portfolios relative to cap-weighted portfolios can be quite large indeed!

When we look at Figure 7.3, it's all too easy to worry that the gains have been good recently, so perhaps we're due for another dip, like the ones that we saw in 1971 through 1972, 1991, and 1999 through 2000. Indeed, 2007 was a one-year dip. Often, a different perspective can help us to understand the two-faced Janus head of risk and opportunity. Much of the reason the Fundamental Index concept is so controversial is that the investment industry is a world in which most people think capitalization weighting is the right way, and perhaps the only way, to index. Consider Figure 7.4. Suppose the industry began with the idea that weighting companies by their fundamental economic scale is the norm and capitalization weighting is the new kid on the block—the discussion would be very different. Almost no one would seriously consider a new indexing approach that outperforms only during infrequent speculative bubbles, no matter what the theoretical merits of the concept!

Furthermore, academics would immediately try to understand why their elegant theories, which prove that capitalization weighting should be unbeatable, fail so miserably. Instead, because cap-weighted indexes have gained so much traction over so many years, the situation is the opposite: Established indexers dismiss weighting by fundamentals, and too many academics dismiss the empirical evidence that contradicts their theories and the theoretical challenges that this work poses to the finance world. Instead of trying

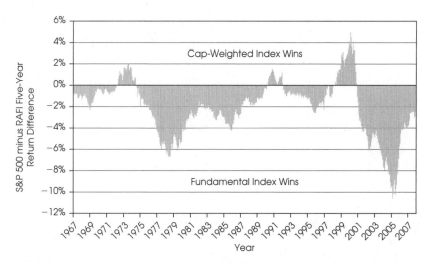

Figure 7.4   Rolling Five-Year Annualized Excess Returns: Cap-Weighted Index versus Fundamental Index Portfolio, 1962 through 2007
Source: Research Affiliates, LLC.

to understand why the theories don't match the real world, and so improve the theories, many people prefer to turn a blind eye to this new line of work and stick with the accepted dogma.

An Equal Comparison: Fundamental Index versus Equal Weighting

One might expect the performance of the Fundamental Index strategy relative to an equal-weighted portfolio to be more or less equivalent. After all, both approaches are indifferent to price. Neither is vulnerable to the cap-weighted performance drag. Both methodologies should randomly place roughly equal amounts in overvalued and undervalued stocks. Sure enough, they both produce meaningful excess returns vis-à-vis the cap-weighted S&P 500. However, the results show that the Fundamental Index strategy outperforms the equal-weighted strategy, at least since Standard & Poor's began publishing its SP EWI.

As Table 7.2 shows, over the 18-year period from January 1990 through December 2007, RAFI U.S. Large bests the SP EWI by 0.9 percentage points per year with considerably less risk. On a risk-adjusted basis, the RAFI U.S. Large dominates by achieving

Table 7.2   Performance Statistics: SP EWI versus RAFI U.S. Large, 1990 through 2007

Measure	RAFI U.S. Large	SP EWI
Annual return	12.9%	12.0%
Annual volatility	13.2%	14.8%
Sharpe ratio	0.68	0.56

Source: Research Affiliates, LLC.

a Sharpe ratio of 0.68, 20 percent better than the SP EWI's figure of 0.56. But, how can this be? Both indexes break the link between portfolio weight and over- or undervaluation. And, the SP EWI has a stark small-cap bias that should have helped its performance over this span. Shouldn't SP EWI be the grand winner? It's not, for a simple reason.

This comparison shows the importance of *selecting* and *weighting* stocks by using fundamental measures of size. Given our earlier discussion of the Standard & Poor's committee-driven approach, one would hardly expect to encounter large companies trading at low enough valuation multiples to become small-cap stocks in the S&P 500. These are the companies that get booted out, frequently in favor of small companies trading at sufficiently lofty valuation multiples to become large-cap growth stocks. The Fundamental Index strategy, in contrast, includes the large companies trading as small-cap value stocks and excludes the small companies trading as large-cap growth stocks. Historically this difference in *selection* provides a tremendous performance boost above and beyond the benefits of reweighting the stocks in our index. So, we should not be surprised that simply equal weighting the growth-biased S&P 500 would fail to match the returns of a more balanced price-indifferent approach such as the Fundamental Index strategy.

So, does an equally weighted Fundamental Index portfolio perform even better still? But, of course! It enjoys the benefits of decoupling the weight from a stock's over- or undervaluation *and* loading up on small companies (introducing a stark small-cap tilt) that historically outperform larger companies. Unfortunately, if the SP EWI is a difficult portfolio to manage, because of turnover and trading costs, the RAFI EWI would be a notch more difficult still. Accordingly, we leave this exploration to others.

Out-of-Sample Results: Small Companies

With the scientific method, we start with an idea and then test it. All subsequent refinements are, to one extent or another, data mining. Data mining is the antithesis of the "scientific method." Any historical research, if based on past data, is subject to concerns about "data mining." We are data mining whenever we scour through past data to find ideas that work—at least in historical simulation. All too often the result is a method that doesn't work on live data.

Our first idea was to consider weighting an index by sales rather than market capitalization. We recognized that weighting companies by size in the economy, rather than market capitalization, would break the link between our portfolio allocations and over- and undervaluation and so would eliminate the performance drag associated with an overreliance on overvalued companies. We expected our approach would add value. That simple idea, subjected to its very first test spanning just over 30 years of data, showed over a 250-basis-point margin of advantage. This test was in full accord with the scientific method. We went on to find large gains, with ample statistical significance, for every measure of company size that we tested, so long as it wasn't linked to price. All of our subsequent research on U.S. large companies represents, to at least some modest extent, data mining.

A strong refutation of any suggestions of data mining requires testing a new idea on data that were not used to develop the idea. We dug deeper into the aggregate performance results and expanded our universe to show that these results are not merely the result of hitting isolated home runs that could easily be dismissed as "luck." The results in almost all markets tested are robust.

Still, some might argue that our expectations were shaped by living through the span we used for our tests and, therefore, that the results are a soft form of data mining. This critique is fair, so in this section, we provide the results of additional tests of the Fundamental Index concept—*unaltered in methodology and so in no way fitted to the new data*—on other sets of data.

Thus far, we have described the results of the Fundamental Index strategy in large U.S. companies. This market is heavily researched by institutional investors and mutual funds. Stocks such as Exxon Mobil, General Electric, Microsoft Corporation, and Citigroup have an army of sell-side analysts covering their every move, dissecting earnings reports, ripping apart balance sheets, and interviewing company managers and suppliers. And let's not forget all the analysts at each of the top global investment management and mutual fund firms. With this blizzard of coverage, the opportunity to profit on a fact or insight about the company, in the hopes that others haven't stumbled across the same idea, is limited at best. For this reason, the cap-weighted index portfolios, with their tremendous cost advantages, are formidable adversaries to an actively managed portfolio and receive sizable new fund flows every year. Even against these Sisyphean barriers, the Fundamental Index portfolios win handily.

Small U.S. companies receive far less research attention. Many such companies fly somewhat under the radar of the comprehensive research activities applied to their larger-cap brethren in the United States and other developed markets. Some 40 Wall Street analysts follow Intel with its market capitalization of $150 billion; only 14 are responsible for covering Jack in the Box with its $2 billion capitalization. Companies with less than $1 billion in market value may be covered by only one or two analysts, or none at all. With fewer competitors seeking profit-generating information, skilled practitioners should be able to add more value in the small-company segment.

As shown in Figure 7.5, the total return of the Morningstar Small Blend peer group beat the small-cap benchmark Russell 2000

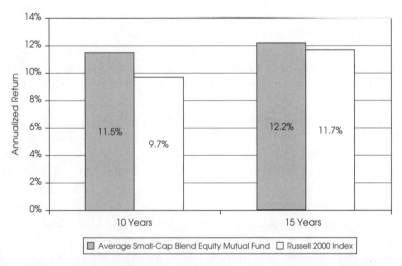

Figure 7.5   Active Managers in Small-Cap versus Benchmark Ending May 31, 2007
Source: Research Affiliates, based on data from Morningstar.

Index by 1.8 percentage points annually over the 10 years ended May 31, 2007. The ground in the small-cap domain is arguably more fertile for active managers than it is in the large caps. It is very important to note that these managers were the *survivors* over the past 10 to 15 years. Presumably, most of the funds that failed were underperformers, so this picture is probably somewhat too rosy.

In such a bountiful space for active management, how does the Fundamental Index strategy stack up? By applying the Fundamental Index methodology to the next 2,000 smaller companies (the 1,001st to 3,000th largest companies selected and weighted on their fundamental economic footprint), we constructed the RAFI U.S. Small Company Index (RAFI U.S. Small). As illustrated in Figure 7.6, the RAFI U.S. Small has produced significant excess returns since 1978, the inception of the widely used (and cap-weighted) Russell 2000 (constructed in much the same "next 2,000" manner, based on the available float of each company's stock).

The RAFI U.S. Small outperformed the Russell 2000 by 340 basis points annually for the entire 29-year history of the Russell 2000. This performance can be compared with the long-term 210 basis point excess return of the RAFI U.S. Large over its comparable cap-weighted benchmark. The excess returns also come with

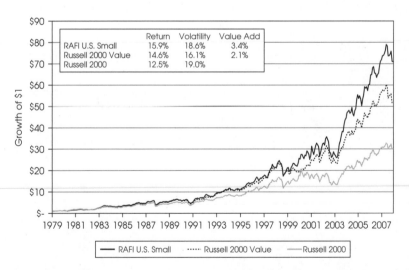

Figure 7.6   RAFI U.S. Small versus Russell 2000 Value and Russell 2000, 1979 through 2007
Source: Research Affiliates, LLC.

less annual volatility—18.6 percent annual standard deviation versus 19.0 percent. Evidently, *the Fundamental Index concept produces larger outperformance as one moves down the capitalization range.*

Recall how the Fundamental Index concept adds value. It doesn't rely on sophisticated models to select stocks for outperformance. It doesn't involve painstaking evaluation of financial ratios. It chooses and weights companies on the basis of economic footprint. In so doing, the Fundamental Index concept largely eliminates the structural link between over- and undervaluation and weight in the portfolio. As a result, pricing errors tend to cancel each other out, largely eliminating the return drag of overweighting the overpriced and underweighting the underpriced.

In a perfectly efficient market, prices equal the enterprise's intrinsic value. If there is any error, it's of a specific sort: Value is randomly distributed around price, rather than price around value. *As the market loses efficiency, the magnitude of any mispricing increases and the cap-weighted performance drag is magnified.* Figure 7.7 illustrates this process. In Chapter 9, where we discuss how the theory may have led us astray, we present new research that finds that the cap-weighting performance drag relative to its opportunity set is proportional to the *square* of the errors in the price. So, if the 2.1 percentage point gain in large companies rises to 3.4 percentage points in small companies, this result is impressive but not surprising.

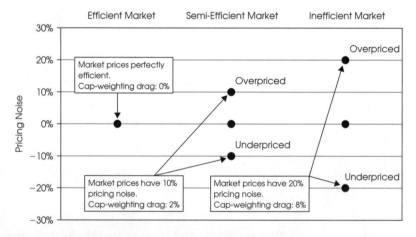

Figure 7.7   Return Drag Rises in Less Efficient Markets
Source: Research Affiliates, LLC.

It may just mean that pricing noise is roughly 30 percent larger in small companies than large.

Using the Fundamental Index with Style: Growth and Value Applications

After exploring the Fundamental Index advantage in smaller stocks, we progressed to an examination of its application on the other major axis of equity categorization, namely, the growth and value continuum. Just as the major traditional cap-weighted index providers segment their broad indexes into style buckets, the RAFI U.S. Large can be split into a RAFI Growth Index and RAFI Value Index.[2] For those investors seeking a pure style play, we can consider how these fundamental style indexes measure up to the widely used Russell style series.

Looking at the growth side of the coin, Figure 7.8 shows that the RAFI Growth has produced an annualized premium over the Russell 1000 Growth Index of 160 basis points since January 1, 1979. This excess return was achieved with much less annual volatility—16.7 percent for the RAFI Growth versus 17.6 percent for the Russell 1000 Growth. The Sharpe ratio received a sizable bump from the 0.32 for the cap-weighted Russell to 0.43 for the RAFI Growth.

Similar excess returns can be earned by implementing the Fundamental Index methodology on the value subset. The RAFI Value beat the Russell 1000 Value Index by 180 basis points per year from 1979 through December 2006 period as shown in Figure 7.8. It did so with an even bigger drop in risk—from 16.7 percent to 14.1 percent. A close inspection of both charts reveals that the vast majority of the reduced volatility was picked up in falling markets, exactly when we most need to cut our risk. And downside retention is exactly what the RAFI Value delivers, with an annual bear market return of −8.5 percent versus more than 13 percent on average for the Russell 1000 Value during such turbulent times.

Why should a RAFI index add 160 basis points for growth, 180 basis points for value, and 210 basis points for the combination of the two? There's a very simple reason. The combined portfolio *also* benefits from contra-trading against the market's excesses, selling growth when it has become progressively more expensive and buying it back as its valuation premium moderates. The individual style portfolios can't enjoy the benefits of this rebalancing!

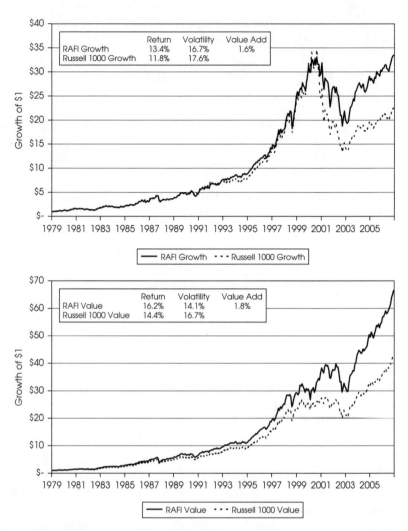

Figure 7.8   RAFI Growth and Value Performance, 1979 through 2006
Source: Research Affiliates, LLC.

Narrowing the Focus

Nasdaq

Of all U.S. equity markets, the Nasdaq is the place where one can reasonably expect the largest pricing errors. Nasdaq stocks are typically small, emerging companies whose prices are based on nebulous long-term prospects. Furthermore, speculators migrate to these companies and shun the often larger, more mainstream stocks. Their speculations are quite likely to make the pricing errors even larger, creating a significant cap-weighted performance drag.

The Nasdaq Composite Index is more than just a roster of young entrepreneurial start-ups and underfollowed stocks, as it also includes a few heavily covered stocks, such as Intel and Microsoft. But it is not a wide-ranging market proxy. Despite the substantial universe and varying sizes of enterprises, the cap-weighted Nasdaq Composite has more than 70 percent of its assets in the technology, consumer services, and health care sectors. Nonetheless, Nasdaq-based index products are extensively used in many investor portfolios. As a case in point, the Nasdaq-100 Index Tracking Stock (often described by its ticker symbol, QQQ), with nearly $19 billion in assets, is the fourth largest exchange-traded fund (ETF) in the United States (State Street Global Advisors, 2007).

The results of our research strongly support the idea that pricing errors are magnified in the Nasdaq market, leading to a significant Fundamental Index advantage over the cap-weighted Nasdaq Composite. As Figure 7.9 shows, the Fundamental Index advantage is very powerful: although the Nasdaq Composite index has delivered 10.5 percent per year since it was launched in 1973, the RAFI

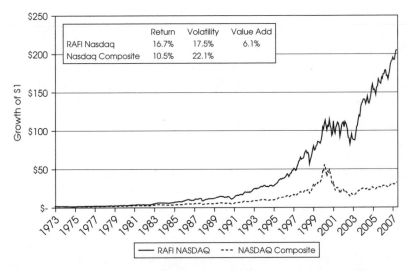

Figure 7.9 RAFI Nasdaq Performance, 1973 through June 2007
Source: Research Affiliates, LLC.

Nasdaq has achieved an annualized return of 16.7 percent over that same span. How important is this 6 percentage point difference? It makes the difference between having 30 times our money or *200* times our money, in just 34 years. The lower volatility observed in large and small U.S. companies also holds.

REITs

Real estate investment trusts (REITs) offer equity investors a way to participate in the real estate asset class in a liquid and transparent manner. These companies own (and often operate) a diversified basket of income-producing real estate properties. The net income is then passed along as a dividend to shareholders. According to the National Association of Real Estate Investment Trusts (NAREIT), there are currently more than 200 publicly traded REITs with more than $475 billion in assets.[3] Although REITs do appear in traditional equity benchmarks offered by such firms as Standard & Poor's and Russell Investment Group, many investors prefer to make a separate allocation to the category because of its diversification benefits and ease of monitoring.

Like stocks, REITs are priced intraday on various exchanges and, like stocks, are valued on the basis of decades of future cash flows. Of course, the future dividends of a REIT are tied to the rental incomes of the underlying properties, whereas stock dividends are linked to corporate earnings. Nonetheless, both rental income and earnings can be significantly different from what is incorporated in prices because of such systematic factors as economic surprises or idiosyncratic surprises at the sector or company level. Thus, one would expect mispricings in REITs. For example, apartments could become overpriced relative to retail properties or hotels could become underpriced as occupancy slumps in a recession. Because REIT indexes are also cap-weighted, one would expect such proxies to also suffer a return drag.

The four-component RAFI methodology can be applied to REITs to create a RAFI REIT Index. Figure 7.10 examines the performance of this RAFI REIT Index versus the widely used and cap-weighted FTSE NAREIT Composite Index. As these results show, REITs do suffer from mispricings in the cross-section: The Fundamental Index strategy adds more than 2.2 percentage points from January 1, 1984, through June 30, 2007. Interestingly, the

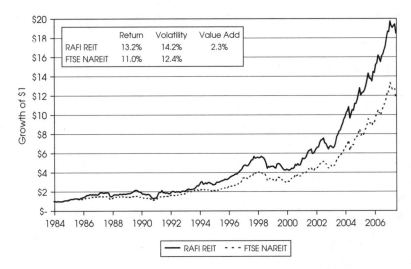

Figure 7.10   RAFI REIT Performance, 1973 through June 2007
Source: Research Affiliates, LLC.

RAFI REIT outperformed during each decade data were available—adding 4.4 percentage points during the 1980s (partial), 0.4 percentage points during the growth/bubble 1990s, and 2.2 percentage points annually—in a major bull market for REITs—over the first 7½ years of this decade.

Sector Performance

Sector index funds and ETFs are being used by advisers and their investors more and more in portfolio construction. Like the broader cap-weighted indexes, our research shows that cap-weighted sector-based indexes will suffer the same type of performance drag as the broader market indexes. A comparison of the excess returns of the RAFI sectors versus comparable cap-weighted sectors for U.S. large companies is presented in Table 7.3.

The Fundamental Index approach produced annualized excess returns in 9 of 10 sectors over the 17½ year evaluation period. Of the 10 sectors, 8 fall in a relatively tight band between 1.7 percentage points and 2.6 percentage points of value added per year. Interestingly, three of the traditional growth stock sectors—consumer staples, health care, and information technology—experienced the largest excess returns. All three beat their

Table 7.3   Excess Returns: RAFI Sectors and S&P 500 Sectors, October 1989 through June 2007

Sector	RAFI Return	Volatility	S&P Return	Volatility	Value Add
Consumer discretionary	9.4%	18.2%	9.8%	16.8%	–0.3%
Consumer staples	14.0%	12.7%	11.5%	13.8%	2.5%
Energy	16.1%	17.2%	14.3%	16.8%	1.7%
Financials	15.6%	18.1%	13.3%	19.1%	2.3%
Health care	15.0%	14.8%	12.6%	16.2%	2.4%
Industrials	13.3%	15.4%	11.3%	15.5%	2.0%
Materials	11.1%	18.8%	9.3%	18.4%	1.7%
Telecommunications	7.5%	21.0%	7.1%	20.3%	0.4%
Utilities	11.7%	14.6%	9.3%	15.3%	2.4%
Information technology	13.5%	25.4%	10.9%	27.4%	2.6%

Source: Research Affiliates, LLC.

cap-weighted counterparts by 2.4 percentage points to 2.6 percentage points, while the least inspired result is found in a classical cyclical value sector—consumer discretionary. A working hypothesis is that the three growth industries frequently contain "next big thing" companies, which often fail to deliver on the high expectations. As the hype intensifies, the stock prices ascend well above any reasonable link to even the most optimistic of operating expectations. Naturally, the cap-weighted sector fund rides the wave of speculation with ever-increasing allocations. Indeed, many of the primary individual equity examples of mispricings outlined at the start of this book fell in these sectors, such as Amgen in health care and Cisco Systems in information technology (IT).

In contrast, the stocks of consumer discretionary companies are inclined to have a noneconomic factor that actually benefits the cap-weighted approach—branding. A powerful brand ensures high customer retention despite high prices (and perhaps even mediocre products). Companies in this sector that enjoy such brands are likely to resist margin-eroding competition longer than companies in more commodity-driven economic sectors. Correspondingly, these favored companies carry high valuation multiples for a long time, delaying the adjustment back to intrinsic value. Additionally, the volatile sales and earnings in this sector may be far less mean reverting than investors might expect.

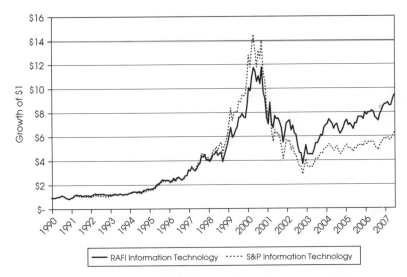

Figure 7.11   Growth of $1: RAFI Information Technology Sector, October 1989 through June 2007
Source: Research Affiliates, LLC.

Examining the tech sector is also instructive. Figure 7.11 shows that the Fundamental Index approach to IT nearly keeps pace with its cap-weighted counterpart during the bubble, softens the impact of the ensuing bear market, and performs strongly in the subsequent bull market upswing of the past few years. Even with this rebound, the RAFI IT sector index is well below the highs posted in 2000 and would require a 30 percent rise to get above water. That's a lot of damage because a 30 percent gain is not easy to achieve, although it's far easier than the *130 percent gain that would be required for the cap-weighted index to erase its losses from the peak.*

The technology example is a particularly instructive illustration of an interesting aspect of a fundamentals-weighted sector fund. The Fundamental Index strategy historically tends to keep pace during strong markets, thereby giving the sector allocator the desired exposure. If the sector falters badly, a Fundamental Index sector portfolio cushions the downside markedly. We have covered this full upside and partial downside phenomenon previously for the broad markets, but it also holds true in sector applications. The right sector choice delivered via fundamental weighting gives nearly full participation in our correct decisions, and the wrong sector bet is cushioned against the full damage of our mistaken choice—an attractive way to play the sector rotation game.

Extending the Analysis Back in Time

Another out-of-sample study of Fundamental Index results focuses on large U.S. companies prior to 1962, the starting point for our own research. Stock market data on individual companies before the mid-1950s is spotty and poor. The inferior quality of the data and the relatively small number of companies are the reasons for our 1962 start date. Jim Davis of Dimensional Fund Advisors applied the Fundamental Index concept to data from 1940 to 1962, an out-of-sample span that predates our 1962 starting point. This was a heroic effort. Davis went to great pains to track down historical prices, returns, market caps, book values, earnings, dividends, and sales for 100 representative companies in the 1940 through 1962 period.[4]

Remarkably, his results for the 1940 through 1962 period mirror our results almost exactly. Our analysis shows 2.1 percentage point average value added by the Fundamental Index. Davis's results in Table 7.4 (Panel A) show excess returns ranging from 0.9 percentage points to 2.6 percentage points for single-metric Fundamental Index constructs with three of the metrics adding in excess of 2 percentage points per year. We took the liberty of averaging the four Fundamental Index portfolios in Davis's study and found that it exceeds the return of capitalization weighting by 2.1 percentage points—identical to our result—and beats equal weighting by 0.6 percentage points per year, as seen in Panel B, again similar to the more recent RAFI results vis-à-vis the SP EWI. In Davis's study, the cap-weighted *value* portfolio does offer two-thirds more value added, but it has 150 percent more value tilt and double the tracking error to achieve this performance.

Two other observations on Davis's work merit mention. First, a cap-weighted index usually uses market cap as the key factor in selecting which companies should be part of that index. A *true* Fundamental Index will typically use company size metrics as a key factor in selecting which companies should be part of the index. In our research, we have found that the nonoverlapping names between these two selection criteria have a nearly 10 percent return

Table 7.4 Results for Fundamental Index Portfolios, July 1940 through June 1962

Panel A. Single-Metric Portfolios*

Metric for Indexing	Annualized Return	Annualized Standard Deviation
Book	18.1%	22.3%
Cash flow	18.1%	22.7%
Dividend	16.4%	19.9%
Sales	17.9%	22.2%
Equal weight	17.0%	22.3%
Cap	15.5%	20.3%
Cap value	18.6%	23.8%

Panel B. Blending into a Composite

	Annualized Return	Annualized Standard Deviation	Cumulative Growth
Average of four	17.6%	21.8%	$24.67
Equal weight	17.0%	22.3%	$22.33
Cap	15.5%	20.3%	$17.13
Cap value	18.6%	23.8%	$27.81

*Based on data from Davis (2007).
Source: Research Affiliates, LLC.

difference per year. Davis's study used the same 100 stocks for all of the indexes. By using the same list of stocks and reweighting them, Davis may have been understating the effectiveness of the fundamental measures and overstating the effectiveness of the cap-weighted indexes by several tens of basis points. Without having access to Davis's raw data, we can't test this hypothesis.

Second, we averaged the results of the four single-metric portfolios because Davis did not create a four-metric composite for weighting the companies. We found that the composite performs better, with much lower tracking error and turnover and a much higher information ratio than the average of these measures for the four constituent indexes. So, the "Average of four" results shown in Panel B are probably understated.

Third, Davis's study relies on 100 companies that were substantial in 1940 and remained so in 1962. This introduces "survivorship bias," which may have affected the various indexes differently.

We cannot know whether this bias hurts or helps the Fundamental Index portfolios relative to the cap-weighted market portfolio.

In short, the results of Davis's study may modestly understate the return advantage for RAFI indexes—and its statistical significance—in the 1940 through 1962 span. Davis and we differ on the interpretation of the data. These varying perspectives will be covered more thoroughly in Chapter 11.

Conclusion

Whether applied to broad sections or narrow swaths of the U.S. equity markets, the long-term outperformance of the Fundamental Index approach confirms our intuition: if there is error in the prices of stocks, the return drag from capitalization weighting is substantial and relatively reliable. And it can be eliminated. The Fundamental Index portfolios add value ranging from a little more than 2 percentage points per year in large U.S. companies to an astounding 6 percentage points annually in Nasdaq stocks.

Allowing such differences to compound, we encounter remarkable advantages in ending wealth. Over 46 years of investing in large companies, the Fundamental Index advantage translates to 2.3 times ending wealth delivered by a cap-weighted index. Similarly, small-company applications result in an ending wealth value over a shorter (28 years) horizon of 2.4 times that of a small-company cap-weighted index. Results in comparison with the Nasdaq Composite over a 36-year span lead to more than a sixfold increase in relative wealth by using a Fundamental Index portfolio.

Time and again, the results confirm a new indexing choice for those dissatisfied with the hollow promise of active management or concerned about the risk that cap-weighted indexes may overload overpriced stocks while chasing fads and bubbles.

CHAPTER 8

Beyond Borders: Fundamental Index Performance in Global Markets

[In scientific controversies,] passion is inversely proportional to the amount of real information available.
—Benford's Law of Controversy
(proposed by physicist and science fiction
author Gregory Benford in his novel *Timescape*)

A testament to the success of any enterprise is its application and effectiveness in other markets. It was one thing for Ray Kroc to sell hundreds of hamburgers and milkshakes a day in Des Plaines, Illinois. The true test of success in today's global economy, however, is whether the McDonald's Corporation strategy—quality, service, cleanliness, and value to every customer—can be repeated around the world. The popularity of McDonald's restaurants across borders and cultures and its 31,000 stores worldwide (the out-of-sample proof), not to mention his legion of imitators, suggest that Kroc's strategy does indeed contain the ingredients for fast-food restaurant success.

The same tests apply to an investment idea, and we are pleased to report that the Fundamental Index concept works globally. In this chapter, we present evidence on how well the Fundamental Index strategy performs in countries outside the United States.

Global Markets

The initial work on applying our simple strategy outside the United States—to eliminate the return drag from capitalization weighting by using fundamental weighting—was done by Nomura Securities, the largest broker in Japan. In 2005, Nomura tested the performance of the Fundamental Index concept in the 23 developed markets in the Financial Times and London Stock Exchange (FTSE) Developed Index series. They chose to test the idea on price-only returns because they did not have reliable global data on ex-dividend dates. Even ignoring the yield advantage of the Fundamental Index portfolios, the same methodology that we tested on U.S. data for 1962 through 2004 produced higher price-only returns than produced by the capitalization-weighted indexes in all 23 countries over the span from 1988 through mid-2005, with no exceptions (Tamura and Shimizu, 2005).

We expanded Nomura's initial work on the non-U.S. markets to include total return data instead of price-only data and a longer time period, 1984 through 2007. As shown in Table 8.1, the new study produced broadly similar results to the initial Nomura study. In the 24 years studied,[1] the Fundamental Index portfolio boosted the average excess return by 260 basis points per year. Adjusted for the lower risk of the Fundamental Index portfolios, this average benefit rises to 310 basis points per year, with over 200 basis points of annual alpha in 19 of the 23 countries. Just one country, Switzerland, fell out of the value-added camp and only barely.

One can see a wide dispersion in these value-added results, ranging from 7.9 percent over 20 years in Ireland to –0.4 percent over the full 24 years in Switzerland. The dispersion occurs for several reasons. First, some of the smaller markets are dominated by one or two single companies (e.g., Royal Dutch Shell in the Netherlands or Nokia in Finland), that disproportionately drive the difference between the indexes and increase the variability of results.

Second, some markets exhibit trends in their willingness to pay a premium for expected growth. Switzerland in the early 1980s was steeped in a culture of skeptical prudence matched by a reluctance to pay a substantial premium for uncertain future growth prospects. Today, as Switzerland has become one of the three global centers for the go-go hedge fund world, that culture has changed

Table 8.1 23-Country Return Statistics, 1984 through 2007

Country	RAFI Return	MSCI Return	Value Added	Risk-Adjusted Alpha	Tracking Error	Risk-Adjusted Info Ratio	Alpha t-Statistic
Australia	16.3%	14.0%	2.3%	3.2%	5.1%	0.63	3.27
Austria	17.8%	12.5%	5.4%	6.4%	9.7%	0.66	3.44
Belgium	15.5%	14.0%	1.5%	2.3%	5.6%	0.42	2.17
Canada	13.4%	10.7%	2.7%	4.0%	6.7%	0.60	3.56
Denmark	12.7%	11.2%	1.5%	2.6%	8.2%	0.31	1.68
Finland[a]	15.8%	14.7%	1.1%	5.1%	20.3%	0.25	1.59
France	16.9%	12.9%	3.9%	4.4%	7.1%	0.62	3.08
Germany	13.8%	10.9%	2.8%	3.8%	5.8%	0.66	4.28
Greece[b]	21.0%	19.1%	1.8%	1.6%	8.6%	0.19	0.82
Hong Kong	22.2%	18.6%	3.6%	3.5%	6.5%	0.54	2.66
Ireland[a]	17.6%	9.6%	7.9%	8.6%	9.1%	0.95	4.50
Italy	15.4%	13.1%	2.3%	2.4%	5.6%	0.43	2.08
Japan	7.1%	4.3%	2.8%	2.8%	5.4%	0.52	2.58
Netherlands	14.0%	12.8%	1.1%	1.5%	6.6%	0.22	1.09
New Zealand[a]	7.2%	6.8%	0.4%	0.4%	8.7%	0.05	0.20
Norway	17.5%	13.3%	4.2%	4.3%	6.5%	0.66	3.23
Portugal[b]	13.2%	9.2%	4.0%	4.6%	8.3%	0.56	2.64
Singapore[a]	13.1%	9.6%	3.5%	3.6%	6.5%	0.56	2.50
Spain[a]	16.8%	13.7%	3.1%	4.2%	5.1%	0.82	4.36
Sweden	17.1%	15.0%	2.1%	3.1%	10.3%	0.30	1.53
Switzerland	11.6%	12.0%	-0.4%	-0.2%	4.3%	-0.05	-0.24
United Kingdom	15.0%	12.1%	3.0%	3.1%	4.4%	0.70	3.45
United States	14.4%	12.4%	2.0%	2.7%	4.7%	0.56	2.90
23-Country average	16.5%	13.9%	2.6%	3.1%	2.9%	1.07	5.52

[a]Start in 1998.
[b]Start in 1989.

Note: Info Ratio = information ratio

Source: Research Affiliates, LLC.

considerably. When the premium paid for growth rises, capitalization weighting enjoys a tailwind because of its growth bias, whereas the Fundamental Index strategy operates into a headwind.

Third, a natural statistical dispersion occurs in results which can lead to outliers. The Fundamental Index strategy is probably far less powerful in Ireland and far more powerful in Switzerland and New Zealand than the historical data suggest. The graphical results in Figure 8.1 show the power of the Fundamental Index concept, both on average and for the individual countries. Here, each line shows the relative wealth of an investor relying on a Fundamental Index portfolio relative to an investor relying on a cap-weighted portfolio for each of the 23 countries in the Morgan Stanley Capital International (MSCI) and FTSE developed world indexes. When the dashed line for Ireland lofts past 200, then passes 300 and off the chart, it means that the investor using a Fundamental Index portfolio has twice as much wealth, then three times as much, and then even more, relative to the investor who has a cap-weighted portfolio of Irish stocks. That extreme outlier on the high end is balanced by the extreme outlier on the low end for Switzerland.

The bold lines are for the G5 countries—France, Germany, Japan, the United Kingdom, and the United States; the dashed lines are for the smaller countries. The heavy gray line in the middle is the average. For the *average* country result, the Fundamental Index investor has 72 percent more wealth than the cap-weighted investor after only 24 years. In other words, the cap-weighted investors lost 40 percent of their wealth relative to the opportunity defined by the average country's Fundamental Index portfolio.

Statistics provide another tool to assess whether results are useful, important, or overwhelming. The *t*-statistic gauges how the average result compares with its uncertainty. Such information allows one to determine the likelihood that the results are a fluke, a consequence of random luck. If a coin is tossed 100 times and comes up heads 55 times, you can't reject the notion that the coin was "fair" and that flipping more heads was just random luck. If you get heads 80 times, however, the likelihood of this particular event's occurring for a fair coin is less than one in a billion. So, in that case, the odds are overwhelming that you've got a "funny" coin; you don't want to bet on tails while that coin is being used!

The finance community generally accepts a 5 percent or smaller probability of random luck as the threshold where results are "significant"—where results are probably not a result of random luck.

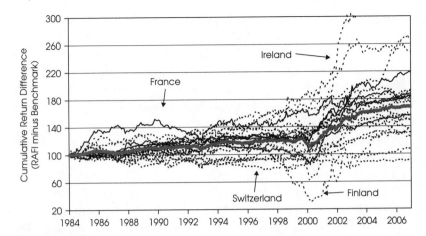

Figure 8.1   Cumulative Value Added in 23 Developed Markets, 1984 through 2006

Note: The bold lines are for the G5 countries—France, Germany, Japan, the United Kingdom, and the United States; the dashed lines are for the other countries.

Source: Research Affiliates, LLC.

The statistical significance of the performance of the Fundamental Index concept in the developed markets is quite strong. For 16 out of 23 countries—more than two-thirds the results are powerful enough that the risk-adjusted Fundamental Index "alpha" is statistically significant. In other words, for each of these countries, there is less than a 5 percent chance that the results are mere random luck. If 1 out of 23 countries were statistically significant at this level, then the whole result could be a fluke, but because 16 out of 23 pass this test, we should not dismiss the results lightly.

The average return across the 23 countries (with a *t*-statistic of 5.5) indicates less than one chance in a million that the results are due to luck. The fact that Fundamental Index portfolios outpace cap-weighted portfolios in 22 out of 23 countries would happen less than three times in a million by random luck. Building on Benford's Law of Controversy, quoted at the beginning of this chapter, we believe that these results are far too powerful to dismiss.

Multicountry Portfolios

A portfolio based on the Fundamental Index methodology will trade against the fads and bubbles in the *country* weights of a multicountry portfolio just as it does in the individual stocks of a single-country portfolio. When we combine countries into an international portfolio, a global portfolio, a pan-European portfolio, and so forth, we find that the Fundamental Index portfolio generates additional value beyond the value added on the individual-country portfolios.

Looking at the country weights in a cap-weighted portfolio (Figure 8.2) versus a Fundamental Index portfolio (Figure 8.3), we can see more stability and *much* tighter ranges for the Fundamental Index portfolio. This stability would have helped investors sidestep the Japanese malaise of 1989 through 1999 when the cap-weighted allocation to Japan dropped from a peak of 51 percent of the developed world stock market value in 1989 to a low of 8 percent 10 years later. To this day, we can't definitively know that the 51 percent was wrong or that the 8 percent was wrong. But obviously both allocations cannot have been right. However, weighting Japanese companies by their share of world sales, cash flow, book value, and dividends—and ignoring price—narrows the range of allocations to Japan in a global equity portfolio to 13 percent to 22 percent, reining in the allocation extremes to a range only one-fifth as wide as the cap-weighted range.

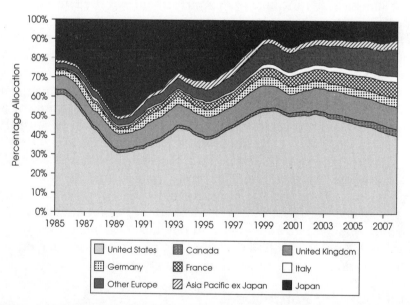

Figure 8.2   Country Allocations: Cap-Weighted Portfolio, 1985 through 2007

Source: Research Affiliates, LLC.

The country rebalancing in a Fundamental Index approach is additive to the bottom line. In our tests, the average result in countries was 260 basis points value added per year over a 24-year span. When we globalized that process to span all 22 countries outside the United States in a combined "Global ex U.S." Fundamental Index portfolio and compared it with a cap-weighted portfolio, we found that the value added rose to 330 basis points, indicating a 0.7 percentage point *additional* annual boost from country rebalancing.

A quick survey of international mutual fund returns in eVestment Alliance reveals that adding 3.3 percentage points to the cap-weighted global and international indexes is impressive. In the 10 years ended June 30, 2007, the Lipper International Large-Cap Core mutual funds achieved a median return of 6.9 percent per year, trailing the MSCI EAFE (Europe, Australasia, and the Far East) Index benchmark's annualized 7.7 percent. Assuming an additional 3.3 percentage points on top of the benchmark from the Fundamental Index concept, the result is an international portfolio delivering results well in the top 5 percent of the international

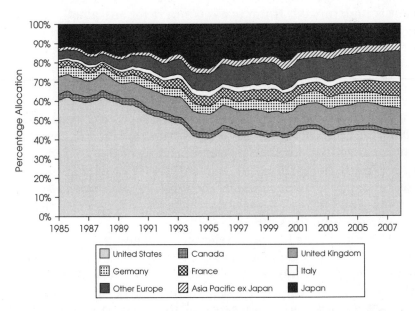

Figure 8.3   Country Allocations: Fundamental Index Portfolio, 1985 through 2007
Source: Research Affiliates, LLC.

mutual fund universe. For an active manager or a brilliant stock picker, this would be an admirable result. For a naïve, mechanistic, simplistic index strategy, it's downright remarkable.

Emerging Markets

The developed markets receive the bulk of institutional and mutual fund research activities. But if the Fundamental Index concept works better in small companies than in large companies (presumably because the pricing errors are larger in the small-company market) and works even better in Nasdaq stocks (presumably because the errors are even larger there), then the concept ought to be very powerful in the emerging markets, where the errors may be enormous.

Consider a simple thought experiment. Suppose a market has two stocks, both ultimately worth $50 and both companies currently the same fundamental economic size. The Fundamental Index portfolio holds the two companies equally. Suppose the markets erroneously view one company as worth $60 and the other as worth $40. The cap-weighted portfolio invests in the two with a 60/40 blend. That is, 60 percent of the portfolio is overpriced and 40 percent is underpriced. If the markets revert to fair value in the next five years, the cap-weighted portfolio will have zero return (–17 percent earned on the overvalued 60 percent of the portfolio just offsets +25 percent earned on the underpriced 40 percent). The Fundamental Index portfolio, however, will earn 4 percent, or 0.8 percent per year. Not bad.

Now, assume the errors are twice as large: Stocks worth $50 are erroneously valued by the market at $70 and $30. In this case, again, the cap-weighted portfolio provides no return. But a Fundamental Index portfolio returns 19 percent, or 3.5 percent per year. Impressive. The value added by the Fundamental Index concept—assuming that the errors are uncorrelated with fair value—rises with the square of the size of the error.

This experiment has direct relevance in applying the Fundamental Index concept to emerging markets, an asset class marked by meteoric ascents and mind-numbing declines. If the errors are twice as large as in the developed markets, then the value added should rise from 200 to 300 basis points per year to perhaps 1,000 basis points per year.

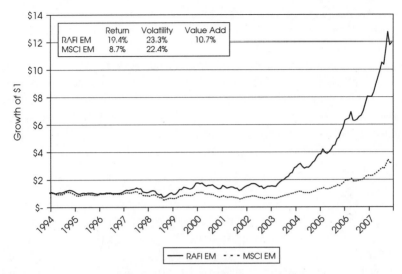

Figure 8.4   RAFI Emerging Market Performance, 1994 through 2007
Source: Research Affiliates, LLC.

Intuition suggests that so large a gain from changing our frame of reference for indexing is implausible. Figure 8.4 shows, however, that an emerging-market Fundamental Index portfolio outpaces the cap-weighted MSCI Emerging Markets (MSCI EM) Index by this very margin! The gap measures up to the theoretical expectations. Superior performance of the Fundamental Index concept is, in fact, what we found in the historical data.

The extraordinary excess returns achieved in emerging markets deserve further exploration. How can a simple, mechanistic Fundamental Index strategy add more than 1,000 basis points of value without trying to pick stocks? Recall how the Fundamental Index concept adds value. It is not by choosing companies that will outperform. It weights companies in proportion to their economic footprint and so *avoids* the return drag associated with systematically overweighting the overpriced and underweighting the underpriced.

In a perfectly efficient market, prices match the enterprise's current fair value, and any subsequent price changes, are symmetrical around price. But are the markets efficient? To assume prices and true value are locked together for securities of the world's developed stock markets is a stretch. To think this condition could hold in the emerging markets is doubtful. Many of the mechanisms designed to maintain fluid and rapid price adjustments associated with market efficiency are lacking in emerging markets. So, the friction—higher trading costs, shareholder restrictions, financial reporting issues—is huge in these markets. Many are new to the use of liquid capital markets, so speculation and simplistic thinking about investments will abound. Furthermore, the odds of political upheaval are much higher in emerging markets. Regime changes, fiscal flip-flops, loss of property rights, and even war create the risk of massive adjustments in fair value for local enterprises.

For all of these reasons, most investors embrace the notion that these markets *should* be inefficient. There *should* be mispricing opportunities. None of this changes the basic fact that if the indexes match the performance of the overall emerging markets' stock markets, then all nonindexed assets (active managers!) must and will collectively have essentially the same return. So, while most investors seek to exploit these inefficiencies by seeking the most insightful active manager, a simpler answer may be to own a Fundamental Index portfolio in these markets. Let the active managers jockey for advantage and, in so doing, create noise in the prices and profit from the dissipation of that noise!

Consistency Counts

As one moves into the less efficient equity markets, not only does the long-term return from capitalization weighting suffer an ever larger drag relative to the Fundamental Index opportunity, but the consistency of that drag increases. Figure 8.5 shows the rolling three-year excess returns of the RAFI U.S. Large, the RAFI U.S. Small, the RAFI Emerging Markets Index (RAFI EM), and the RAFI Global ex U.S. Index (RAFI Global ex U.S.) in relation to their cap-weighted counterparts.

Breaking these data down into "batting averages," we find that the RAFI U.S. Large beat its cap-weighted benchmark in 70 percent of the three-year periods covered in Figure 8.5—an impressive result considering that virtually all of the misses occurred in bubble markets. How many active managers win in 70 percent of all three-year spans? Over the past 15 years, we find that fewer than 3 percent of all active mutual funds won at least 75 percent of the rolling three-year spans.[2]

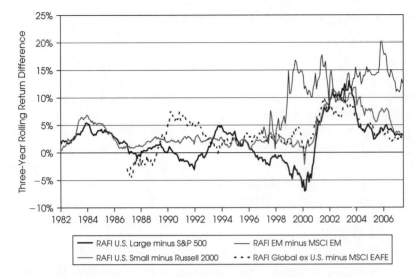

Figure 8.5 RAFI Indexes versus Cap-Weighted Indexes: Rolling Three-Year Excess Returns, 1979 through June 2007

Notes: Beginning dates are as follows: RAFI U.S. Large (1979), RAFI U.S. Small (1979), RAFI EM (1994), RAFI Global ex U.S. (1984).

Source: Research Affiliates, LLC.

A Fundamental Index portfolio for the international developed markets shows an improvement on this standard, with a batting average of 88 percent over the widely used MSCI EAFE. Not to be outdone, a Fundamental Index portfolio applied in the small U.S. companies market comes in at 99 percent. Emerging markets remarkably show no three-year periods of underperformance—a 100 percent batting average—albeit for a much shorter time span than the other markets.

What creates the consistency of excess returns in the international, U.S. small company, and emerging markets segments? The answer is simple. Not only are the mispricings larger in these markets, but the mispricings are also more numerous and frequent. The frequency with which individual stocks are significantly mispriced rises outside the U.S. large company market. A greater number of mispriced stocks generally reverting toward their true values translates to a more consistent return drag in the cap-weighted index over intermediate periods and, consequently, more reliable value added from the Fundamental Index approach.

Concluding Lessons from the Global Markets

The past global evidence is overwhelming. Furthermore, the widespread individual-country outperformance indicates not only that it can apply *to* any country or region but also *from* any country or region. For example, a European investor can seek a Japanese Fundamental Index solution and vice versa.

The case for applying the Fundamental Index concept overseas is only strengthened if investors strongly believe in the relative inefficiency of stock prices in international markets and, in particular, emerging markets. An index methodology, adding particularly large value in the less efficient markets, is an exciting development for passive investors. But let's not forget that the Fundamental Index portfolios merely capture the return available in the markets in a fashion that doesn't link over- or underweighting to over- or undervaluation. In other words, *the result comes not so much because the Fundamental Index portfolios have positive alphas but because cap-weighted indexes have negative alphas—relative to the fundamentals-weighted opportunity set.* Another way to put this is that the Fundamental Index concept offers a "better equity beta." We explore this idea in depth in Chapter 14.

Previously, standard practice was to adopt indexing first in the U.S. large-cap space, where prices were believed to be relatively efficient, and to avoid indexing in the relatively less efficient markets, such as small-cap domestic stocks or emerging markets. The less efficient backwaters of the equity world were reserved for the active fund managers and their teams of analytical sleuths. Indexing in these active-manager-friendly areas was the domain of only the most orthodox of passive believers or was followed only as the last resort by investors who persistently failed to find superior active managers. The results we have shown using the Fundamental Index strategy in small companies and emerging markets open up the possibility that the standard index fund practice can arguably be reversed: One can make the case that indexing in a fundamental construct should be *first* applied in the least efficient markets.

The robust results achieved through the extension of the Fundamental Index concept to global markets underscore the negative alpha of capitalization weighting that, consistent with our hypothesis, prevails in nearly all markets. The recipe to correct the associated return drag is simple, requiring only two ingredients—mispriced stocks and a weighting scheme that is uncorrelated with those errors. The Fundamental Index approach weighting companies by their economic scale is the first such idea that is scaleable, liquid, and matches our company allocation to something which sensibly represents the company's size. In Chapter 13, we explore whether these pricing errors can be relied upon into the future.

9

Has Theory Led the Profession Astray?

In theory there is no difference between theory and practice. In practice there is.

—Attributed to Yogi Berra

The Fundamental Index concept is simple and historically powerful. So, one of the biggest mysteries in this research is that it took almost 50 years after the launch of the S&P 500 Index to explore index weightings that reflect the size of an enterprise rather than its market capitalization. Was the industry blinded by theory or, in the words of *Institutional Investor* magazine, trapped by "An Overwrought Orthodoxy"?[1] Theory does a marvelous job of explaining how the world *ought* to work. Often, the best models and theories offer powerful qualitative insights and some quantitative guidance, abstracted from the full complexity and minutiae of the real world. But no model or theory is so complete as to fully describe reality, especially on matters confounded by human behavior, with its rich contradictions, emotions, and eccentricities.

Understanding assumptions and the consequence of ignoring them can be illustrated with perhaps the most famous experiment in all of physics—Galileo's work on falling bodies. Aristotle, using a rock and a feather as examples, taught that heavy objects fall faster than light objects. For nearly 2,000 years, this hypothesis remained unexamined, untested, and universally accepted. Galileo hypothesized that all objects fall at the same rate regardless of their mass. To prove it, he ostensibly dropped various objects from the Leaning Tower of Pisa.[2] Sir Isaac Newton later codified this conclusion with his Universal Law of Gravitation, which stated that the gravitational force pulling objects down is proportional to the masses of the objects. Because more massive objects are being pulled harder by gravity, exactly in proportion to their larger mass, they accelerate toward earth at the same speed as less massive objects, which experience lower gravitational pull.

Although Aristotle, Galileo, and Newton's ideas were each in their own way elegant, all three theories usually fail—at least a little bit—in the real world. Consider dropping a bowling ball and a feather. No matter how many times you repeat the experiment, the bowling ball slams into the ground long before the feather. Of course, the reason is the resistance or friction of air acting to slow the feather. The same interference holds true, although to a lesser extent, for a large rock and a pebble. And yet, even allowing for motion in a vacuum, seeking to understand the interaction of matter at the atomic level—or on the scale of the universe at large—by using intuitions gleaned from classical mechanics governing planets and stars would be a severe misapplication of Newton's theories.

Many financial practitioners and theorists tend to embrace popular and convenient theories and cling to their predictions in the face of overwhelming evidence that the theories are imperfect. The CAPM is one of the most useful theories for understanding how the capital market prices assets, and for demonstrating how risk and reward should be linked in equilibrium. Its quantitative predictions, however, have relentlessly failed empirical tests. To insist that all CAPM predictions must be true would be a gross misapplication of one of the most important theories in modern finance.

Will the *Real* Active Strategy Please Step Forward?

Adherents of indexing resent the notion that the Fundamental Index approach is referred to as an "index" and even more fervently resent the notion that it might be considered a "passive" strategy. Much of this controversy hinges on nothing more than semantics: How should one define *index* or *passive?* Nowhere in any dictionary we've perused is "capitalization weighting" mentioned in the definitions for *index* or *passive*.

Using a pragmatic definition, an index is a portfolio that is objective, formulaic, transparent, historically replicable, and has low turnover. The Fundamental Index portfolios qualify using these criteria. If a purist CAPM definition of index is used (if it's not cap-weighted, it's not an index), our indexes flunk the test. Interestingly, the purist definition came to the fore only after we introduced the Fundamental Index concept! Before that, there was no vocal criticism of the SP EWI or for those who referred to the price-weighted DJIA as an "index."

We think that much of this controversy stems from a "fundamental" difference in one's frame of reference between those with a capitalization-centric perspective and those with an economy-centric world view. The stock market *is* cap-weighted. So, to measure the performance of the market, one must use capitalization as the weighting metric. But the economy is *not* cap-weighted. So, to measure the performance of the average stock on the basis of companies' economic footprints, one must use something with a more fundamental basis than capitalization for the weighting metric. Capitalization weighting is utterly neutral relative to the market, whereas a Fundamental Index portfolio is blissfully neutral relative to the composition of the publicly traded economy.

Which is the "right" way to index? In their own terms, both are right. Which has structural biases and style tilts? In their own terms, neither. But from the other's frame of reference, both.

The market pays a premium for companies with consensus expectations for above-average growth and prices companies with below-average growth expectations at a discount. Relative to the economy, the market (hence, capitalization weighting) has a clear growth bias, investing most of our money in companies with above-average growth expectations, while a Fundamental Index portfolio is studiously neutral, ignoring valuation multiples, price, or future expectations.

Reciprocally, relative to the market, the Fundamental Index portfolio has a value bias, while capitalization weighting is inherently neutral. The more premium the market is willing to pay for expected future growth, the more value bias the Fundamental Index portfolio will exhibit relative to the market. In a very real sense, they are simply mirror images.

Which is more "active"? Again, the answer depends on one's frame of reference. With capitalization weighting, not much trading is required except to accommodate changes in the list of companies included in the index. But the weights assigned to those companies bounce—sometimes madly—as a consequence of the shifting preferences, expectations, and speculations of the markets, which show up in the form of relative price movements. With the Fundamental Index concept, the weights assigned to companies change gradually and deliberately to reflect their gradually changing economic scale. But a Fundamental Index investor must trade more than a cap-weight investor in order to contra-trade against the market's relative price movements whenever prices and objective fundamental metrics of success diverge. That trading can far exceed the concurrent changes in the fundamental scale of an enterprise.

In short:

- From a market-centric view of investing in *stocks*, the Fundamental Index concept appears to be a value-oriented active strategy because of the trading that's required to rebalance company weights back to the company's economic footprints.
- From an economy-centric view of investing in *companies*, a Fundamental Index portfolio is studiously neutral, while capitalization weighting seems to be an active strategy because of the wide swings in company weights in the index relative to company weights in the economy.

Both views are right, in their own frame of reference. We cannot fairly say that either frame of reference is the only correct one.

The Origins of Cap Weighting

From its launch in 1957 onward, the goal of the S&P 500 was to proxy the performance of the aggregate U.S. stock market. The "index" began with the S&P in 1926 with only 90 constituents. It was cap-weighted, but it was hardly representative of the aggregate market. Reconstituted in 1957 with its expansion to 500 stocks, the S&P 500 represented more than 80 percent of the value of NYSE-listed stocks (on a cap-weighted basis) at the time.[3] Given this wide coverage, the new S&P 500 served as an excellent proxy for the performance of the overall U.S. stock market, which was its stated purpose.

Suppose there had been a dissenting opinion at the table in 1957 suggesting a different orientation. This nonconformist committee member might have asserted that weighting stocks by capitalization, although assuredly representing the *overall market,* might not give investors an accurate representation of the *average stock* in that market. "This cap-weighted list of 500 will be placing the majority of its emphasis on stocks with the highest prices and valuation multiples, focusing on growth companies, not on the broad economy," our dissenter argues. "The index will chase every fad and bubble that comes along, and if a company doubles in price, we'll own twice as much of it *after it's already gone up.* Why should we invest most of our money in companies that have gone up the most or that are priced at the highest multiples? Won't we be assured of investing disproportionately in the companies with the biggest errors in their price?"

If that skeptic had been at the table in 1957, it's quite possible that the S&P 500 might have been weighted by fundamental measures of the size of the 500 companies. If so, not only would the Fundamental Index concept fail to stir controversy today, but cap weighting could never have gained any traction, except as a quaint academic abstraction, because of its relentless underperformance.

Or the skeptic might have been dismissed with a counterargument that would have been compelling at the time: "Our index is a barometer of the stock market. The only way to accomplish this goal for our index is to cap weight it, because the market is cap-weighted. No one would want to invest this way, for the very reasons you cite. It certainly isn't an *investment portfolio.*" The S&P 500 achieved its goal, and the hypothetical fundamental-weighting advocate was never heard.

Our hypothetical rebel's argument, however, is worth exploring. If an investor wishes to get a sense of how the average stock or even a basket of stocks with random weights performs, capitalization weighting is not the most appropriate benchmark because the larger-cap stocks dominate the performance of the set. Instead, when statisticians attempt to ascertain the average of a large range of outcomes, they frequently use the *median*—that is, the middle value of a set. The simple *mean* (or "average") is often inaccurate because it can be significantly skewed by outliers.[4]

Suppose the committee members in 1957 realized that the S&P 500 would in due time morph from a measure of market returns into a performance benchmark and, eventually, an investment portfolio. If there had been a glimmer of expectation that these evolutions were going to take place, it is quite likely that someone at that table would have raised exactly the arguments of our hypothetical skeptic, and the history of the past 50 years would have been very, very different.

Validation of Cap Weighting by Theory

In 1957 as the S&P 500 was being launched, portfolio risk was still primarily determined by "rules of thumb and folklore," as Peter Bernstein, author of *Against the Gods,* noted in a *Financial Analysts Journal* article (Bernstein, 2005a). The situation changed by the end of the 1950s and 1960s. First, in 1952, Harry Markowitz introduced Modern Portfolio Theory (MPT), which proved that combining multiple risky assets with low correlations can reduce overall portfolio risk (Markowitz, 1952). Today, this is common knowledge, but at the time, the concept was revolutionary. With only three sets of inputs—expected return, expected standard deviation, and correlation, across all of the assets being considered—investors now had a tool to effectively allocate their investments in a way that would deliver the highest return per unit of risk.

From a process known as mean-variance optimization or "quadratic programming," the entire range of efficient mixes across the risk and reward spectrum is the *efficient frontier.* Furthermore, although the mathematics was unwieldy before the commercial use of computers in the 1960s and 1970s, Markowitz showed investors how they could largely eliminate the unique, individual risk of each security (later designated by Sharpe and others as "idiosyncratic risk") in the market portfolio, leaving only the risk of the market itself (the "systematic risk").

By the late 1950s, another line of research had produced the efficient market hypothesis (EMH), which posits that the crowd is wiser than any single investor (which is probably true most of the time!). In effect, Adam Smith's "invisible hand" of capitalism governs securities trading. Through this process, the price of any security reflects all available information and analytics, and investors cannot identify investment strategies to achieve superior returns (Samuelson, 1965;

Fama, 1965). If the EMH holds, investors cannot add value through security selection. Accordingly, neither fundamental analysis of individual securities nor technical analysis will be able to discover opportunities to outperform the market.

Twelve years after Markowitz's pioneering work in 1952, and a mere seven years after the 1957 launch of the S&P 500, Bill Sharpe, Jack Treynor, and others advanced a groundbreaking theory describing the link between market equilibrium and the pricing of assets. This theory is known as the capital asset pricing model, or CAPM.[5] In it, the concept of the "market clearing portfolio" was introduced. The market-clearing portfolio is the portfolio for which supply equals demand at any given instant. It is, of course, the cap-weighted market portfolio. This cap-weighted market index was validated as an "efficient portfolio," meaning that one could neither achieve higher return without higher risk, nor achieve lower risk without lower return. Furthermore, the best higher-risk portfolio is this selfsame market portfolio on steroids; that is, the same portfolio with leverage. And, the best lower-risk portfolio is again the same portfolio, but blended with cash. The investor's optimal *equity* portfolio, then, is the cap-weighted market index; no other investment makes sense.[6]

The CAPM states that the expected return on any stock is solely related to its market or systematic risk (better known as "beta"). In theory, high-beta stocks expose the investor to greater market risk and provide higher expected return for the greater risk exposure. Low-beta stocks provide lower expected return but also lower risk. Any extra risk that's uncorrelated with this market portfolio can be diversified away and should carry no reward at all.

Neither the CAPM nor the EMH of classical finance theory, although elegant in their simplicity and powerful in their qualitative insights into the capital market, precisely reflects reality. Most economists, financial practitioners, and academicians, *including the originators of these theories,* agree that the CAPM and EMH are abstractions, not 100 percent correct. Finance theories are useful in their ability to offer powerful intuitions through parsimonious models based on simplifying assumptions. These theories allow us mere mortals a shortcut to understand the invisible hand that guides the financial markets without having to examine the full complexity of the system and without having to fret about the overwhelming body of data that contradicts our theories.

Unfortunately, the simplifying assumptions are just that—assumptions that are not entirely realistic. Therefore, some of the quantitative predictions that result from theory are more speculations on how the world *should* work. Those who mistake theory for reality suffer the unintended consequences of a model that was never meant to be used as a unifying theory of how the world actually works.

The best finance theoreticians are quite open about the limitations of their theories. We don't find the originators of these theories confusing their theories with reality. Many will agree that the world continues to overuse and misuse their theories without proper intellectual rigor. For example, the CAPM involves a list of assumptions that ignore the frictions that exist in any dynamic environment:

- There are no taxes or transaction costs.
- All investors are rational and fully informed.
- All investors are concerned only with expected risk, return, and correlations for their investments (in finance parlance, view stocks only in mean-variance space), ignoring all other considerations (e.g., companies social responsibility).
- All investors can borrow without limit—at the same risk-free rate.
- Lenders are willing to lend—without limit—to any borrower that comes their way at that same risk-free rate.
- The risk-free rate is precise and well defined. Tacitly, then, all investors define risk in the same way, so they view the same asset as risk free.
- All investors have the same general "utility function" (a measure of an investor's risk aversion).
- The markets are efficient: Price equals fair value.

With these assumptions in place, the CAPM is a powerful tool. Unfortunately, none of these assumptions—not one—is found in the real world! As with most top academics, Bill Sharpe has been far more open about its limitations, from the early days of CAPM, than many of his disciples in the indexing community.

Take the third assumption, for example. It appears sensible, but it may be the most unreasonable of all. It states that all market participants choose investments solely on the basis of their risk and reward profiles, which are formed *on rational expectations*. Evaluating a potential sale, they are indifferent to whether the security in question has an unrealized loss or gain. In this rational world, stockholders—assuming no taxes—are not concerned about whether the company pays out profits in dividends, buys back stock, or retains its earnings. Whether to hold a tobacco stock is decided solely on the stock's investment merit, not the product it sells or its track record on social responsibility. A profitable gun-runner or cocaine cartel is judged *solely* on its investment merits. The portfolio managers' clients are assumed to be rational and thus uninterested in what stocks rank near the top as long as they offer the highest risk-adjusted returns.

Unfortunately for those who like to think that the real world conforms perfectly to the model, investors, on the whole, do a poor job of following through on this assumption of mean-variance rationality. Behavioral finance research confirms that investors are more hesitant to realize losses when the sale confirms that the initial purchase was a poor investment decision whereas holding the losing stock holds out some hope of a positive outcome in the future (Statman, 2005). Similarly, dividend policy is not irrelevant to investors. Dividend-payout ratios tend to be excellent predictors of future earnings growth and stock price performance.[7] Moreover, the $2 trillion invested in socially screened portfolios is clearly not invested solely on the basis of risk and return expectations. In the CAPM world, economic participants would be apathetic about corporations' social, environmental, or religious practices. And in mean-variance expectations, the last few days of a quarter would be no different from other trading days. In the real world, however, CNBC coverage is filled with descriptions of mutual funds tidying up their portfolios for quarter-end.

Peer-group and liability considerations are two additional risk dimensions not captured in the CAPM. Yet, both significantly influence investment decisions and risk taking. Peer-group comparisons receive considerable emphasis from consultants and financial advisers, who bombard their investment committees quarterly with universe percentile rankings. The focus on one's peers has become so widespread that for many investors, particularly institutional investors, it may well be the primary risk that we seek to minimize. A study of 19 large defined-benefit pension plans found their asset mixes best minimized peer-group risk while allowing much higher levels of portfolio volatility and mismatch between assets and their pension liabilities (Arnott, 2004).

Speaking of liabilities, since the disastrous funding results of 2000 through 2002, plan sponsors are paying more attention to opportunities to better match the assets of pension portfolios to the return characteristics of their liabilities. Attempts to steer a portfolio's risk posture in that direction comes into direct conflict with the mean-variance approach of the CAPM. In an asset/liability framework, long-duration bonds most closely match the long-term liabilities of a pension plan, so from that viewpoint, these bonds are a risk-minimizing asset class. But in a mean-variance framework, unless we redefine risk to be based on the asset/liability mismatch (often called "surplus risk"), long-duration bonds look terrible, with marginally higher returns than short-term bonds but considerably more annual standard deviation. Figure 9.1 shows how long-duration bonds shift from being a relatively low-risk asset class to being a moderately high-risk one. Absolute return investors would view bonds in the context of the left-hand portion of the chart, whereas pensions would assess their "riskiness" on the right. *Not all investors have the same risk aversion.* This issue is explored further in Chapter 12.

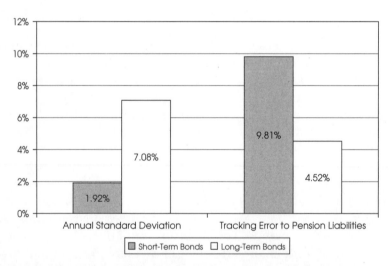

Figure 9.1   Different Measures of Investor Risk Aversion, 10 Years Ended September 2007

Notes: Short-term bonds represented by Lehman Brothers 1–3 Year Government/Credit Index. Long-term bonds represented by Lehman Brothers Long Government/Credit Index. Liabilities calculated by using the Ryan Liability Index.

Source: Research Affiliates, based on data from eVestment Alliance.

40 Years Later: Empirical Results of the CAPM

With so many evident inconsistencies in the CAPM's underlying assumptions, it shouldn't come as a surprise that the CAPM is woefully inadequate in explaining security returns. Some academic studies have empirically demonstrated that high-beta stocks underperform low-beta stocks—*the exact opposite of what the model specifies* (Fama and French, 2004). Others show a link that is, at best, far weaker than the CAPM would predict. Figure 9.2 is one such analysis. It illustrates annualized returns of various beta groups/deciles from 1928 through 2003. The relationship between beta and security returns is essentially nonexistent for a 75-year span in the U.S. stock market.

The CAPM fails to perfectly explain asset pricing in the real world because none of its many assumptions is factually correct. Even in theory, the model has holes. Markowitz, 40 years after the publication of the CAPM, penned a piece showing that if individual share prices are efficient, the market portfolio must be mean-variance *inefficient*: "Thus, in this world that is like the CAPM but has realistic constraints, the market portfolio is typically not an efficient portfolio" (Markowitz, 2005). Sharpe previously acknowledged as much in his 1970 book. With so much practical and theoretical evidence to the contrary, why does the profession cling to

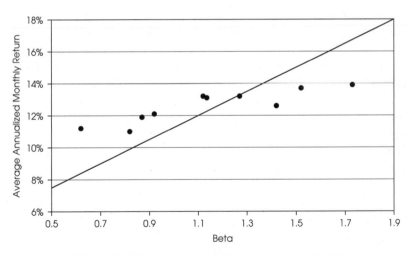

Figure 9.2   CAPM Empirical Results: Beta and Stock Performance
Source: Fama & French (2004).

its conclusion that the market-clearing portfolio, the cap-weighted market portfolio approximated by indexes such as the S&P 500 or the broader Wilshire 5000 Index, efficiently offers the highest return per unit of risk? Is it stubbornness, ignorance, laziness, or financial self-interest? We can't know the answer to these questions, but we can know that the originators of these theories admit that their theories are only approximations of the real world and that their conclusions are only approximately correct.

Ockham's Razor Applied

Many anomalies—that is, results not predicted by our most important theories—cast large shadows over classical finance theories and the assumptions on which they are built. One is the size effect: Small-cap and mid-cap stocks have produced higher returns than large-cap stocks over the past 80 years, albeit with extended dry spells. Another is the value effect: Companies that exhibit low P/Es, low price-book ratios, low price-sales ratios, and higher dividend yields have outperformed growth stocks, again with extended dry spells. A third is the long-horizon mean-reversion effect: Even though short-term "winners" of the prior month tend to repeat, longer-term winners (those of the past decade) tend to revert into laggards, and the long-depressed stocks tend to outperform. A fourth is the January effect: Stocks (especially small-cap and deep-value stocks) tend to rally significantly in the first few days of January as investors readjust their portfolios after year-end tax planning or for portfolio window dressing have run their course. The size effect is vividly demonstrated in Figure 9.3. And there are many more.

In the hard sciences, many (if not most) scientists and academics rejoice in the opportunity to improve theory. The world of finance, however, often reacts to data that contradict its elegant and simple theories with skepticism. It's as if they are saying, "The theory is too elegant to be wrong, so there must be something wrong with the data." Instead, complex and tortured hypotheses and formulas relating to hidden risk factors are used to explain the small-cap premium, the value effect, the relationship between the two, and the mean-reversion effect.

Which brings us to Ockham's Razor. William of Ockham was a fourteenth-century logician and friar whose principle states that "entities should not be multiplied beyond necessity." In the twentieth

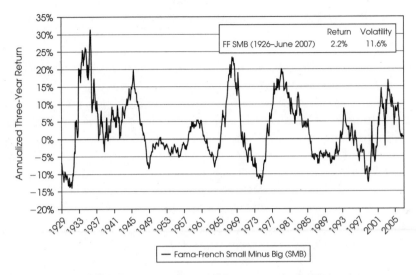

Figure 9.3   Size Effect: Three-Year Rolling Returns, 1926 through June 2007

Sources: Research Affiliates, based on data from Kenneth French. (http://mba.tuck.dartmouth.edu/pages/faculty/ken.french/).

century, Albert Einstein echoed Ockham in his famous advice to "make everything as simple as possible, but not simpler."[8] Today, the idea can be found on a bumper sticker as "KISS: Keep it Simple, Stupid." As strong believers in Ockham's Razor, we set out to find a single, simple reason for these anomalies between data and conventional finance theory. We found that simple pricing errors would account for most of the so-called anomalies (Arnott and Hsu, 2008; Arnott, Hsu, Liu, and Markowitz, 2007).

Pricing errors muddy the clear assumptions underlying the CAPM and EMH, and they complicate the mathematics, perhaps beyond closed-form solution. Instead of assuming efficient markets (and accurate pricing, with errors symmetric around price), we can alternatively assume that every stock's price is equal to its fair value plus or minus an error term, which we will call "noise" (with errors symmetrical around value). The market is constantly attempting to correct these errors so that prices reflect fair value. Because we cannot know today's "fair value" for decades of future cash flows, the noise may well persist, so correcting the errors may take years or even decades. And as corrections are gradually recognized by the markets and incorporated into the price, new surprises come along, keeping the aggregate mispricing relatively steady over time.

Most investment professionals—and many academics—readily acknowledge that the pricing error phenomenon we have just described is a sensible alternative view of the markets and offers a compelling alternative to the notion of efficient markets. Real world frictions, whether behavior based, agency based, or driven by real-world costs and real-word differences in investor needs, circumstances, and preferences, may impede the incorporation of information into prices and, therefore, discovery of fair value in market transactions (the same way the resistance of air causes the feather to fall slower than the bowling ball, even though they would fall at the same pace in a vacuum). The market imperfections, like frictions on the feather, may lead to deviations, sometimes wide, between price and fair value.

This simple change of allowing for pricing errors allows us to explain many of the anomalies documented in the financial literature. Consider the following: The stocks that are priced above their fair values will have lower *eventual* returns as the mispricing is corrected. They will, of course, have a higher capitalization and valuation multiple than if they were priced at fair value. These same companies presumably have enjoyed positive momentum as their price has risen above fair value.

- Overvalued stocks will be a bit overrepresented among large-cap stocks and will underperform in the long run. *Voilà: the size effect!*
- Overvalued stocks will be a bit overrepresented among the growth stocks with higher multiples and lower dividend yields and will underperform in the long run. *Voilà: the value effect!*
- Overvalued stocks will frequently have achieved their overvaluation by dint of past outperformance and will underperform in the long run. *Voilà: mean reversion in long-term returns!*
- Overvalued stocks will be a bit too prevalent in the top of the cap-weighted indexes, leading to a return drag versus price-indifferent weighting methodologies. *Voilà: the drag of capitalization weighting, relative to its opportunity set, as illustrated by the Fundamental Index concept!*

Each of these is a variant on an economic principle known as "order bias." If our samples (e.g., prices) have random errors, then the outliers will often have an error in the opposite direction. As long as prices deviate from fair value, these market anomalies should persist in the future, which raises the question: Why should investors want to cap weight their passive equity exposure? As evidenced throughout this book, *any weighting methodology that ignores price* will lead to better average risk-adjusted results, both in theory and in practice. The obvious exception is when bets are so very concentrated that they create large idiosyncratic risk, which swamps the benefits of taking price out of the weighting scheme. Still, the Fundamental Index concept provides a more elegant solution than previous rudimentary approaches, such as equal weighting. The result is a representative, low-turnover portfolio without the return drag of capitalization weighting.

Concluding Comments: Theory and the Profession

We do not wish to be seen as "bashing" the giants of finance theory. They made immense contributions to our understanding of markets—the function and the behavior of markets. The pioneers who developed financial theories deserve all of the acclaim that has been showered upon them. Rather, we are critical of those who mistake theory for fact, those who misapply the theory in inappropriate areas or contexts, and those who are married to convenient modeling frameworks and their requisite assumptions as if they were fact, rather than welcoming advances which can improve our understanding of the real world. This simplistic abuse of our elegant theories is nothing more than a shortcut to avoid the burden of thinking.

The responsibility of advisers and fiduciaries is to achieve the best return they can for their clients. They do clients and themselves a disservice by accepting theories—no matter how brilliant or elegant—as fact, especially in the face of overwhelming empirical evidence to the contrary. When noise, or pricing error, is added to the pricing models, the mathematics of finance quickly become complicated. Accordingly, academia prefers to assume that, although stock prices may not equal intrinsic value, they are close enough that the error doesn't matter. But error does matter. The quicker the profession acknowledges the cracks in theory, the quicker we can go about seeking the next evolution in our theories. Meanwhile, we can exploit the gaps between theory and reality to identify better (higher return *and* lower risk) solutions for clients.

The cap-weighted S&P 500—the granddaddy of all index funds—was not initially designed to be the basis for an investment strategy. It's reasonably likely that its designers would have been shocked at the very suggestion, because this would mean deliberately owning more of an asset *after* it has soared and less *after* it has tumbled. It was merely intended as a measure of the performance of the broad stock market. Its other uses came later, first as a benchmark to gauge the success of our investment managers and strategies, and later—once the failings of many managers and strategies were revealed—as a management strategy in and of itself.

We can now see that the simple fact of overweighting the overvalued and underweighting the undervalued is not a necessary evil structurally and irrevocably embedded in index fund investing. Nor do we need to tolerate the resulting return drag from capitalization weighting. With due respect to the pioneers of modern finance and the cap-weighted indexes that they spawned, a better alternative now exists.

CHAPTER

10

The Basic Criticism:
Our Style and Size Tilt

Nothing is more apt to deceive us than our own judgment of our work. We derive more benefit from having our faults pointed out by our [critics] than from hearing the opinions of friends.[1]
—Leonardo da Vinci

From the outset, the Fundamental Index methodology stirred considerable discussion and debate among money managers, academics, and other stakeholders in the investment game. Oftentimes, one's skeptics can be dismissed as competitors with a vested interest in the status quo or even uninformed grandstanders. This is not the case in the Fundamental Index debate. Many of the questions are fair and are being asked by some of the brightest lights in the investment world, including such luminaries as Vanguard Founder Jack Bogle; the author of *A Random Walk Down Wall Street* and professor at Princeton, Burton Malkiel; hedge fund manager Cliff Asness; and Harvard Business School professor André Perold. These critics raise important points that can help us gain valuable insights to improve the profession's collective understanding and ultimate benefits from the Fundamental Index concept.

151

In this chapter, we seek to address the main criticisms of the Fundamental Index idea, including the most common critique: The Fundamental Index strategy is nothing more than a repackaged value-tilted small-cap portfolio.

Merely a Value Tilt

Critics contend that the Fundamental Index strategy derives its benefit from a value tilt. They cite the large body of academic research that confirms the existence of a value premium: Stocks with low price-book ratios and high dividend yields outperform over long periods. We don't disagree with the notion that a value bias relative to a capitalization-weighted portfolio historically boosts returns in most markets, nor do we dispute the fact that the Fundamental Index strategy has a structural value tilt relative to the cap-weighted market. We prefer to frame the discussion in a different light, however. The cap-weighted portfolio has a growth tilt—favoring companies with above-average growth expectations for which the market pays a premium multiple—*relative to their economic scale.* But what is the nature of that growth tilt? Does a tilt that shifts from one sector to another and from one company to another with the shifting expectations and preferences of the broad market have an economic meaning beyond simply reflecting those preferences? Those premium multiples too often are more than subsequent events can justify, which means that portfolios that don't have this growth tilt tend to outperform.

The structural growth orientation of the cap-weighted portfolio can be illustrated by looking at two hypothetical stocks. They have the same economic scale as measured by sales, book value, cash flow (CF), and dividends, but they differ in their market capitalizations. One trades at twice the market multiple because of its outstanding recent operating results, rapid recent growth, and the resulting high expectations for its future growth. The other has suffered serious setbacks and sells at half the market multiple. *Capitalization weighting doubles the weight of the former and halves the weight of the latter relative to their identical economic scale.*

The result is a structural growth bent for cap-weighted portfolios relative to the companies' scales in the economy. Of course, growth stocks have a higher multiple than distressed stocks for a reason: They are expected to build revenues faster, thereby earning more for shareholders. In effect, the market reflects the *future expectations* for the economic footprint of these companies, for which the market is prepaying as if that future growth were a *fait accompli*. In an efficient market, the market will correctly gauge future prospects and prepay for expected future growth exactly the right amount to assure that the growth and value stocks offer the same risk-adjusted return!

By contrast, a Fundamental Index portfolio is neutral relative to the economy, weighting companies in accordance with their current economic footprint. So it doesn't share the tilt toward growth. Nor does it structurally assure that its portfolios are over- and underweighting the over- and undervalued companies (relative to their eventual fair value weights). *In an efficient market, no advantage accrues to the cap-weighted portfolio for its decided growth bias relative to the economy. And no material disadvantage is borne by the Fundamental Index portfolio for its value bias relative to the cap-weighted market.*

From an economic perspective, the cap-weighted market has a growth tilt while the Fundamental Index portfolio is neutral. And, from a capitalization-centric point of view, the Fundamental Index portfolio has a value tilt while the cap-weighted market is (of course) neutral. Indeed, in any snapshot in time, the large-company Fundamental Index portfolio is, in the words of some critics, "pure value and nothing but value." As can be seen in Table 10.1, a sales-weighted Fundamental Index strategy will assign a weight to any company equal to its capitalization weight divided by the relative price-to-sales ratio for the stock. That's a "pure value" measure and nothing but pure value.

But . . . that value tilt of a Fundamental Index portfolio is dynamic. The larger that the premium the market is willing to pay for growth, measured in relative price/sales, the larger the

Table 10.1   Fundamental Index Weights and Value Measures

Weightings

RAFI Sales Weight = Cap Weight / Relative Price-Sales Ratio
RAFI Book Weight = Cap Weight / Relative Price-Book Ratio
RAFI CF Weight = Cap Weight / Relative Price-CF Ratio
RAFI Dividend Weight = Cap Weight × Relative Dividend Yield

Source: Research Affiliates, LLC.

value bet the sales-weighted Fundamental Index portfolio makes. Therefore, the value bet will be large when the market pays a large premium for perceived future growth opportunities, and the bet will be modest when the market pays a small premium for future growth.

The critics overlook the fact that growth and value are not types of companies; they are mere manifestations of whether the market is paying a premium or a discounted valuation multiple for a company. So, the rosters of companies on these growth and value lists constantly change. Today's growth stock may be tomorrow's value stock, and vice versa. The market's perceptions of growth opportunities are constantly shifting. As expectations shift, so too does the price relative to the economic scale of a company.

In 1982, Bob Shiller pointed out that the stock market is far more volatile than the fundamental underpinnings of value. Specifically, he observed that because market levels should reflect the net present value of the future dividend distributions of all stocks, prices are vastly more volatile than dividends. This means that either expectations of future dividend growth are pogo-ing up and down or the discount rate for those future dividends must be pogo-ing down and up. The same observation applies for individual stocks. When a company dives deep into the growth camp, does that mean that the discount rate has changed materially relative to the discount rate for the average company, or that growth expectations have changed? Because a large change in the discount rate for one company relative to others makes no economic sense, growth expectations for this company have changed.

Valuation multiples do *not* follow a random walk! They mean-revert, which means that when they're high, they tend to fall and when they're low they tend to rise. In an efficient market, as a growth company succeeds in accordance with expectations, its valuation multiple will retreat so that its return over time matches that of the value companies. But, in an inefficient market, the multiples can deviate from their true value. Indeed, the Fundamental Index portfolio trades against *whichever* companies, sectors, styles, or even countries are receiving the most extreme bets from the cap-weighted markets. And that's a constantly shifting roster. The dynamic shifts that the Fundamental Index strategy makes over time—in the value tilt and in other "bets"—contribute the lion's share of the value added.

Although the degree of the Fundamental Index value tilt will fluctuate, determining where the Fundamental Index portfolio falls, *on average*, on the value continuum is useful. The average value bias can be measured by using standard style analysis, first developed by Bill Sharpe, that measures the degree to which a portfolio "tracks" a predefined set of style portfolios.[2] Figure 10.1 shows the style analysis for the RAFI U.S. Large Company Index (RAFI U.S. Large), Russell 1000 Value, and the S&P 500 Index. The vertical spectrum of the style map illustrates where a portfolio falls in terms of size from

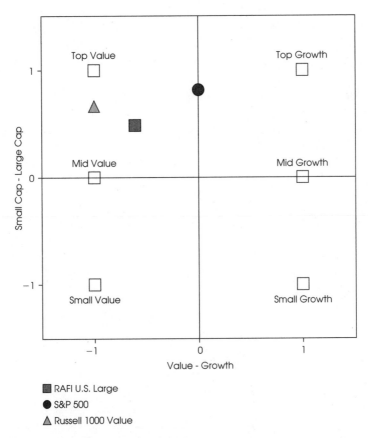

Figure 10.1 U.S. Equity Style Map: Total Average since Inception
Source: eVestment Alliance eA-MPI Style Analysis.

the large-cap (top) to the small-cap (bottom) category, and the horizontal spectrum shows the style bias of the portfolio, with value on the left and growth on the right.

According to this analysis, the S&P 500 is style neutral on the value-versus-growth dimension and at the upper end of the large-versus-small dimension. Not surprisingly, the RAFI U.S. Large is 50 percent more value than the S&P 500. It plots about halfway between the S&P 500 and the Russell 1000 Value Index. This outcome is not surprising because style is being measured relative to a cap-weighted portfolio that has a natural growth bias relative to the economic exposure of these companies. Furthermore, the fact that it shows half as much value tilt as the value index is not surprising. After all, the Russell 1000 Value eliminates most of the growth stocks. Unlike the Russell 1000 Value, the RAFI U.S. Large *includes the growth stocks,* albeit at their current economic scale rather than at the market's perceptions of their *future* scale.

If the RAFI U.S. Large exhibits half the value tilt of the Russell 1000 Value, on average over time it should capture about half the value premium over long periods. Figure 10.2 shows the performance of the RAFI U.S. Large versus the Russell 1000 Value and the

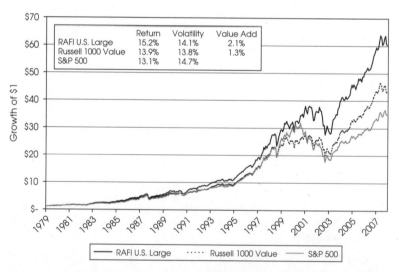

	Return	Volatility	Value Add
RAFI U.S. Large	15.2%	14.1%	2.1%
Russell 1000 Value	13.9%	13.8%	1.3%
S&P 500	13.1%	14.7%	

Figure 10.2   RAFI U.S. Large versus S&P 500 versus Russell 1000 Value, 1979 through 2007

Source: Research Affiliates, LLC.

S&P 500. The data confirm the existence of a long-term value premium, with the Russell 1000 Value outpacing the S&P 500 by 80 basis points annually over this 29-year period. If the Fundamental Index advantage is solely attributable to its value tilt, as critics contend, the Fundamental Index premium should be about half that, or about 40 basis points. Instead, the RAFI U.S. Large more than doubles the incremental return—to *210 basis points.* If the average value tilt—half that of the Russell 1000 Value—contributes value-added half as large as the Russell 1000 Value adds, then the other 170 basis points of value added came from other sources. Empirically, much of this additional value added is attributable to the dynamic shifts in stock selection, style, or sector. Clearly, something more than the traditionally accessed value premium is at work here.

If the Fundamental Index portfolio has a value tilt relative to the cap-weighted market, it should be at its best in markets favoring value stocks and it should be facing a headwind in markets favorable to growth stocks. We find that this is true. If we have a powerful growth market (in which growth stocks are sharply outpacing value stocks), then the value added from a Fundamental Index portfolio can easily swing negative. Why? Because a Fundamental Index portfolio lacks the growth tilt of the cap-weighted market. It does not enjoy the tailwind from a growth market, so relative to the cap-weighted market, it faces a headwind in growth markets.

By the same token, if we have a powerful value market (growth stocks are sharply underperforming value stocks), the cap-weighted index faces a headwind and the Fundamental Index portfolio will enjoy the benefits of a powerful tailwind.

But, there's a fascinating asymmetry. A Fundamental Index portfolio typically wins more in a value market than it loses in a growth market. In fact, we find that much of the incremental return comes from its dynamic contra-trading against whatever active bets the cap-weighted market is making relative to the economic scale of companies, not from the average value tilt of the Fundamental Index portfolio. Consider that the Fundamental Index portfolio has a substantial value tilt after growth has outpaced value on a sustained basis. But, if the market pays an erroneously large premium at these times, then the Fundamental Index portfolio has its largest value tilt when value is poised to be most rewarded. Likewise, growth is most likely to be profitable when the market is paying a small premium for growth; that is, when the value tilt of the Fundamental Index portfolio is smallest.

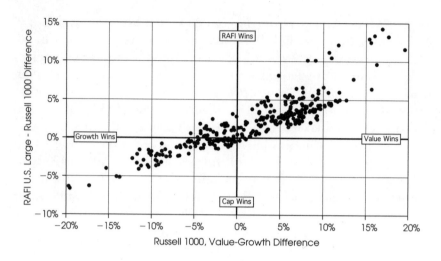

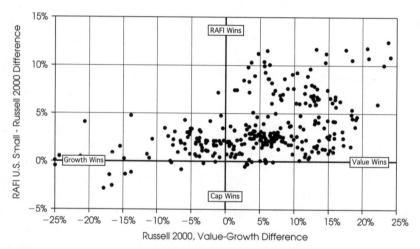

Figure 10.3   Rolling Two-Year Excess Returns in Growth and Value Markets, 1979 through June 2007

Source: Research Affiliates, LLC.

Figure 10.3 illustrates this dynamic using rolling two-year excess returns, with the vertical axis representing the excess returns of RAFI over capitalization weighting and the horizontal axis displaying the excess returns of value over growth. As the top panel shows for U.S. large companies, when value is beating growth by 10 percentage points to 20 percentage points, the Fundamental Index portfolio wins by 4 percentage points to 14 percentage points, but when growth is beating value by 10 percentage points to 20 percentage points, the Fundamental Index portfolio loses by 1 percentage point to 7 percentage points. This surprising asymmetry is remarkable in small companies, as can be seen in the lower panel where the RAFI portfolio is brilliant in value markets and yet holds its own even in a strong growth market. This result is further evidence that, at least over time, "it's not just value."

What happens if we "detrend" the result? If we have half as much value tilt as the Russell 1000 Value, on average over time, then the RAFI U.S. Large should lag the Russell 1000 Index by 5 percentage points if Russell 1000 Value loses by 10 percentage points and should win by 5 percent if Russell 1000 Value wins by 10 percentage points.

How do we perform relative to a portfolio that is half Russell 1000 and half Russell 1000 Value? Table 10.2 tells the story. The Russell 1000 Value beat the broad Russell 1000 by a respectable 1 percentage point per year over the past 28 years. *But* the variability in that margin of victory was substantial, more than 5 percent in the typical year. So, the results fail the most basic statistical tests. The RAFI portfolio beat the broad Russell 1000 by 2.4 percentage points per year, with a more modest 4 percent risk. The significance rises to one chance in 1,000 that this is a fluke. Adjusted for its average value tilt over time, the RAFI portfolio adds a still respectable 1.8 percentage points, *net of its average value tilt,* with only 2.1 percent

Table 10.2 Netting Out the Value Tilt, January 1979 through March 2007

Portfolio	Average Margin of Win	Standard Deviation of Win	*t*-Statistic (and *p*-Value[a]) of Win
Russell 1000 Value − Russell 1000	1.00%	5.00%	1.01 (0.16, not significant)
RAFI − Russell 1000	2.40%	4.10%	3.09 (0.001, highly significant)
RAFI − Average Tilt[b]	1.80%	2.10%	4.54 (0.000003)

[a] The *p*-value is the probability that this value added could happen by random chance.

[b] Here, we're taking the difference of RAFI return and the return of a portfolio which is half the Russell 1000 and half the Russell 1000 Value.

Source: Research Affiliates, LLC

uncertainty. This sort of consistency is remarkable over so long a span: There is one chance in 300,000 that this could be happenstance. In small companies, the value added of 3.6 percentage points with only 4 percent volatility, achieves one-in-a-million statistical significance.

Given this evidence, the Fundamental Index strategy, not surprisingly, outperforms the cap-weighted markets during a strong value period, such as the past seven years. Surprisingly to many critics, it also outperforms the value indexes. From March 2000 through June 2007, while the Russell 1000 Value climbed 101 percent, the RAFI U.S. Large soared by 117 percent. What makes this performance impressive is the number of growth stocks with bleak performance over this span—even some Nasdaq high flyers such as Amgen, AOL, Cisco Systems, Intel, and Oracle—held in the Fundamental Index strategy (but not in the value indexes because of their high multiples). Much like a thoroughbred saddled with additional weight can still beat most horses, even pretty fast ones, the RAFI U.S. Large has been able to produce larger excess returns than *the relevant value indexes* despite holding many of the plunging growth stocks.

Compared with a cap-weighted portfolio, a large-company RAFI portfolio will have a decidedly value orientation, but that's just a reflection of the overwhelming reliance in our industry today on cap-weighted indexes. A Fundamental Index portfolio will be neutral relative to the composition of the current economy (or at least the publicly traded portion of the economy). A cap-weighted portfolio will be neutral relative to the market (if broad enough, it *is* the market).

For investors who see no compelling evidence to structurally favor growth companies just because they command premium valuation multiples, the Fundamental Index methodology provides a diversified and economically representative equity choice that achieves much higher returns than achieved by existing narrowly focused value or broad cap-weighted indexes. This makes it an interesting choice, well worth our consideration, even if we don't share the view that capitalization weighting may overexpose us to the overvalued companies.

Small-Cap Bias

Small-cap stocks, like value stocks, have also proven to be winners over the long-term relative to their larger-cap brethren. Although the statistical evidence on a "small-cap effect" is even weaker than for the "value effect," academics assert that this small-cap premium exists to compensate investors for the additional risks of owning smaller companies. After all, they are less able to weather economic downturns and are less liquid than large-cap stocks. An alternative view is that the premium returns have been earned because (and when) small-cap stocks have been priced at a discount to the large-cap stocks, a condition that no longer prevails at this writing. As in the value case, detractors of the Fundamental Index strategy claim much of the concept's advantage is derived from a tilt toward small-cap stocks.

In our opinion, this critique is a clear miss. The small-cap bias of the Fundamental Index concept comes and goes and is seldom material. The average company in the RAFI U.S. Large portfolio in June 2007 was virtually identical in capitalization to the average company in the Russell 1000 and only slightly smaller than the average company in the S&P 500, an index lacking 500 of our smaller names. As Figure 10.4 shows, the average weighted capitalization of the RAFI U.S. Large was $84 billion as of June 2007 versus an $83 billion figure for the Russell 1000.

When the markets assign a lower valuation multiple to small companies than to large companies, a valuation-indifferent index will restore these stocks to their large economic weight. It will seemingly "overweight" the stocks of small companies (relative to the

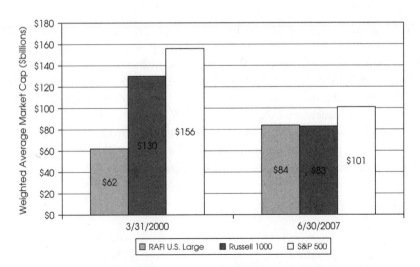

Figure 10.4   Average Weighted Capitalization for RAFI U.S. Large, Russell 1000, and S&P 500
Source: Research Affiliates, LLC.

classic cap-weighted indexes), thereby creating a small-cap tilt relative to the cap-weighted market. But one could as easily say that the market has a large-cap tilt relative to the economy. When the markets assign higher valuation multiples to small companies, as they did in the United States in 2007, the Fundamental Index portfolio, because it is valuation indifferent, invests less in these stocks than do the cap-weighted indexes, leading to a larger-cap profile for the Fundamental Index portfolio.

Only in rare instances, when large-cap and small-cap companies command starkly different valuation multiples, will the size profile of the Fundamental Index portfolio materially diverge from a relatively confined range. At the peak of the tech bubble, the average weighted market capitalization of the RAFI U.S. Large was $62 billion, roughly half that of the Russell 1000. The reason for this gap is simple. The market was paying an immense premium to some of the era's highest-priced (hence *largest-cap*) stocks, even though the companies themselves were not very large. Names such as AOL, Cisco, Intel, and Lucent Technologies, weighted according to their modest economic scale, caused the Fundamental Index portfolio to *seem* considerably smaller than the Russell 1000 or its cap-weighted cousin, the S&P 500. Of course, such a period is exactly the time investors would not want significant stakes in these large-cap high flyers!

The bottom line for investors and their advisers is whether a Fundamental Index portfolio can outperform in a large-cap dominated market. Probably the best way to answer such a question is to examine the remarkable run large-cap stocks enjoyed during the second half of the 1980s and throughout most of the 1990s. From 1984 through 1998, as shown in Figure 10.5, the Russell 1000 bested the Russell 2000 Index in 11 of 15 calendar years, for a cumulative annualized return of 17.5 percent versus the Russell 2000's 11.2 percent. Meanwhile, the RAFI U.S. Large outperformed the Russell 1000 by an average of 60 basis points per year, *during the best extended large-cap relative performance period in recent history.*

Fama and French Factors

The value and size effects were exquisitely documented by Eugene Fama and Kenneth French in their *Journal of Finance* masterpiece (1992). They found that, in addition to broad market exposure, exposure to value stocks and small-cap stocks increases a portfolio's expected

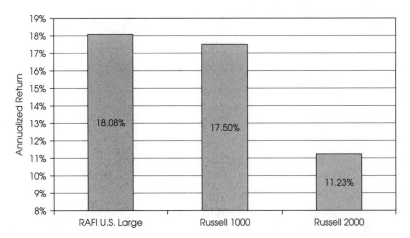

Figure 10.5   Fundamental Index Performance in Large-Cap Cycle, 1984 through 1998

Source: Research Affiliates, LLC.

return. That is, diversified portfolios of value stocks and small-cap stocks can earn more than a large-cap portfolio of similar market beta! Fama and French subsequently posited that value and small-cap exposure must be substantially more risky than what is suggested by their market betas (as measured by the CAPM). After all, in a rational and efficient market, additional return can be had only through taking on more risk.

Critics of the Fundamental Index strategy argue that the RAFI concept does not create economically significant alpha; it just takes on more value and small-cap risk. If so, the Fundamental Index strategy is nothing new. It is just a way of embedding value and small-cap exposure into a portfolio in an intelligent and dynamic way (by contra-trading against the market's largest excesses). *We agree.* In fact, we pointed out this nuance in the article (Arnott, Hsu, and Moore, 2005) that introduced the Fundamental Index concept.

The Fama-French model is a long-short model. To mirror the behavior of a portfolio very different from the cap-weighted market while using the Fama-French factors, one must be prepared to have some short positions. For the RAFI U.S. Large at the peak of the bubble, the Fama-French mirroring portfolio (the Fama-French portfolio that precisely matched the beta and style tilts of the Fundamental Index portfolio) was approximately 115 percent long and 15 percent short. The investor willing to take long and short positions can replicate the characteristics of the Fundamental Index strategy by (1) complementing an S&P 500 or Russell 1000 core port-folio with an overlay of long-short satellite portfolios that are long in deep-value and small-cap names and short in high-growth and mega-cap names; (2) shifting the composition of these long-short port-folios as the constituent holdings change; (3) shifting the size of these long-short overlay portfolios monthly, to match the changing style tilts of the RAFI program over time; and (4) frequent rebalancing. That's a lot of work to match a dumb old index that just selects and weights companies by their fundamental footprint in the economy!

When applied to the Fundamental Index concept, not surpris-ingly the Fama-French model shows an exposure to the value effect and, to a modest extent, to the size factor. Surprisingly, even net of these factors, the Fundamental Index portfolio earned an estimated alpha of 30 basis points from 1979, when Russell style portfolios were first available, through 2006. In contrast, most indexes, par-ticularly those with a value tilt, exhibited a negative Fama-French alpha in that period, as shown in Table 10.3. In fact, as far as we are aware, *no other existing indexes offer a value tilt relative to the cap-weighted markets while avoiding large negative Fama-French alphas.*

The Davis analysis (2007) for 1940 through 1962, which we covered in Chapter 7, had similar Fama-French results for the Fundamental Index strategy. He focused on the lack of a signifi-cant alpha, net of the Fama-French three factors, and the consist-ent value tilt of the Fundamental Index portfolios. Unlike Davis, we focus on the raw return difference of more than 200 basis points per year in his results, leading to 40 percent more wealth after just 22 years. After all, few investors would be happy with a poor rate

Table 10.3   Fama–French Alpha Comparison, 1979 through 2006

Portfolio	Annual Return	Fama-French Alpha	Adjusted R^2	Small	Value	Beta
RAFI U.S. Large	15.8%	0.3%	0.97	−0.10	0.36	1.03
Russell 1000	13.5%	0.4%	1.00	−0.15	0.01	1.01
Russell 1000 Value	14.6%	−1.1%	0.96	−0.15	0.44	1.02

Source: Research Affiliates, LLC.

of return and a positive Fama-French alpha if the alternative is a higher rate of return with no Fama-French alpha!

Mark Carhart extended the Fama-French model by observing that price momentum also carries unexpected rewards. It's interesting to note that a Fundamental Index portfolio will sell winners if their economic success hasn't risen commensurate to the rise in share price. Because momentum strategies add value and because a Fundamental Index portfolio trades against momentum, we should have been hurt by the anti-momentum character of our portfolio. It's striking to note that the 0.3 percent Fama-French alpha on Table 10.3 *soars* to 1.1 percent in the Fama-French-Carhart analysis. This is 1.1 percent of return, which is utterly unexplained in a Fama-French-Carhart model!

We find the relatively neutral results for the Fundamental Index concept relative to the Fama-French factors not at all surprising. A well-specified risk model ought to be able to explain the differential returns of simple indexes constructed in a formulaic fashion with no overt stock selection. The Fundamental Index concept is nothing if not simple, and the Fama-French three-factor risk model is obviously a well-specified risk model. That being said, it's clear that the Fundamental Index portfolio captures these factors more efficiently than existing commercially available benchmarks and products. It is far simpler to implement than a core-satellite approach, in which we create a core of market-replicating equities plus Fama-French long-short factor portfolios. The complexity of the replication, the cost associated with managing the Fama-French factor portfolios, and the potential need to hold short positions that at times will be quite large make the Fundamental Index approach more attractive from an implementation perspective.

Some Big Surprises in Small Companies

If the Fundamental Index strategy is just the result of value and size tilts, we might expect to see even greater value and size bets in the Fundamental Index strategies that generate the largest alphas. We'd be wrong! The RAFI U.S. Small, which comprises the 2,000 companies ranked from 1,001 to 3,000 by the fundamental measures of size, provides a good test of this contention. From 1979 through 2007, returns of the RAFI U.S. Small exceeded the returns on the small-cap benchmark Russell 2000 by 340 basis points annually. Moreover, it did so with larger companies than the Russell 2000 and a surprisingly modest value tilt, on average.

To properly assess this seemingly illogical result, we examine the construction of comparable fundamental and cap-weighted indexes (see Figure 2.1 in Chapter 2). In a comparison of the top 1,000 companies weighted by capitalization versus those weighted by fundamentals, an average of 700 to 800 names will be the same (the weights will, of course, differ). Toward the bottom of the cap-weighted list, however, more and more companies are seen that are relatively small on an economic scale (cash flow, sales, etc.) but are trading at lofty enough multiples to leap onto the large-cap list. These stocks are not large companies, so they appear in the RAFI U.S. Small. As a result, they boost the valuation multiples and average weighted market capitalization of the RAFI U.S. Small portfolio.

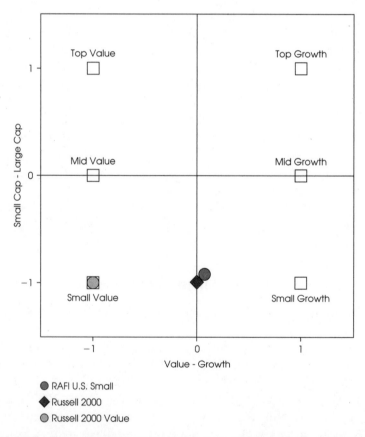

Figure 10.6   Style Analysis: RAFI U.S. Small, 1979 through June 2007
Source: eVestment Alliance eA-MPI Style Analysis

This point can be best illustrated by an example. Salesforce.com was such a company in June 2007: With a market capitalization of nearly $5.0 billion and a P/E higher than 4,000, it is large, but with trailing annual revenue of slightly less than $400 million, it is fundamentally small. As a result, Salesforce.com is big when capitalization is used as a criterion and small when fundamental size is used as a criterion. It lands in the Russell 1000 and the RAFI U.S. Small.

At any point in time, there are scores of these high-multiple stocks (like Salesforce.com). All of them raise the average capitalization of the RAFI U.S. Small higher than the comparable Russell 2000. These high-multiple, small-company stocks also largely offset the natural value tilt of the Fundamental Index portfolio. In fact, at times, the RAFI U.S. Small has a growth tilt! It should not be surprising, then, to learn that the RAFI U.S. Small falls close to the center of the value continuum and is a trace larger than the Russell 2000 on the size continuum in the style analysis based on Sharpe's methodology, as shown in Figure 10.6. Yet, with a negligible value bias and no cap tilt it still dramatically outperforms the Russell 2000. Unlike the gains of the RAFI U.S. Large, the RAFI U.S. Small outperformance is achieved without any assist from a small-cap tilt (indeed, quite the contrary) and with hardly any assist from a value tilt. Furthermore, it even outpaced the Russell 2000 Value Index by 130 basis points annually. Clearly, the value and small-cap arguments are irrelevant to the value added from the Fundamental Index concept in small companies.

A Proof Statement in 2007

The fact that Fundamental Index portfolios scored impressive wins in 2005 and 2006 is unsurprising. These were "value years." Value stocks beat growth in most of the major markets around the world. Capitalization weighting, with its growth tilt, therefore faced a headwind and Fundamental Index portfolios, value tilted relative to the cap-weighted markets, enjoyed a tailwind. The real test comes when this situation reverses.

In 2007, the markets rewarded growth and punished value all over the world. Small companies were especially hard-hit. Growth beat value by an impressive 12 percentage points in U.S. large-cap companies, by 10 percentage points in developed non-U.S. markets, and by a whopping 17 percentage points in U.S. small-cap companies. Large-cap beat small-cap by 7 percentage points in the United States and by 10 percentage points in developed non-U.S. economies.

Against this hurricane-force headwind, which crushed many value strategies and "quant" managers, how did the Fundamental Index portfolios fare? As shown in Figure 10.7, just fine. In emerging markets, they won by over 9 percentage points in an immense growth-dominated bull market year. In developed non-U.S. small and large companies, they won by 5 percentage points and 3 percentage points,

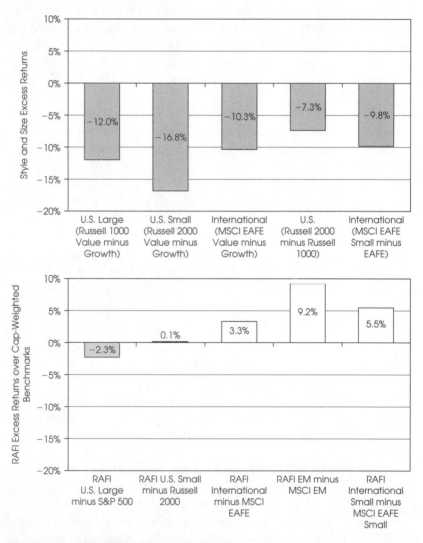

Figure 10.7   RAFI Performance in 2007
Source: Research Affiliates, LLC

respectively. And, after big wins in 2005 and 2006, they matched the cap-weighted index for U.S. small companies and suffered a mild 2.3 percentage point haircut in U.S. large companies. A remarkable outcome in a relentless growth year.

Conclusion

The Fundamental Index concept, in any snapshot in time, is value—pure value and nothing but value. But the value is of a very specific sort. The weight of each stock is the same as its capitalization weighting divided by its relative valuation multiple (whichever combination of size metrics one chooses to use). Why? *Because it neutralizes whatever growth bets the market is making at that time.* Because growth companies are priced by the market at a premium and value companies are priced at a discount—precisely enough in an efficient market to equalize their expected future risk-adjusted returns—the growth tilt of the cap-weighted indexes doesn't really do anything for us. Because a Fundamental Index portfolio restores the weights back to the economic scale of the companies, the Fundamental Index strategy neutralizes the constantly changing growth bets made by the market.

The issue becomes more interesting when the bets and the results over time are examined. Because the market is constantly reassessing future growth prospects for every single stock, it constantly shifts its preferences: The most extreme growth (and value) bets of the cap-weighted markets are always changing. Bets shift at all levels: individual stocks, sectors, growth versus value, large versus small, beta, and so forth (importantly, for international portfolios, also at the country level). A Fundamental Index portfolio will trade against *all* of the extreme bets. Because fundamentals change far more slowly than prices, many of these trades ultimately prove rewarding (Shiller, 1981). As a consequence, a Fundamental Index portfolio adds roughly four times as much value relative to its tracking error against the cap-weighted market as a simple value portfolio. Over time, the Fundamental Index concept is far more than "pure value and nothing but value."

CHAPTER 11

Other Common Critiques: Hits and Misses

A wise skepticism is the first attribute of a good critic.
                              —James Russell Lowell

BUT

It is much easier to be critical than to be correct.
                              —Benjamin Disraeli

Common criticisms of the Fundamental Index concept are that we are data mining, that the strategy is costly, that the index is not an index, that no one knows *ex ante* which stocks are overvalued, and finally, that even if the strategy works, unexplained excess returns will disappear as others implement the strategy. We deal with each in this chapter.

Mining the Data?

The human mind is marvelously adept at finding patterns and positive affirmations of their preconceptions when, in fact, the experience and the associated feedback are nothing more than random data. Depending on their personal experience, investors may find seemingly reliable strong support for certain investment strategies and return patterns in the stock market. The natural ebb and flow in performance of the equity market and of its various styles and industries almost guarantees that *any* strategy will have its day in the sun. The key to finding a winning strategy is, of course, being able to identify the strategy's sunny days. If one gets the starting and ending points in one's analysis just right, almost any strategy, no matter how ridiculous—buying small-cap stocks after the American League wins the World Series—can be demonstrated to outperform. Tunnel through enough data and you will find investment gold.

Skeptics of the Fundamental Index concept suggest that we have just burrowed through enough historical data to identify a time period and a strategy that worked. Worse, the back-test results conveniently end with the strongest period in the history of Fundamental Index relative performance. The critics suggest that the majority of the long-term premium is attributable to the past seven years. They ask, "Where were the fundamental indexers in 1998 and 1999 when the strategy was getting clobbered?"

This claim has some merit. As Figure 11.1 shows, the rolling one-year and rolling five-year returns of the RAFI U.S. Large in excess of the S&P 500 Index returns validate both the disappointments of 1998 through 1999 and the strength of recent results. Since the technology bubble burst in March 2000, the Fundamental Index portfolio has enjoyed a remarkable seven-year run. Indeed, it was precisely the unprecedented nature of the run-up and subsequent dramatic destruction of wealth from capitalization weighting that initiated our first conversations about building a better index.

Another criticism related to data mining is that we picked a starting point for our research that optimizes the cumulative results. Why start in 1962? The simple answer is that our process involves five-year averages of fundamental data—to reduce turnover—and our test is on a 1,000-stock portfolio. The databases first included fundamental measures of company size on 1,000 stocks in 1957.[1] Accordingly, 1962 is the first year for our series. The choice of beginning date is a case of being pragmatic (and careful), not one of cherry picking a starting date. As noted in Chapter 7, Jim Davis (2007) reported nearly identical results for 100 stocks from 1940 through 1962.

Little can be done about the start date for examining the historical efficacy of the Fundamental Index concept, but beginning with 1962, we can measure results for the concept over spans *shorter* than 46 years. This approach allows us to test whether the results are much

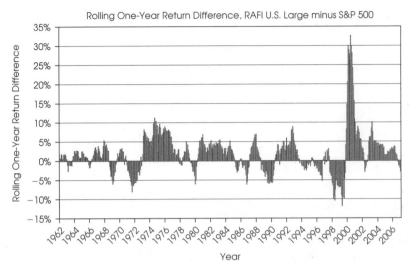

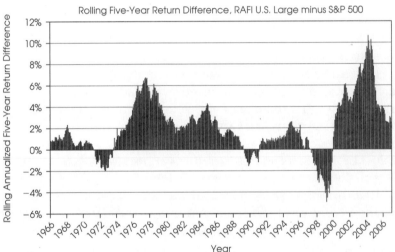

Figure 11.1   Rolling One-Year and Five-Year Excess Returns, 1962 through 2007

Source: Research Affiliates, LLC.

better (or worse) than if we had chosen to start the analysis later. Figure 11.2 shows that the cumulative annualized excess return from the Fundamental Index concept is surprisingly insensitive to start date except for the period surrounding the tech bubble. Starting our analysis any time other than the 1997 through 2001 period leads to

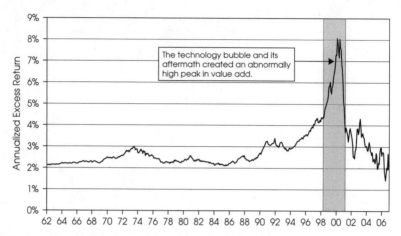

The technology bubble and its aftermath created an abnormally high peak in value add.

Figure 11.2 Annualized Fundamental Index Premium versus S&P 500 for Various Start Dates, 1962 through June 2007

Note: Inception through June 2007.

Source: Research Affiliates, LLC.

200 basis points to 400 basis points value added. Of course, the most recent results are volatile because we are dealing with ever-shorter time spans, so dropping a few months can make a big difference.

We can also try to appease the detractors by cutting out the bubble and post-bubble years. Critics point out that the aftermath of the bubble was extraordinary—and it was—but so was the bubble itself. Table 11.1 displays the excess returns of the RAFI U.S. Large over the S&P 500 over three time periods—the entire date range excluding 1998 through 2001 (this span includes *both* the best two years and the worst two years for the index's performance—the last gasp of the bubble and its early aftermath) and 1962 through 1997. Excluding these periods, the excess returns fall into essentially the same range: The Fundamental Index portfolio achieved a value-added premium of 1.7 percentage points versus a 2.0 percentage points for the entire testable time horizon. So, perhaps 20 percent of the cumulative Fundamental Index advantage might be traced to the effects of contra-trading against the largest bubble in U.S. capital market history. Even if we *include* 1998 and 1999—the worst two-year span in the historical record for the Fundamental Index portfolio— and *exclude* 2000 and 2001—the best two years—the Fundamental Index portfolio still produces excess returns of 130 basis points above the S&P 500, more than half the long-term 200 basis points for

Table 11.1 RAFI Excess Returns, 1962 through 2007

Period	RAFI U.S. Large Return	S&P 500 Return	Excess Return
1962 through 2007	12.3%	10.3%	2.0%
1962 through 2007 ex bubble	12.5%	10.7%	1.7%
1962 through 1997	13.1%	11.5%	1.6%

Source: Research Affiliates, LLC.

the entire evaluation period. Accordingly, the claim that most of the excess return came from this recent seven-year surge for value strategies has little merit.

The successful performance of the Fundamental Index concept in other markets—outside the originally tested large-company U.S. domain—is perhaps the strongest counterargument to the data-mining criticism. As discussed in Chapters 7 and 8, the Fundamental Index concept has been tested in many, many markets, and it works in almost all cases. In the United States, depending on how we measure our results, we find up to one-in-a-million statistical significance. In global applications, where results are mostly even stronger than the U.S. results, the significance jumps to one in 35 million. This finding invites the question: How much out-of-sample evidence do our data-mining critics need?

Despite the broad out-of-sample support for the Fundamental Index concept, however, we must acknowledge that back-tests *always* work. We never see products based on back-tests that do not work. Many observers won't accept the validity of a new idea until they see live performance.[2] Although the live performance record for the Fundamental Index concept is still short, the results are consistent with those predicted by our research. Table 11.2 illustrates how the Fundamental Index idea has fared in six major asset classes since the original launch date in late 2005, showing outperformance in all six relative to their capitalization-weighted counterparts, with four adding more than 2 percentage points of value annually.[3] Emerging markets, consistent with our theory and historical results, leads the way with an annualized premium of 7.1 percentage points followed by FTSE RAFI Japan at 3.8 percentage points in excess returns.

The Fundamental Index strategy is moving from back-tested theory to real-world success, and the results are encouraging. To be sure, longer time horizons are needed to fully judge live results. Critics remain,

Table 11.2   FTSE RAFI Indexes versus Cap-Weighted Indexes, December 2005 through 2007

		Return	Volatility	Value Added	Risk-Adjusted Alpha	Beta	Correlation
U.S. Large	FTSE RAFI U.S. 1000	10.7%	7.8%	0.6%	0.7%	0.99	0.98
	S&P 500	10.1%	7.7%				
U.S. Small	FTSE RAFI 1500	8.2%	11.8%	0.8%	1.1%	0.91	0.99
	Russell 2000	7.4%	12.8%				
International	FTSE RAFI Developed ex U.S.	23.1%	9.5%	2.0%	2.5%	0.97	1.00
	MSCI World ex U.S.	21.2%	9.8%				
Europe	FTSE RAFI Europe	27.6%	10.2%	2.6%	2.1%	1.02	1.00
	MSCI Europe	25.0%	9.9%				
Japan	FTSE RAFI Japan	5.4%	12.8%	3.8%	3.8%	0.97	0.96
	MSCI Japan	1.6%	12.6%				
Emerging	FTSE RAFI Emerging Markets (EM)	45.3%	18.6%	7.1%	6.1%	1.03	0.99
	MSCI EM	38.2%	17.9%				

Source: Research Affiliates, LLC.

however and always will. For some, neither historical evidence nor live experience will ever persuade them—some because of vested interests in the status quo, some because of a stubborn adherence to convention, and some because of a deeply held belief in classical finance theory. For others, the data mining argument eventually goes away, but other concerns remain. As John Steinbeck asserts in *On Critics* (1977), "Time is the only critic without ambition."

Costs

Controlling costs is a critical element of any successful investment program. The power of compounding combined with the levering effect of time transform even modest savings to greater ending wealth values, *all else being equal.* In comparing ending wealth for the Fundamental Index strategies versus those for cap-weighted index strategies, however, precost results are not equal.

Critics of the Fundamental Index concept point out that, despite the high returns of these portfolios, Fundamental Index products carry higher costs than their cap-weighted counterparts. A direct comparison of expenses is somewhat difficult because of today's plethora of traditional and Fundamental Index portfolio choices—mutual funds, exchange-traded funds (ETFs), managed accounts, and so on. Furthermore, in this book, it is not our goal to zero in on specific products. Comparison is further complicated by each investor's unique circumstances, such as account size, vehicle preference, brokerage channel, and custodial arrangements.

Even so, we can perform a simple comparison: Compare the respective expected returns net of all expenses. Suppose we choose to invest in index funds via an ETF. We can invest in an S&P 500 portfolio with a fee of 0.10 percent or a Fundamental Index portfolio with a fee of 0.50 percent. The incremental cost difference is 40 basis points—enough to cost us 4 percent of our end-point wealth in just 10 years, assuming the two strategies have identical returns before costs. Jack Bogle is right: costs matter!

But suppose the incremental value added from the Fundamental Index strategy is 210 basis points per year, matching the 46-year record of the RAFI U.S. Large returns, against a comparable 1,000-stock cap-weighted portfolio. The investor has the opportunity to earn a net return of 160 basis points a year more than the cap-weighted index and 170 basis points more than the cap-weighted index fund investor, which compounds to almost 20 percent more wealth in 10 years. Not bad! Less expensive Fundamental Index variants would look even better.

This comparison can be applied for the ETF investor, the mutual fund investor, the financial adviser, or the pension executive. Simply line up the available vehicles for the anticipated account size, examine the fees, make an informed decision on forward-looking returns, and calculate. On this measure, the services of the great majority of active managers look overpriced: Most of them don't *even* beat the market *before* fees! But the Fundamental Index portfolio looks like a favorable investment, unless we want to assume far less future value added than the historical evidence would suggest. Indeed, in some markets (international, small-company, emerging), it appears to be very inexpensive when measured against historical return benefits.

Management fees or mutual fund expense ratios are the most obvious expenses to track because they are listed on financial web sites and in periodicals. But what about the stealthy, hidden areas of costs, such as brokerage commissions and market impact? Perhaps the greatest strength of a cap-weighted index is its infrequent trading. Critics of the Fundamental Index strategy claim that our approach will result in higher portfolio turnover, and so higher trading costs, than a cap-weighted index. They are right and they are wrong.

Compared with the low turnover of a cap-weighted index fund, the RAFI U.S. Large has a slightly higher turnover (10 percent versus 6 percent). As discussed in Chapter 6, much of this additional trading is buying companies that have recently faltered and selling those that outrun their underlying economic size. Because the Fundamental Index approach is contra-trading against investor sentiment, the costs may be surprisingly low.

Furthermore, much of the trading for a RAFI portfolio is in the largest and most liquid companies, where the trading costs are demonstrably lower than in the smaller companies. In contrast, trading for a cap-weighted portfolio is concentrated in smaller, less liquid companies. Accordingly, the cost of rebalancing a Fundamental Index portfolio may very well be no higher than the cost of rebalancing a cap-weighted portfolio. These critics also prefer not to note that for small companies and other niche strategies, this trading cost argument backfires. The turnover, and associated trading, of small-company Fundamental Index portfolios is *less* than for small-cap indexes.

Time will tell whether trading costs for Fundamental Index portfolios are measurably higher or lower than for cap-weighted indexes, but no serious observer would suggest that the trading costs of a Fundamental Index portfolio can even remotely approach the costs of an average active strategy. In the words of *The Economist* Buttonwood column (2006):

> Fundamental indices should not be compared solely with traditional index funds but also with active managers who can run up expenses of two percentage points a year. In contrast to them, as Bogey would say, fundamental-index expenses do not amount to a hill of beans.

The RAFI U.S. Large annual turnover of 10 percent to 12 percent is much closer to the turnover associated with indexing than it is to that of active management, which often averages 100 percent per year or more. As far as costs go, we agree with the traditional indexers: Lower costs are one of the real advantages of index funds, including Fundamental Index portfolios.

Is It an Index?

Some indexers and academics protest that a fundamentals-weighted index is not a true index, arguing that the term *index* applies only to capitalization weighting. In our view, this disagreement is a simple matter of semantics and frame of reference. By the purist's definition of indexing, only cap-weighted portfolios are macro consistent with the market, and, therefore, only cap-weighted portfolios can be referred to as *indexes*. By this definition, the Fundamental Index approach is an active strategy. On the other hand, no law dictates that all indexes must be weighted by market capitalization.

As we have stated throughout the book, we prefer to define the word *index* in a more pragmatic, less academic way as something that is formulaic and objective (rules based, with no subjectivity), replicable (by others and historically), transparent, and of reasonably low turnover. By this definition, the Fundamental Index construction produces an index. And by these criteria, few of the widely accepted cap-weighted indexes qualify. For instance, the S&P 500 misses on several counts: It is selected by a committee, so it is not formulaic or objective. Decisions cannot be replicated, nor is its construction transparent. But it does have reasonably low turnover. The Russell Investment Group keeps the float methodology for its indexes secret, so it cannot be replicated. The SP EWI flunks on all criteria. Not only does it fail the same tests that the S&P 500 fails, but its turnover is rather high.

It is fair to say that the Fundamental Index portfolio is a nice passive replication of the overall look of the economy, at least the publicly traded parts of the economy. From the macroeconomic frame of reference, cap-weighted indexes aren't just active, they are *very* active.

Do We Know Which Stocks Are Overvalued?

Despite the Fundamental Index concept being elementary and its construction crystal clear, more so than some traditional indexes, the concept has still been labeled *active management* by some. Jack Bogle, for example, claims that the Fundamental Index approach is based on some "ability" to discern which stocks are undervalued and which are overvalued:

> This new breed of indexers—not, in fact, indexers, but active strategists—focuses on weighting portfolios by so-called fundamental factors. . . . They argue, fairly enough, that in a cap-weighted portfolio, half of the stocks are overvalued to a greater or lesser extent, and half are undervalued.

> The traditional indexer responds: "Of course. But who really knows which half is which?" The new Fundamental Indexers unabashedly answer, "We do." They actually claim to know which is which. (Bogle, 2007)

This criticism is not valid. The Fundamental Index strategy is valuation indifferent. It makes no determination of the relative attractiveness of one security over another. It is not a "smart index" that seeks underpriced stocks. It is a "dumb index" that reflects the composition of the economy rather than the composition of the cap-weighted market. Nor is it an active strategy, in the traditional context, weighting companies based on assessments of where the values are and which way share prices of individual stocks are heading. Rather, it is an index designed to eliminate the structural flaw in capitalization weighting whereby the weights in the portfolio are linked to the price—hence, to the pricing error—of each stock.

Some of these critics point to the fact that Fundamental Index portfolio weights are directly linked to the cap-weighted index weights *divided by a company's valuation multiple.* Doesn't this mean, they argue, that it's an active strategy that pays explicit attention to a company's valuation multiples relative to the market? Again, the answer depends on one's frame of reference. From a cap-weighted worldview, this is a fair interpretation. From the perspective of a company's economic scale, the opposite holds true. Capitalization weighting weights a company's stock in direct proportion to its valuation multiple relative to the market. The Fundamental Index portfolio pays no attention to price or to valuation multiples, only to the economic scale of a company's business. It simply takes the over- or underweighting in the cap-weighted market portfolio and corrects it back to the economic scale of the company.

A cap-weighted index will, as a matter of course, overweight stocks that are overvalued and underweight stocks that are undervalued, relative to their unknowable fair value weights. Fundamental Index portfolios will, as a matter of course, overweight some stocks and underweight others relative to their unknowable fair value weights. But in the Fundamental Index portfolio, these errors are no longer explicitly linked to over- or undervaluation and should be reasonably random. Therefore, the over- and underweighting will cancel, and the performance drag of the cap-weighted portfolio will be eliminated— all *without knowing which companies are over- or undervalued.*

To emphasize this point, we return to a consideration of the first major valuation-indifferent index—the SP EWI. Because it holds 0.2 percent in all 500 stocks, the SP EWI may appear to have severed the link between over- and undervaluation and the weight each stock has in the portfolio. After all, every company, depending on whether it is in the S&P 500 or not, has either 0.2 percent weight or no weight. Because membership in that index ostensibly has no bearing on whether the company is over- or undervalued, this approach should work at least as well as the Fundamental Index portfolio. But as we showed in Chapter 7, it has failed to do so since the 1990 inception of the SP EWI, despite the deep small-cap tilt of the equally weighted SP EWI portfolio. Why not? Because almost all new additions to the S&P 500 are high-multiple, popular growth companies at the time they are added to the index. Companies that are deleted, apart from those that are dropped as a result of corporate actions (mergers or bankruptcies), are generally out-of-favor, low-multiple, deep-value companies. So the list from which the SP EWI is constructed is a biased list.

Even so, the SP EWI produces handsome excess returns relative to the cap-weighted S&P 500. Relative to the SP EWI, about 100 stocks in the S&P 500 have larger weights than 0.2 percent. By choosing the SP EWI over the S&P 500, is the investor saying that all of these 100 large-cap stocks are overvalued in the S&P 500 and all the 400 smaller cap names are undervalued? Of course not! Such an assertion would imply that every leading U.S. company— Exxon Mobil, Microsoft, Pfizer, Citigroup—is overpriced and every smaller-cap company is undervalued! Clearly, an investor adopting an equal-weighted approach is making no such assertion.

Neither is the advocate of a Fundamental Index portfolio. The goal of price-indifferent indexing is *not* to identify underpriced securities. It is to break the link between over- and undervaluation and over- and underweighting in the portfolio.

How Long Can It Last?

Some critics argue that the Fundamental Index performance edge cannot last forever. This criticism of the Fundamental Index concept is perhaps the most ironic. Traditional indexers assert that if the Fundamental Index strategy does produce some unexplained excess return, then the market will arbitrage it away. Because of the concept's success, all investors will switch to Fundamental Index portfolios and it will become the cap-weighted portfolio. The value added by the concept will disappear.

The irony arises in two ways. First, these skeptics of the Fundamental Index concept are setting forth an argument based on the premise that the concept not only works but works so well that everybody will use it. The second irony is more subtle. Consider the transition from current markets to a hypothetical market in which much of the indexed assets in the world are in Fundamental Index portfolios. This transition would involve a flow of investment capital that would artificially boost those same Fundamental Index portfolios while hammering the cap-weighted indexes!

This argument is reminiscent of an old joke on Wall Street. An investor and a professor are walking down the street. They see a $100 bill on the sidewalk. The investor bends down to pick it up. The professor rolls his eyes and says, "Why are you wasting your time? If that $100 bill was really there, it would have been picked up a long time ago."

Another puzzling aspect of this critique is the credit given to the market—professional managers, individual investors, advisers, 401(k) participants, or anyone ponying up a dollar for stocks or equity mutual funds—that all would eventually recognize this opportunity and act to exploit it.

There is remarkable inertia in the ways that people think about their investments. In Chapter 4, we noted that equity investors have two basic choices—index funds and active management. Given the index funds' virtually unchallenged long-term performance advantage, shouldn't it be the dominant form of equity investing by now? Not even close. After 30 years of trampling most active managers, index funds still represent a little less than 20 percent of the total assets invested in the U.S. stock market and barely 10 percent worldwide. This simple fact demonstrates that despite long odds of success, an overwhelming majority of equity investors still prefer to play the active management game. They refuse to give up on the notion that they can beat the market (as, we would cheerfully acknowledge, do we!). Indeed, apart from the meteoric growth of ETF assets, the penetration of the index fund has steadied in recent years, despite recognition by the financial press and investing public of its long-term superiority.

A good portion of the Fundamental Index concept's most diehard opponents come from supporters of the EMH, which assumes that investors are collectively so very rational that the broad markets will make well-informed decisions that maximize all investors' collective risk-adjusted returns. Is the market so very efficient? When given all available and relevant information on two distinct investments, do investors collectively always make the right choice? Most academics and almost all practitioners would answer: "Of course not." There's precious little evidence for the rational and well-informed investors posited by the EMH, given the modest penetration of the index fund.

Shouldn't investors at least be savvy enough to be fee conscious? If market participants—knowing they face a slim probability of achieving above-index returns—are to be enticed into active management, it would be by low investment fees, right? Again, not true. Consider a piece by Richard Ennis (2005), a principal at institutional consulting firm Ennis Knupp + Associates, that outlined the trend in investment management fees:

> Since about 1975, however, we have witnessed another pronounced trend, one that at first blush appears to be at odds with vigorously efficient markets and with the evidence on manager performance—namely, the steady rise of the price of active investment products. . . . Since 1980, the average equity mutual fund expense ratio has risen from 0.96 percent to 1.56 percent.

The relentless upward march in mutual fund expense ratios is striking. For the past 30 years, active portfolio managers haven't collectively done a good job, yet these nonperformers ask for greater and greater compensation. And the market gives it to them! For those who are troubled about their opportunities to earn double-digit returns in a low-yield world, we even see immense sums of money flowing to hedge funds, where fees are several times the costs of actively managed mutual funds, despite historical returns that aren't notably better!

What does this discussion indicate about the speed at which investors will universally adopt a better equity choice like the Fundamental Index strategy? If history is any indication, the pace of change will be gradual. Investors are likely to benefit for some time by making the simple and intuitive switch. Early progress has been, paradoxically, both startlingly fast and startlingly slow. In the three years since we introduced the idea, more than $20 billion has flowed into the Fundamental Index concept. That amount is remarkable in so short a span. But it is still far less than 1/1000th of the value of equity markets worldwide. If this pace continues, our idea should be the dominant form of stock market investing in a few thousand years.

Suppose the switch to the Fundamental Index approach occurs more quickly, and we reach a point where all indexed money is in a Fundamental Index portfolio. In this implausible scenario, the cap-weighted index and Fundamental Index portfolios become essentially the same. But, during the transition from here to there, the excess returns of Fundamental Index portfolio investing *temporarily* would be more potent than in the past because of the very flow of funds from classical index funds to Fundamental Index strategies. With the transition to universal implementation, the historical annual value added of 200+ basis points would be increased, by the very adoption of the idea, before the advantage disappears because of universal adoption. In this unrealistic scenario, the early adopters will presumably reap outsized benefits.

Conclusion

The scrutiny of the Fundamental Index concept is intense for several reasons. One is because this modest idea—weighting companies by their scale in the economy—produces such startling results. It is a simple, elegant idea that calls into question 50 years of informed opinion, finance theory, and investment practice.

Presumably, some of the controversy is provoked by the perceived threat that this idea may represent for those with a vested interest in the status quo. Doesn't that cover most of the investment community? Accordingly, the results of the Fundamental Index idea have been dissected thoroughly and run through a battery of portfolio analytics by both its proponents and its skeptics. *In all of these tests, no one has pointed to significant, lasting performance failures.*

The naysayers point to a host of concerns, because the idea strikes at their core belief that the markets are reasonably efficient and their cap-weighted index funds cannot be beaten reliably by any strategy. Some of the critics are indiscriminate and miss the target, while others' arguments have merit. Perhaps the greatest source of histrionics is the debate over whether it is active or passive, an index or a strategy, a debate over more semantics. We view the Fundamental Index concept as a new, transparent, and powerful choice to add to the investors' tool kit. In this context, we shouldn't care a whit what people choose to call it.

CHAPTER 12

Why Trust the Fundamental Index Concept?

Performance data represents past performance, and may not reflect future investment returns.
> —U.S. Securities and Exchange Commission[1]

Thus far, the case for and against the Fundamental Index concept has centered on *past* investment results, both retrospective and live. Of course, using past performance to make a forecast for the future is fraught with peril. Past is not prologue. Maybe history occasionally rhymes, as Mark Twain once quipped, but it rarely repeats. For this reason, the most successful investors—whether top pension executives, chief investment officers of major endowments, or the major investment consulting firms—try to place a rather small emphasis on performance when evaluating an investment strategy. Of course, this goes against human nature, even for the best investors.

One of the most respected investment professionals, David Swensen (2000) of the Yale University Endowment, in his book *Pioneering Portfolio Management*, stated succinctly: "Instead of examining critically the factors driving past performance, investors frequently simply associate superior historical results with investment acumen." Gary Brinson (2005), who, together with his colleagues, taught us the importance of strategic asset allocation, is even more adamant about the pitfalls of performance:

> Investment results are largely random noise. This statement is true even for extended periods, but it has particular applicability in short-term intervals. By definition, random noise offers no predictive information which is why past investment performance has no predictive value.

Accordingly, for the coming pages, we set aside the numbers, power down our analytical software, close our spreadsheets, and lay out the philosophical groundwork for the Fundamental Index concept. We follow this with a few more analytically oriented points to illustrate why we think the *future* efficacy of the Fundamental Index concept will differ little from the past, probably for many years to come (though not for *every single one* of those years!).

Stock Logic

The Fundamental Index concept is built on a simple but logical foundation. If markets are efficient—which few observers believe—capitalization weighting is optimal and *modest departures from it are essentially harmless.* But if noise—events, disruptions, shocks, and other stimuli—causes prices to deviate from underlying fair values, capitalization weighting will hurt us by concentrating our money in the most overvalued assets, while the Fundamental Index concept won't do that. If the noise is temporary, stocks that are overvalued or undervalued today may become more fairly priced in the future, which gives Fundamental Index relative returns a tailwind. In a capitalization-weighted construct, weights are positively correlated with these mispricings, so the resulting portfolio will have a higher proportion of overpriced stocks than any portfolio where the weights are *not* correlated with these mispricings.

Intuitively, we know that mispricing occurs. We saw evidence of the mispricing in earlier chapters. The impact of these pricing errors on a portfolio can be illustrated by the changes in the list of top 10 companies by capitalization over long periods of time. The list changes significantly and quickly. This phenomenon mirrors, at the individual stock level, Robert Shiller's (1981) seminal work demonstrating that stock market volatility drastically exceeds the volatility of the underlying fundamentals of the very same market portfolio. Shiller's findings may be a function of fast changing investor risk preferences at the aggregate level. After all, a mere half percent drop in the average investor's demand for real returns will boost the market by 15 percent or more, even if expectations for the future haven't changed. But this shouldn't hold true for individual companies, where the demand for real returns from stocks "A" and "B" shouldn't be very different. So the observed turbulence in the top 10 stocks by market capitalization suggests quick shifting expectations and preferences for individual companies far in excess of the likely changes in the underlying fundamentals for the companies.

Table 12.1 shows many of the familiar companies in the 1965 list of top 10 companies by capitalization—such as General Motors, AT&T, Standard Oil of New Jersey (now Exxon Mobil Corporation), and DuPont. In 1965, DuPont was the sixth largest company in the United States by capitalization. But by 1970, it was no longer on the top 10 list. For a cap-weighted investor in 1965, DuPont was the biggest disappointment because over the next five years, DuPont's stock price cratered; it severely underperformed the average stock. It can be considered a "fallen angel"—that is, a company that was once in the top 10 list of the "angels" of Wall Street and is no more. Over the past 42 years, 26 angels have fallen from the list when their stock prices underperformed. Each of these 26 would have hurt the cap-weighted index fund investor.

Index fund investors were also hurt by the "flip-flops," a special kind of fallen angel, one that comes onto the top 10 list but leaves as fast as it arrived. Xerox replaced DuPont in 1970 and was gone five years later. It disappeared from the elite as fast as it had arrived, never to return to the top 10. There were 15 flip-flops during the past 42 years. Each of the flip-flops hurts index investors in two ways: The investment before the company takes off is too small to help materially and is then too large when the stock peaks and tumbles from the top 10 list. Table 12.1 shows that pricing changes cause unexpected large and rapid changes in the largest holdings, all of which prove wealth destroying because some of the largest positions underperform enough to fall off the list.

An index based on fundamental measures of company size experiences far less movement in the top 10 ranking over time and will be much more stable than a cap-weighted index, as Table 12.2 shows. The economic size of a company changes at a more measured

Table 12.1 Top 10 Companies by Capitalization, 1965 through 2007

Rank	1965	1970	1975	1980	1985	1990	1995	2000	2005	2007
1	AT&T	IBM	AT&T	IBM	IBM	EXXON	GENERAL ELECTRIC	MICROSOFT	GENERAL ELECTRIC	EXXON MOBIL
2	GENERAL MOTORS	AT&T	IBM	AT&T	EXXON	GENERAL ELECTRIC	AT&T	GENERAL ELECTRIC	EXXON MOBIL	GENERAL ELECTRIC
3	STANDARD OIL CO. NJ	GENERAL MOTORS	STANDARD OIL CO. NJ	EXXON	GENERAL ELECTRIC	IBM	EXXON	CISCO	CITIGROUP	CITIGROUP
4	IBM	EASTMAN KODAK	EASTMAN KODAK	GENERAL MOTORS	GENERAL MOTORS	AT&T	COCA-COLA	WAL-MART	MICROSOFT	MICROSOFT
5	TEXACO	STANDARD OIL CO. NJ	GENERAL MOTORS	STANDARD OIL CO.	AT&T	PHILIP MORRIS	PHILIP MORRIS	EXXON MOBIL	PFIZER	BANK OF AMERICA
6	DUPONT	SEARS ROEBUCK	SEARS ROEBUCK	MOBIL	SHELL OIL	MERCK & CO.	WAL-MART	INTEL	BANK OF AMERICA	PROCTER & GAMBLE
7	SEARS ROEBUCK	TEXACO	PROCTER & GAMBLE	GENERAL ELECTRIC	AMOCO	BRISTOL-MYERS SQUIBB	MERCK & CO.	LUCENT	JOHNSON & JOHNSON	JOHNSON & JOHNSON
8	GENERAL ELECTRIC	XEROX	GENERAL ELECTRIC	STANDARD OIL CO. CA	DUPONT	DUPONT	IBM	IBM	IBM	PFIZER
9	GULF OIL	GENERAL ELECTRIC	AMOCO	ATLANTIC RICHFIELD	SEARS ROEBUCK	AMOCO	PROCTER & GAMBLE	CITIGROUP	AIG	ALTRIA
10	EASTMAN KODAK	GULF OIL	CHEVRON	SHELL OIL	EASTMAN KODAK	BELLSOUTH	DUPONT	AOL	INTEL	JP MORGAN CHASE

New to top 10   Falling off top 10   Flip Flop

Summary: Fallen Angels: 26; Changes: 38; Flip-Flops: 15; Leads RAFI: 23; Lags RAFI: 41

Source: Research Affiliates, LLC.

Table 12.2 Top 10 Companies by Fundamental Size, 1965 through 2007

Rank	1965	1970	1975	1980	1985	1990	1995	2000	2005	2007
1	GENERAL MOTORS	AT&T	AT&T	AT&T	AT&T	EXXON	EXXON	EXXON MOBIL	EXXON MOBIL	EXXON MOBIL
2	AT&T	GENERAL MOTORS	GENERAL MOTORS	GENERAL MOTORS	EXXON	IBM	IBM	FORD	CITIGROUP	GENERAL ELECTRIC
3	STANDARD OIL CO. NJ	STANDARD OIL CO. NJ	STANDARD OIL CO. NJ	EXXON	IBM	GENERAL MOTORS	GENERAL MOTORS	GENERAL ELECTRIC	GENERAL ELECTRIC	CITIGROUP
4	FORD	FORD	IBM	IBM	GENERAL MOTORS	FORD	FORD	GENERAL MOTORS	WAL-MART	MICROSOFT
5	TEXACO	IBM	TEXACO	MOBIL	MOBIL	AT&T	GENERAL ELECTRIC	GENERAL MOTORS	FANNIE MAE	BANK OF AMERICA
6	DUPONT	TEXACO	FORD	FORD	TEXACO	EXXON	AT&T	AT&T	BANK OF AMERICA	WAL-MART
7	GENERAL ELECTRIC	GULF OIL	GULF OIL	TEXACO	AMOCO	GENERAL ELECTRIC	MOBIL	PHILIP MORRIS	AT&T	VERIZON
8	SEARS ROEBUCK	MOBIL	MOBIL	GENERAL ELECTRIC	CHEVRON	DUPONT	PHILIP MORRIS	FANNIE MAE	CHEVRON	CHEVRON
9	IBM	GENERAL ELECTRIC	STANDARD OIL CO. CA	GULF OIL	GENERAL ELECTRIC	CHEVRON	DUPONT	WORLDCOM	GENERAL MOTORS	ALTRIA
10	STANDARD OIL CO. CA	SEARS ROEBUCK	SEARS ROEBUCK	STANDARD OIL CO. CA	DUPONT	AMOCO	CHEVRON	IBM	AIG	PFIZER

New to top 10   Falling off top 10   Flip Flop

Summary: Fallen Angels: 10; Changes: 17; Flip-Flops: 2; Leads Cap: 41; Lags Cap: 23

Source: Research Affiliates, LLC.

pace than Wall Street's rapidly shifting future expectations for that same company.

Not surprisingly, the names in the top 10 lists in Tables 12.1 and 12.2 for 1965 are similar; eight companies make both top 10 lists. Interestingly, DuPont placed sixth in both fundamental size and cap weight in 1965 and fell off of both lists in the next five years. Not only did the stock price crater, but the business also went off the rails. DuPont's aggregate operating results failed to keep pace with the growing economy.

Over the 42-year period, however, the Fundamental Index top 10 list is far more stable than the cap-weighted top 10 list. The Fundamental Index strategy will have some exposure to companies whose business deteriorates, such as DuPont in the 1960s, but there are only 10 fallen angels on the Fundamental Index top 10 lists over the past 42 years. Only 10 of the 20 are gone; only 10 of the 20 hurt the Fundamental Index performance by tumbling off the list.

Only two flip-flops have occurred in the past 42 years for the Fundamental Index top 10 list: AIG (American International Group) and WorldCom. One got on the wrong side of a powerful regulator; the other got on the wrong side of the law. A company can artificially inflate fundamental measures of company size—sales, cash flow, and book value—through aggressive accounting or, in the case of WorldCom, outright fraud. The Fundamental Index process is not a fraud detector. Such companies can wind up with a larger Fundamental Index weight than they deserve. But the small number of flip-flops during 42 years underscores the stability of economic size. Better one fraudulent top 10 holding in 42 years than 15 companies that got to that lofty level and promptly crashed as a result of fads, bubbles, and shifting expectations.

An index that suffers a minimum of fallen angels and flip-flops should suffer less performance drag from having large investments in companies that fall off the list. The RAFI U.S. Large Company Index (RAFI U.S. Large) has been burned only 10 times since 1962 by having major stakes in businesses that shrunk enough to leave the list versus 26 instances for the cap-weighted index. Of course, this discussion is focused solely on the top end of the indexes, but heavyweight underperformers and lightweight outperformers are prevalent from top to bottom. The Fundamental Index concept is intended to neutralize their wealth-eroding effect.

One nuance in these results was unexpected. Suppose a company's rank by capitalization is five on the list and its Fundamental Index rank is eighth. If the capitalization ranking subsequently rises, then we might say that capitalization weighting *leads* the Fundamental Index weight; it is more predictive of where the stock is going than the Fundamental Index weight. If the capitalization ranking subsequently falls, then we might say that the Fundamental Index weight *leads* the capitalization weight; that the Fundamental Index weight is more predictive of where the stock is going than the cap weight. If the market is efficient, this should be a random draw. If the Fundamental Index concept is counterproductive in steering us away from growth opportunities, then it should not be a random draw—capitalization weight should lead Fundamental Index weight far more often than vice versa.

What do the data suggest? The Fundamental Index weight is more predictive in 41 cases in which a company's rank has changed, and cap weight is more predictive in 23 cases. The chance of a coin toss coming up heads 41 times in 64 tries is less than one in 100.

The Present versus the Future: How Often Is Wall Street Right?

The Fundamental Index and cap-weighted index portfolios, by design, represent different "views" of the economy. The Fundamental Index portfolio mirrors the look of today's economy. By allocating to each stock in accordance with its current financial size, the resulting weight broadly reflects its current economic importance. It is by no means a perfect match, however, because the publicly traded companies are only part of the economy. Privately held companies and the government also contribute to the size of the economy, but their contributions aren't captured in Fundamental Index portfolios. Also, the economic scale of a company is imperfectly measured by any single metric of company size (nor even a combination like the one that we favor). Nevertheless, the Fundamental Index strategy and its four fundamental measures of company size form a pretty accurate portrayal of the composition of the publicly traded parts of today's economy.

In contrast, a cap-weighted index reflects Wall Street's best guess of tomorrow's economy. Companies with bright prospects and high price-earnings (P/E) multiples are expected to be much larger in the future. Indeed, because share prices should match the discounted net present value of *decades* of future cash flows, it's fair to say that the cap-weighted market is a best guess of the look of the future economy, not tomorrow or next year, but decades into the future. The market pays for these anticipated future successes today, as if those growth expectations are assured. This leads to higher valuation multiples and, therefore, larger capitalizations for these growth stocks. The resulting emphasis is on the projected large companies of the future, at the expense of the portion of the current economic leadership with less optimistic growth expectations.

On the surface, building a portfolio that reflects the future seems more sensible than building one that reflects the present. Investors see the innovative, useful products and services of growth companies, and have confidence in the companies' expanding role in the economy in the years ahead. Of course, investors want to capture the fruits of these expanding enterprises in their portfolios. Furthermore, the share price contains a wealth of information about investors' collective views of a company's forward-looking long-term prospects.

This future-oriented view has two problems, however. First, if the market is doing its job right, investors pay *exactly* enough to prepay for the growth company's superior future growth. They pay as if that growth is a *fait accompli* and pay exactly enough to bring the future risk-adjusted return on the company's stock down to match the broad market *and even that of the unloved value stocks!* Second, the market's estimates of the future—for individual companies, industries, markets, and countries—are often in error. These errors can be large or small, and they can exist for short periods or very long periods. Many studies have shown that our collective ability to predict the future for a company's profits beyond the next couple of years is pretty poor.[2] Our crystal ball is cloudy for the one-year outlook and pretty much opaque beyond two or three years.

It's fair to point out that share prices are supposed to discount all future cash flows from our investments for decades into the future. In draft research by Arnott and Li (2008) exploring the implications of "clairvoyant value," we examine the top 10 names in the original S&P 500, and find that cash flows of the past 50 years account for only about 80 percent of the "clairvoyant value" of 1957! Today's share price, as a best guess of the value of today's future cash flows, discounted all the way back to 1957, comprises about 20 percent of the 1957 value of these 10 companies. The market's valuation of a company is an estimate of a long period of future cash flows. Anyone care to guess how large GE, Microsoft, Exxon Mobil, or Citigroup will be as a percentage of the U.S. economy in 2058? History suggests that some of these won't even be in the top 25 companies 50 years hence! Large errors in today's price relative to the "clairvoyant value" of all future cash flows will be the norm, not the exception.

Examining the historical sector allocations of cap-weighted and Fundamental Index portfolios is insightful in this regard because, cumulatively, the "today versus tomorrow" weighting discrepancies often manifest themselves in industry composition. Figures 12.1 and 12.2 illustrate the relative stability of these sector allocations over time for the two types of index. (Note that we smoothed the data in these graphs over a centered two-year window. If we hadn't done this, the cap-weighted graph would be so jagged as to be almost unreadable.)

In the cap-weighted sector allocations, shown in Figure 12.1, two large bulges stand out. The most recent is the technology and telecom bulge that peaked in 2000. The combined weight of these three sectors soared from less than 20 percent of the cap-weighted

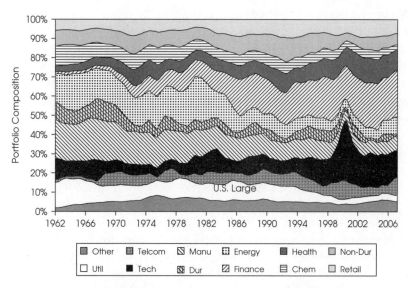

Figure 12.1 Cap-Weighted Sector Allocations, 1962 through June 2007

Source: Research Affiliates, LLC.

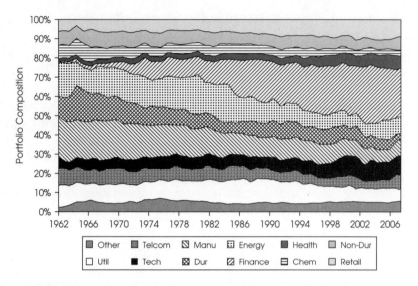

Figure 12.2 Fundamental Index Sector Allocations, 1962 through June 2007

Source: Research Affiliates, LLC.

market in the mid-1990s to more than 40 percent at the top of the bubble. In the late 1990s, there was widespread discussion of a "new paradigm," where technology would exert accelerating economic growth beyond anything ever seen before. In effect, the startling sales growth of the internet and broader tech sector convinced many investors that these companies would grow so rapidly in the years ahead that, on the basis of net present value of future cash flows, they would represent more than half the economy in the coming decades. When these companies' profits and sales failed to grow fast enough to sustain this illusion, technology stock prices dropped significantly, bringing the sector weight down with them.

The weight of the energy sector in the cap-weighted index in the early 1980s is also instructive. A combination of high inflation, a seemingly unbreakable OPEC (Organization of Petroleum Exporting Countries) coalition, and rising commodity prices led many to suspect that crude oil prices would rise to $100 per barrel. These prognosticators were eventually right in 25 years rather than a few months! Energy stocks rode a wave of speculative sentiment. In only three years, rising share prices more than doubled the sector's weight—to an immense 30 percent in 1981. But by the peak of the tech bubble, oil was below $10 per barrel, investors thought of energy stocks as a boring backwater, and these companies made up less than 5 percent of the market, *even though their sales and profits had grown handily in the intervening decades!*

As sector allocations surge in a cap-weighted index, a natural side effect is a more concentrated index portfolio. In extreme instances—such as during the tech bubble or energy bubble—the expected diversification of traditional index funds is severely compromised. In the 1990s prior to 1999, the largest sector concentration in the cap-weighted index ranged from 16 percent to 22 percent of the market, which is consistent with the diversification expected of passive investing. As the decade came to a close, however, technology stocks rose to a 31 percent allocation. In effect, the market was saying that almost one-third of all future U.S. profits would be earned in the technology sector, which accounted for well under 10 percent of all sales at the time! With no rebalancing mechanism inherent in capitalization weighting, such a portfolio is subject to significant return-chasing behavior—with most of our money invested in recent past winners and far less in the recent losers—while suffering its negative effect on portfolio diversification, as we discussed in Chapter 3.

The impact of the swings in sector weights is significant. A lot of money is at risk if the market's forecasts prove faulty. Even if Wall Street gets the forecasts right, sectors just meet expectations and there are no net benefits: The favored sectors become much larger over time, but *because investors have already paid for that growth today, they derive no real benefit.* They simply earn the market returns. The payoff is decidedly asymmetrical. If the market calls heads and it turns up, the investor ties; but with tails, investors lose, and can lose significantly. As the Red Queen says in *Alice in Wonderland,* "Now, *here,* you see, it takes all the running *you* can do, to keep in the same place. If you want to get somewhere else, you must run at least twice as fast as that!" Better, perhaps, to avoid playing this stacked game of chasing hot sectors.

The Fundamental Index sector weights change gradually over time in a way that mirrors the evolution of the economy. Figure 12.2 shows no sudden spikes in sector allocations nor any subsequent crashes. To be sure, spikes in sales or profits will show up as modest wiggles in this chart, as some of these trends persist and some don't. Still, the annual rebalance ensures discipline and avoids the return-chasing behavior inherent in traditional cap-weighted indexes. Even while rebalancing against the most extreme bets in the cap-weighted markets, the Fundamental Index portfolio still keeps turnover at a low level. Outperformers are rebalanced back to their economic sizes, and the proceeds are invested in companies that have recently fared better fundamentally than in their share prices. The strategy elegantly captures the major secular changes, the evolution of the overall economy—for example, the rising importance of the financial, health care, and technology sectors and the significant decline in U.S. manufacturing, basic industries (e.g., chemicals), and consumer durables—the "creative destruction" of Joseph Schumpeter. By capturing the economic footprint of hundreds of companies, the Fundamental Index strategy avoids the periodic speculative runs in hot sectors and dives in out-of-favor sectors; more importantly, it thereby avoids the significant return drag caused by the all-too-common reversals of those fads, bubbles, and crashes.

Take another look at these two figures. Many people in the academic and indexing communities refer to the Fundamental Index portfolio as an active strategy, even though its sector mix, shown in Figure 12.2, shows remarkably steady change reflecting the gradual evolution of the broad economy. They refer to capitalization weighting as a passive strategy, even though its sector mix, shown in Figure 12.1, reflects rapidly shifting expectations and constantly changing active bets on which segments of the economy will grow most and which segments will decline. Figure 12.1 reflects no rebalancing of our portfolio, while Figure 12.2 is constantly rebalancing back to the economic weights of companies and sectors—contra-trading against the sometimes extreme optimism and pessimism of the cap-weighted markets.

Why Does Wall Street Get It Wrong?

Companies expected to be large tomorrow will be overrepresented in a cap-weighted index relative to their economic scale. On the other hand, the expected losers of tomorrow will have a smaller weight that reflects their diminished expected economic role in the future. In the past, these expectations often failed to materialize, and the cap-weighted index was punished as a result. But is there a rationale for expecting the same errors in the future? This question is crucial because these errors *structurally* impair the return of the cap-weighted index.

The finance profession has various theories as to why pricing errors persist and sometimes blossom into bubbles.[3] Unfortunately, the worlds of classical finance and behavioral finance have exhibited a rather icy indifference to one another for many years. The classicists disdain behaviorists' lack of mathematical rigor and the fact that behavioral finance has no model for how markets should behave in equilibrium. The behaviorists disdain the classicists' reliance on efficient markets and a raft of other simplifying—but factually incorrect—assumptions. We submit that simply introducing noise into the classicists' models—even though it complicates the elegant mathematical simplicity of these models—may go a long way to bridging this gap. Because classical finance theory relies a great deal on efficient markets, most theories that purport to explain pricing errors are rooted in behavioral finance, a body of theory and knowledge that explains the lack of rationality or consistency in the methods people use to reach investment decisions.

One explanation lies in the human tendency to pay a premium for the potential of a huge payoff. Willingly accepting poor odds for the slim chance of a huge award is not restricted to the world of finance. Each week, millions of Americans visit the corner grocery to buy lottery tickets. The odds against winning a $12 million Powerball prize in California are more than 175 million to 1 (Carey, 2007). And, on average, most states return to the players only about 50 cents of every dollar paid to play. But motivated by the potential of the huge jackpot, players turn a blind eye to the horrendous odds standing in their way.[4]

In the stock market, the desire to find the "next Microsoft"—a fast-growing company that exceeds even the highest of expectations—is powerful. Peter Lynch called such companies 10-baggers because they rise 10-fold in a few short years. Of course, the stocks that fail to become "the next big thing" are often big disappointments. Many stocks have appeared at both extremes, especially in the Nasdaq indexes. Buying 20 such companies in order to find one 10-bagger is usually folly. *But, that's what the market is collectively doing at the top of the valuation multiple ranges!* A lottery ticket mentality may afflict the investors (speculators?) who feverishly seek such companies.

Yet the cap-weighted markets treat such investors, and the resulting prices, as rational elements of an efficient market.

Overemphasizing the recent past and the likelihood that it will continue can also explain irrational investor behavior. It may apply to mutual fund investors (recall our discussion of the performance game, with our chasing of the recently successful funds, strategies, and asset classes) as well as professional analysts and portfolio managers. In the case of the technology and energy sector bubbles, which were unrelated and separated by 20 years, immediate past results were extrapolated, *by investment professionals*, to shape future expectations. At the peak of the tech bubble, investment professionals were also guilty of extrapolating the recent *weak* results of the energy and manufacturing sectors!

A striking correlation is often visible between the recent past results of a company and consensus expectations for its future. This rather consistent forecasting error may spring from the deluge of financial information that cascades onto us all, professionals and amateurs alike. With so many (often conflicting) decision-making variables, analysts may understandably focus on (in behavioral finance terms, "anchor on") the most recent historical results. Behavioral finance calls this psychological phenomenon *representativeness*. Rules of thumb—shaped by recent experience and incorrectly deemed "representative" of normal conditions—replace comprehensive and rational analysis of potential outcomes. Despite having taken shortcuts, the decision maker tends to maintain a high degree of confidence in the representative forecast.

Finally, agency issues can shed light on how stocks with perceived strong growth prospects wind up with large positions in a cap-weighted index fund. Keep in mind that active portfolio managers have two primary responsibilities: running their clients' money and running their own businesses. These responsibilities can be in conflict. To remain in business, managers need clients. When performance is good, client retention is easy. When performance is bad, it's not. So, interests seem outwardly aligned. But wait a minute! When results are bad, managers may be tempted to make decisions that are easier to defend rather than those that may be harder to explain, even though the markets will typically reward *discomfort*, not comfort. Often, underperforming managers find it far easier to review with clients top holdings in exciting and recently successful growth companies than to go over the "bad news" stocks with their negative publicity. Being out of step with the "crowd" takes a lot of courage, which may explain why we see so many portfolio managers owning the "popular" companies. An old adage among portfolio managers is: "You never get fired for owning IBM" (with the implication that you could be fired for owning stocks that are not well known and fail to deliver).

Many clients encourage this behavior by confusing "good companies" with solid investment opportunities. Consider the following comparison of Intel and Unisys set forth by famed behavioral finance professor Hersh Shefrin (2007) of Santa Clara University:

> The information provided about these two stocks most likely would lead an investor to conclude that Intel has been a better company than Unisys for this period, particularly based on the past five-year sales, market cap, and retained earnings. Suppose that investors form their judgments about risk and return by relying on representativeness. They thus believe that better stocks feature higher expected returns. In addition, they associate safe stocks with the stocks of financially sound companies. They would tend to judge Intel as a better *stock* than Unisys because they would think Intel is a better *company* than Unisys. So, they would end up viewing Intel as featuring a higher expected return than Unisys, but they *also* would view Intel as being a *safer* stock than Unisys. (p. 5; emphasis added)

Hersh's specific example is just one of a multitude that lends credence to John Maynard Keynes's (1936) famous quote, which is too often quoted only in its closing sentence:

> . . . it is the long-term investor, he who most promotes the public interest, who will in practice come in for most criticism, wherever investment funds are managed by committees or boards or banks. For it is in the essence of his behavior that he should be eccentric, unconventional and rash in the eyes of average opinion. If he is successful, that will only confirm the general belief in his rashness; and if in the short run he is unsuccessful, which is very likely, he will not receive much mercy. Worldly wisdom teaches that it is better *for reputation* to fail conventionally than to succeed unconventionally. (emphasis added)

Business success depends as much on reputation as results. When results are poor, what retains clients best is a good reputation. Investments that seem rash (e.g., doubling up on our long-term losers) may sully our reputation enough to lose us our business, even if they prove to have been shrewd choices. This dynamic provides an artificial boost in allocation to those stocks that have done well recently and are expected to do so in the future.

Dynamic Style and Size Exposures: When Do We Want Value and Small Cap?

Tying portfolio weights to the economic scale of an enterprise delivers a stable and disciplined portfolio that eschews chasing the hot sectors, styles, or individual stocks or selling out of those that have disappointed. This contra-trading process, inherent in the Fundamental Index methodology, is a powerful element of its advantage.

To gain an intuition into how the Fundamental Index methodology leads to excess returns, Figure 12.3 shows the dynamic nature to the value tilt for the RAFI U.S. Large strategy relative to the growth-versus-value performance differential from 1979 through December 2007. For the solid line, a level of 50 percent on the left-hand vertical axis means that growth has cumulatively outpaced value by 50 percent in the prior 10 years, while –25 percent means that it has underperformed by 25 percent. The dashed line measures the value tilt of the RAFI U.S. Large over time; a value of 1 on the right-hand vertical axis indicates a value tilt approximately equal to that of the Russell 1000 Value Index, whereas a value of 0 indicates a neutral bias, one approximating a blended broad-market cap-weighted portfolio like the Russell 1000 Index. Of course, because the Fundamental Index concept has an inherent value tilt relative to the cap-weighted market, this "value tilt" can never reach zero.

Notice the powerful link between the growth stock outperformance and the resulting value tilt of the RAFI U.S. Large portfolio. This is not surprising. Consider the late 1990s. As growth stocks took off in 1998 and 1999, the RAFI U.S. Large portfolio steadily trimmed the hot growth stocks back down to their economic scale and topped the slumping value stocks back up to their economic scale. Because the market was paying more and more of a premium for expected future growth, the Fundamental Index portfolio

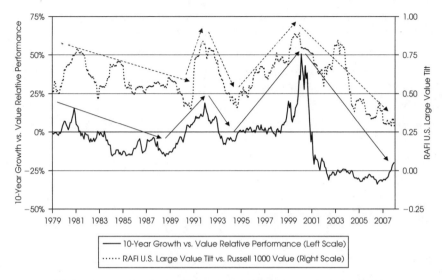

Figure 12.3   Dynamic Value Exposure, 1979 through June 2007
Source: Research Affiliates, LLC.

seemed to be taking on an ever-larger value tilt—so much so that at the bubble's peak, the RAFI U.S. Large had a value tilt almost as large as the Russell 1000 Value, *even though the Fundamental Index portfolio still held most of the growth stocks.*

This exhibit vividly shows that, as the market pays more and more for growth, a Fundamental Index portfolio will be paring growth stocks back to their economic weight again and again, leading to a substantial value tilt in the portfolio at the height of a growth stock cycle, just in time for that speculative excess to reverse course. Alternatively, one can just as fairly see this situation as one in which the market itself has taken on a substantial growth tilt, by paying an ever-higher premium for expected future growth. Both perspectives are accurate!

To understand this dynamic, think back to what was occurring at that time. The stocks of the era's high flyers—Cisco Systems, Intel, Lucent Technologies, AOL—were appreciating rapidly, thereby taking up a larger and larger portion of the Russell 1000 Growth Index and pushing many less extreme growth stocks into the Russell 1000 Value. Meanwhile, the RAFI U.S. Large also held most of these glamorous growth stocks, but at the lower weights reflective of their economic scope. Compared with a cap-weighted index, the RAFI U.S. Large had a much higher allocation to "value" stocks than to "growth" stocks, but only because the market was paying an unprecedented premium for perceived future growth prospects. This combination led to a deep-value orientation on the part of the RAFI U.S. Large portfolio right before value took off.

When value stocks experience sustained outperformance, as they did in 1981 through 1988 and again in 2000 through 2006, a Fundamental Index portfolio winds up with an ever-diminishing value emphasis. In such environments (e.g., 2007), growth stocks will be trading at only slightly elevated multiples to their value counterparts. At these times, immune to the effect of multiples on portfolio weights, the Fundamental Index portfolio looks and feels much like a core cap-weighted portfolio. In fact, many Russell 1000 Growth stocks are *overweighted* in a recent snapshot of RAFI U.S. Large holdings. Top Russell 1000 Growth holdings—General Electric, Wal-Mart, and Altria Group—are all in the RAFI U.S. Large with larger positions than in the cap-weighted Russell 1000. Indeed, the last time the RAFI U.S. Large had a value tilt comparable to 2007 was at the start of 1991. In both 1991 and 2007, growth trounced value by more than 1,000 basis points. In this bleak environment for the Fundamental Index portfolios, how hard hit were they relative to the cap-weighted indexes that enjoyed the tailwind of a growth-dominated market? In 1991, the RAFI U.S. Large portfolio earned a 31.3 percent return against 33 percent for the Russell 1000. In 2007, the comparison was 3.2 percent versus 5.8 percent. Shortfalls? Yes. Disasters? Hardly.

In the second half of 2007, many quantitative value managers experienced massive underperformance—on a scale that they had not seen before. Because the RAFI U.S. Large entered this period with such a modest value bias (or capitalization weighting entered with a modest growth tilt), it lagged the performance of the Russell 1000 by just 2.6 percentage points, in a large-growth year, when the Russell 1000 Growth beat the Russell 2000 Value Index by a staggering 22 percent. During this period, several hedge fund managers and hedge fund-of-funds managers (managers who pick other hedge fund managers) went out of business. Others struggled.

Why did quantitative value managers get hammered while Fundamental Index portfolios got lightly clipped? Many managers, seeing their value strategies win for seven years with ever-diminishing volatility and ever-increasing consistency, had ramped up their leverage to 10-fold and beyond. So, when value underperformed with a vengeance, they were crushed. During this period, the Fundamental Index portfolios had been making smaller and smaller value bets. One large hedge fund manager, under fire in the press for his flagging results, described this market experience as "a deleveraging of historical proportions." Perhaps not. Perhaps it was the largest deleveraging of quantitative value-tilted market-neutral strategies in their brief history. Perhaps it was triggered by their use at the highest-ever leverage ratios when the market was paying a historically low premium for growth.

The changing value exposure of the RAFI U.S. Large strategy—which resembles a deep-value portfolio after strong growth runs and has a mild value orientation after value outperformance—is self-evident in Figure 12.3. Note that the value tilt of the Fundamental Index strategy not only becomes most pronounced after growth has soundly outpaced value, it also now has a pronounced value tilt ahead of a winning period for value. Reciprocally, the value tilt becomes modest after value has won, when growth may take center stage. Certainly, this pattern would seem to add to portfolio returns. As we show shortly, this dynamic tilt contributes almost as much to the performance of the Fundamental Index portfolio as its average value bias does.

The Fundamental Index methodology leads to a dynamic exposure to company size as well. As in the case of the dynamic value tilt, the Fundamental Index methodology tends to have its greatest small-cap exposure right before those stocks surge and a neutral stance regarding larger-cap exposure at the end of a long small-cap run. In 2000, the RAFI U.S. Large had a dramatically smaller-cap bias relative to the Russell 1000 than it did in 2007. Throughout the 1990s, the RAFI U.S. Large was continually rebalancing the highest priced (and largest cap) shares back to their fundamental weights, whereas the cap-weighted markets let them run to lofty weights just before they crashed.

After the bubble burst in 2000, market leadership shifted in favor of smaller-cap stocks with the Russell 2000 cumulatively outperforming the Russell 1000 by over 50 percent as shown in Figure 12.4. As the multiples of these stocks increased, they began to constitute a growing portion of their respective cap-weighted indexes. A natural consequence of the higher allocation to small-cap is that the average weighted capitalization of the Russell 1000

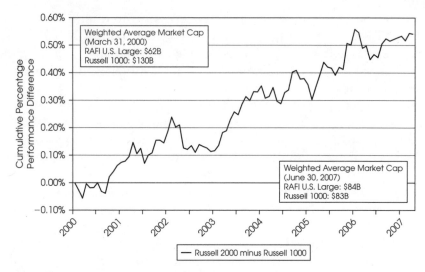

Figure 12.4 Cumulative Outperformance of Russell 2000 over Russell 1000, March 2000 through June 2007
Source: Research Affiliates, LLC.

has decreased—in fact, it has decreased to the point where the average capitalization of the RAFI U.S. Large is now about even with the average capitalization of the Russell 1000. As in the case of the dynamic value tilt, the Fundamental Index methodology tends to have its greatest small-cap exposure after those stocks have been hammered often right before they surge, and a mild large-cap bias at the end of a long small-cap run.

Show Me the Numbers

Blissfully unconcerned with the shifting favorites in the cap-weighted indexes, the Fundamental Index portfolio is immune to the effects of valuations on index construction and avoids the trap of allocating great percentages to the recent darlings of the market. If the market were efficient, if prices matched fair value, this immunity would *neither help nor hurt* the Fundamental Index portfolio. But in an inefficient market, contra-trading against the fads, bubbles, and shifting expectations of the market is very profitable.

A traditional performance attribution analysis parses the success of an investment strategy into three separate areas: the economic sectors, the value-growth and size exposure, and the individual stocks. It is instructive to use this construct to compare the performance of a RAFI portfolio with that of a cap-weighted portfolio like the S&P 500. Before looking at the numbers, let's review the recent experience of these four factors:

- *Economic sectors.* The examination of historical sector allocations showed that the market often incorrectly gauges which sectors will be important in the future, has too lofty expectations for some industries, and has too bleak expectations for others. Often, the market wrongly extrapolates the successes of rapidly growing industries and the disappointments of mature or stagnant industries. As these perceptions are corrected, the price-weighted index suffers.
- *Value and size exposure.* The past 10 years were instructive about how the growth and value styles and large companies and small can take turns in market leadership. In capitalization weighting, the index investor, riding the current style wave, absorbs a growing percentage of assets in the hottest style.
- *Individual stocks.* The snapshot of top 10 holdings of the past 42 years illustrates the frequency with which security prices overshoot the fair value of the underlying enterprises. In capitalization weighting, any of these top 10 that are overpriced will eventually fall out of the top 10. Keep in mind that over the past 80 years, only 3 of the top 10 stocks, on average, beat the average stock in the S&P 500 in the subsequent decade. And there are many large companies trading at deep discounts that the cap-weighted indexes will miss altogether.

The importance of each of these elements as drivers of the Fundamental Index return is shown in Table 12.3, which presents a dynamic attribution analysis—a modified version of the standard Brinson Attribution Analysis that shows both the static and dynamic element of each component of the value added—of the RAFI U.S. Large compared with the S&P 500.

In this analysis, sector allocation of the RAFI U.S. Large added 0.50 percentage points annually beyond the returns for the benchmark S&P 500. The average RAFI U.S. Large sector exposure was slightly negative relative to the S&P 500, costing the portfolio

Table 12.3   RAFI U.S. Large Dynamic Attribution Analysis, 1962 through June 2007

Total Value Added	2.12%	
Sector Allocation	0.50%	
Average sector exposure		-0.05%
Dynamic sector exposure		0.54%
Style: Growth vs. Value	1.03%	
Average growth/value exposure		0.53%
Dynamic growth/value exposure		0.50%
Style: Small vs. Large	0.33%	
Average size exposure		0.13%
Dynamic size exposure		0.20%
Stock Selection	0.26%	

Note: The methodology used differs from the standard Brinson Analysis by separating the allocation component into two variables, dynamic allocation and static allocation, as described in the working paper "Research Affiliates Dynamic Value Added Attribution Model" (April 9, 2007).

Source: Research Affiliates, LLC.

0.05 percentage points. This very neutral result should come as no surprise because over the very long term, as Figures 12.1 and 12.2 showed, the two portfolios have similar *average* allocations over the 45 years. But over certain intermediate spans, the cap-weighted indexes will ramp up exposure to some industries following price run-ups and ramp down exposure to others after price declines, far away from the economic scale of these enterprises. By not chasing the supposed sectors of tomorrow and enduring the ensuing relative losses, by contra-trading against those fads and shifting expectations, the RAFI U.S. Large was able to add 0.54 percentage points of value over the S&P 500 from 1962 to June 2007. Clearly, the RAFI U.S. Large benefited from dynamic sector allocation.

The Fundamental Index strategy typically maintains net value exposure over time. This tilt shows up in the *static attribution* analysis, where the average value tilt adds 0.53 percentage points. In other words, in a world in which value has historically tended to materially outpace growth over long spans of time, the Fundamental Index strategy benefits by always having some value exposure. However, as this attribution analysis shows, the dynamic value exposure of the Fundamental Index strategy is just as important to our returns. When the market is bidding up the price of growth stocks, the Fundamental Index portfolios will be trimming those same holdings. When the market is punishing growth and rewarding value, the Fundamental Index portfolios will be trimming value and buying growth! The strategy tactically increases the value exposure after sustained periods of growth outperformance, often just before those growth stocks reverse course, and decreases the value bias after prolonged cycles of value outperformance. This dynamic value tilt contributed about 0.50 percentage points annually of outperformance for the RAFI U.S. Large vis-à-vis the S&P 500.

It's well worth pointing out that the worst situation for a Fundamental Index portfolio relative to the cap-weighted markets is *not* when value has been on a long winning streak and the market shifts to favor growth, as it did in 1991 and 2007. In this circumstance, our value tilt is too slight—unlike many value-tilted quant strategies—to do us much harm. The worst situation for a Fundamental Index strategy is when *growth* has been on a long winning streak, so that the Fundamental Index portfolio's value tilt has already become pronounced *and growth keeps on winning!* This was the situation in 1998 and 1999, when the RAFI U.S. Large had its worst two years ever. But, the good news in this circumstance is that this kind of market cannot persist indefinitely. The worse a hit we take in the growth market, the stronger our benefit from the subsequent reversion toward the mean.

On the size spectrum (small-cap versus large-cap), the story is similar to the value tilt, but on a smaller scale. As we noted in Chapter 10, the RAFI U.S. Large has a modest exposure to the small-cap premium, mainly because the market has historically priced small-cap stocks at discounted valuation multiples. RAFI responds by reweighting them *up* to their economic scale. Confirming this assertion, the static analysis reveals that the RAFI U.S. Large benefited only slightly (0.13 percentage points per year) from having a modest small-cap bias on average. The dynamic size tilt of the Fundamental Index strategy that is trading opposite to the market preferences for large or small companies, contributed 0.20 percentage points annually. In 2007, of course, the market priced small-cap stocks at a premium, so the RAFI U.S. Large reweighted them *down* to their economic scale, thereby taking on a modest large-cap tilt *relative to the cap-weighted market portfolio!*

Although not a deliberate part of the Fundamental Index approach, stock selection added 0.26 percentage points per year to the RAFI U.S. Large outperformance and completed the total annual excess historical return of 2.12 percentage points. This contribution is interesting. The Fundamental Index portfolio doesn't *do* stock selection! Still, we do find that the approach picks up some out-of-favor companies that are missed by the cap-weighted indexes. As we showed in Chapter 2, these companies, while they may comprise only 2 percent to 4 percent of the Fundamental Index portfolio, have historically outperformed their counterparts—the small companies at lofty multiples that we will miss—by nearly 10 percentage points per year.

Two key lessons can be learned from this analysis. First, a comparison of the Fundamental Index historical allocations to individual stocks, economic sectors, style, and size exposures versus the cap-weighted index reveals *multiple* sources of excess return, not just benefits from a value tilt. Second, the Fundamental Index advantage isn't attributable solely to simple, static tilts to small-cap and value stocks or to out-of-favor sectors. The dynamic components, whether dynamic shifting of sector allocations, along the style dimensions of growth versus value or large versus small, or including large companies at deep discount multiples that the cap-weighted indexes will miss, account for more than two-thirds of the excess returns created by the Fundamental Index concept. The *average* sector, size, and style tilts contribute a bare 30 percent of the total value added.

This straightforward, passive approach of allocating to stocks on the basis of their economic size shifts the portfolio's exposure away from *any* extreme bets in the cap-weighted market, whether these extreme bets are in sectors, styles, or even individual stocks. This dynamic element is a simple and very powerful by-product of fundamental weighting.

Fundamental Index Strategy versus the Crystal Ball

The dynamic nature of the Fundamental Index methodology adds value for investors historically, across many markets and many decades. We have good reason to believe that this benefit is structural and (unlike the predictions of the many indexers who invoke the

Heisenberg Uncertainty Principle) is not likely to disappear just because we have now observed it. The power of shifting away from the market's excesses can be illustrated by examining the results of a strategy with perfect foresight.

Suppose an investment manager that we will label Crystal Ball Asset Management has perfect foresight about the style whims of the market. Its team of strategists can look three years into the future and determine, with 100 percent certainty, whether growth stocks will outperform value stocks or vice versa. With this information, it can invest 100 percent of its portfolio in the "winning" Russell 1000 Growth or Russell 1000 Value.

Starting at the end of 1978, Crystal Ball sets up shop, and it invests its first dollar on January 1, 1979, in the Russell 1000 Growth. Over the next three years, the Russell 1000 Growth outperforms the Russell 1000 Value by 39 basis points annually. In the subsequent three years (1982 through 1984), Crystal Ball is 100 percent in the Russell 1000 Value—the winning strategy for that period. Every three years, the team at Crystal Ball repeats the exercise and is always on target. Note that the triennial reassessment of this portfolio would have caught the top of the bubble perfectly by switching from growth in the six years from 1994 through 1999 to value for the six years from 2000 through 2005! The result is an annualized return of 16.4 percent from 1978 through 2005; by comparison, the figure for the S&P 500 is 13.3 percent. Of course we can't take this analysis up through 2007 because the current three-year span is still under way, so cannot know what Crystal Ball Asset Management would have chosen for 2006 through 2008; at this writing it could easily go either way.

No doubt every adviser, pension board, and endowment investment committee would be lining up to invest with Crystal Ball. Alas, no investor can come anywhere near this forecasting accuracy. But the Fundamental Index strategy has shown some ability to tactically allocate to various market exposures. Of course, the shifts don't imply any judgment on the relative valuations and return prospects of sectors or styles. No team of strategists is retained, nor is any style or company research conducted, in the management of a Fundamental Index portfolio. Nor is the shift ever 100 percent into growth or value; in fact, Figure 12.3 showed us that we use less than one-third of Crystal Ball's full range! Rather, the shifts result from mirroring the extremes in the cap-weighted markets by rebalancing company weight in our portfolio back to the company's

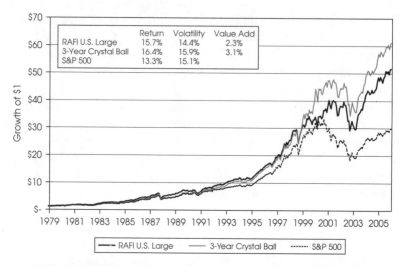

Figure 12.5   RAFI U.S. Large versus the Crystal Ball, 1978 through 2006
Source: Research Affiliates, LLC.

economic scale. In so doing, we avoid the damaging effects that price extremes, and the frequent reversals from those extremes, will have on results. Nonetheless, the exposures do change relative to the cap-weighted alternatives.

So how does the Fundamental Index portfolio compare with the Crystal Ball portfolio? As expected, it underperforms. But it comes startlingly close. As Figure 12.5 shows, the RAFI U.S. Large earned an annualized return of 15.7 percent compared with a return of 16.4 percent for Crystal Ball. The Fundamental Index strategy, with its dynamic portfolio tilts, achieved 74 percent of the value added of a perfect three-year growth/value market-timing strategy. Crystal Ball Asset Management will never exist, but investors wishing to capture *most* of its excess returns may be able to do so with the Fundamental Index strategy.

Does the Fundamental Index Concept Work in Bonds?

A key measure of an investment strategy's staying power is its robustness in other markets. We've shown how well the Fundamental Index concept works in a wide span of equity markets, but a skeptic might argue that equity markets are highly correlated now, so even our out-of-sample tests are not convincing. The bond market, however, is a very different investment category for exploring out-of-sample results.

Most bond indexes are cap-weighted and, if pricing errors exist, can be expected to suffer the same return drag as the equity markets. Some of the largest bond managers are skeptical of the notion of cap-weighted bond indexes for a very simple reason: Companies with the most debt outstanding have the largest positions in the index. So, indeed, if a company floats a new bond, thereby going further into debt, the bond index funds must buy more of the debt of this company. Why, exactly, would we want to own more bonds in a company simply because it's just increased its debt?!

In the bond markets, the opportunity for pricing errors varies by investment grade. Fair values are reasonably deterministic in the investment-grade arena—U.S. Treasuries and highly rated corporate bonds. The cash flows are known, the discount rate is self-evident (it's the yield to maturity or yield to call for callable bonds), so the fair value is known. Thus, pricing errors should be very small. This stands in stark contrast with the vast unknowns of future cash flows of a company stock. Investors in such bonds are largely clipping coupons and hoping to have their principal returned.

Recall that the value added by the Fundamental Index concept is proportional to the square of the pricing errors. If errors are one-tenth as large for bonds as for stocks, the value added will drop 100-fold. If a Fundamental Index portfolio can outpace its cap-weighted counterpart by 200 to 300 basis points, as appears to be the norm in equities, then in bonds it should add 2 to 3 basis points. It's a lot of work for not much benefit. Therefore, we skipped testing the Fundamental Index concept in investment-grade bonds.[5] Instead, we focus on two segments where pricing errors are expected to be larger: high-yield debt and emerging-market debt.

High-Yield Debt

The ability of companies with lower-quality issues to repay their debt hinges on the companies' near-term operating results and the economic environment. This uncertainty leads to significant pricing errors in the cross-section of high-yield bonds. As with stocks, capitalization weighting should leave a high-yield bond index overexposed to the overpriced securities and underexposed to the underpriced. As with stocks, we cannot know which is which. Moreover, as economic environments change, the value of a company's debt is much easier to assess than the value of its equity. Whether the junk bond investor is going to get interest or principal becomes reasonably clear in a few short years, whereas the ultimate fair value of stocks can take decades to sort out. This acceleration of "error discovery" boosts the theoretical gains for a valuation-indifferent index.

How do we test the Fundamental Index concept in high-yield bonds without reviving the whole data-mining issue? By using the same Fundamental Index methodology as we applied to equities. We create a series of fundamental-weighted high-yield bond indexes based on sales, dividends paid, cash flow, and book value of the bond issuer and a Fundamental Index composite that equally weights the four. All four fundamental metrics outperformed the price-weighted Merrill Lynch index. Dividends led the way with an annualized return of 9.9 percent, against 6.6 percent for the Merrill Lynch U.S. High-Yield Bond Index (ML) from 1997 through 2006, followed by sales, cash flow, and book value. Figure 12.6 displays the results of the RAFI High-Yield Bond versus the cap-weighted index. The RAFI High-Yield Bond Strategy finished at 8.4 percent,

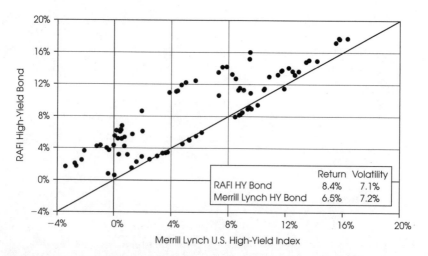

	Return	Volatility
RAFI HY Bond	8.4%	7.1%
Merrill Lynch HY Bond	6.5%	7.2%

Figure 12.6 RAFI High-Yield Bond versus Merrill Lynch High-Yield Master II Index: Three-Year Rolling Returns, 1997 through 2006

Source: Research Affiliates, LLC.

more than 190 basis points better than the Merrill Lynch Index. On a rolling three-year basis, it rarely experiences a shortfall, and, as with equities, the gains for the RAFI index are best when high-yield bond returns are single-digit or worse. The implication is that the performance drag from capitalization weighting is not an equities-only phenomenon.

Some of the same market dynamics that boost the performance of the Fundamental Index equity series are at work in the high-yield bond market. The tech companies whose stocks sold at unprecedented valuation multiples during that bubble were also able to obtain considerable debt financing. The vast majority of these new companies, with no long-term track record of meeting obligations, were rated below investment grade. But the same expectations that drove their stock prices to remarkable highs allowed these companies to pile up considerably more debt than they would have been able to find in a more stable, rational environment. As the debt increased, so did the companies' weight in high-yield indexes—but not in the Fundamental Index portfolios.

Emerging-Market Debt

As with high-yield bonds, prices of the sovereign debt of emerging-market countries react strongly to market noise and to perceived risks of default. The past 15 years has produced several periods of dramatic price swings—the Mexican peso crisis of 1994, the Asian flu of 1997, the Russian default of 1998, and the Argentine default of 2002. If these crises pushed the prices of certain countries' or regions' bonds well below their fair value, the bonds would be underrepresented in the price-weighted emerging-market bond indexes. Based on this volatility, we would expect emerging-market bonds to be potential beneficiaries of the Fundamental Index methodology.

To test this hypothesis, we needed to carry out some additional work. We can't very well weight emerging-market countries by their sales, profits, book values, or dividends! But we can assess the *size* of an emerging *country* in many different ways, both economic and not. We decided that an approximate picture of the fundamental size of a country can be provided by the following:

- Population
- Area

- Gross domestic product (GDP)
- Oil consumption
- Government spending
- Total government debt

As with our stock market measures, we realized that any of the size factors has shortcomings. For this reason, from the outset, we chose to use multiple measures of economic scale in the Fundamental Index methodology.

Most of the relationships between these metrics and economic importance are rather straightforward. A nation's GDP measures the size of its economy as defined by the market value of all final goods and services produced, so it is roughly the equivalent of sales to a corporation. Countries that use more oil per capita than other countries would be expected to engage in greater economic activity. Population, of course, implies the availability of labor. Geographical area deserves additional discussion because its economic significance may be questioned, but land mass may be lightly correlated with natural resources and opportunity for development. And area surely qualifies as a measure of "size" for a country.

As with the equity indexes, the crucial element in applying the Fundamental Index methodology to emerging-market bonds is eliminating the link between price (and pricing error) and index weight. The results for the series are presented in Figure 12.7 and compared with results for a price-weighted portfolio from the same emerging-market bond universe. Each of the six single metric Fundamental Index constructs outperformed. Equally weighting all six metrics into a composite provided an annualized excess return of 370 basis points, more even than the value added in U.S. stocks! We expect that this is not due to larger errors than in U.S stocks but to faster "error discovery" in the bond realm. Furthermore, these bonds are not subject to a value premium or small-company premium, so the argument that style tilts alone make the Fundamental Index approach successful loses substance in this application.

Conclusion

Based on our extensive research across markets and time periods, we believe there are compelling reasons to trust the efficacy of the Fundamental Index methodology. Now it's time for investors to

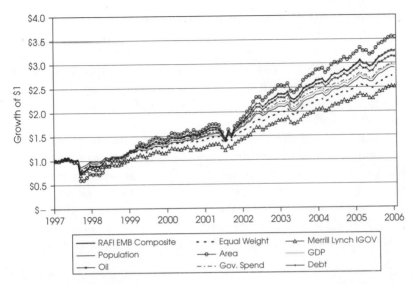

Figure 12.7 RAFI Emerging-Market Bonds, 1997 through 2006

Notes: Research Affiliates (EMG Bond)
Population: U.S. Census Bureau (2005)
Area: CIA World Factbook (2006)
GDP: World Bank Statistics (2004)
Oil Consumption: CIA World Factbook (2005)
Expenditures: CIA World Factbook (2006)
Debt: CIA World Factbook (2005)
Merrill Lynch Emerging Markets Data: IGOV from Bloomberg (Foreign Sovereign debt BBB+ and lower)
Source: Research Affiliates, LLC.

make their decisions. Some investors have already decided, but the embrace of the Fundamental Index concept is still in its infancy. Some $20 billion has flowed into strategies based on the concept. Compared to the $5 trillion in conventional indexes and the $50 trillion in global equity markets, this sum is the proverbial drop in the bucket. Will continued embrace of the idea doom it to failure? We don't think so, although we won't know the answer for years to come (as an aside, this line of criticism would argue against doing anything new—ever). We find plenty of reasons to expect the concept to continue to add value in the years ahead, at least until it has become far more widely adopted than today.

Traditional indexes weighted by capitalization will continue to allocate most of the market portfolio to recent winning stocks, sectors, and styles—whatever is most in favor. Whatever has the loftiest consensus expectations for future success will get the largest allocations. In many cases, the market will be right, but it will have prepaid in full for those growth expectations. Still, in many cases, the markets will be wrong because many of the millions of investors are making suboptimal decisions, paying too much for the potential 10-bagger, anchoring on the recent past, and confusing good companies with good stocks.

As we can see, the Fundamental Index concept is effective in global markets and nonequity categories. The advantage relative to capitalization or price weighting has been examined in bonds with promising early results. We know of no small-cap or value premium in the fixed-income markets. We do know that noise and associated mispricings exist in these markets, as in any markets, and that is enough for the Fundamental Index process to find opportunity.

CHAPTER

13

Finding Opportunity in a World of Lower Returns

Let our advance worrying become advance thinking and planning.
—Winston Churchill

The phrase "timing is everything" applies to most all of life's many twists and turns. The minute we begin our commute, the year we change jobs, and the moment when we meet our soul mate, each choice affects our days, our careers, and our lives. This old adage is every bit as true in the investments arena. Even the very best of investment strategies, begun at an unfortunate starting point, can disappoint over a very long stretch. Although the historical long-term benefits and rationale of the Fundamental Index strategy appear clear, what about the markets next few years?

The technology bubble and its aftermath proved fertile ground for all price-indifferent indexers. But, that exceptional era is history. Some people believe that the Fundamental Index era is over, therefore, almost as soon as it began. We disagree. In this chapter, we examine the likely market environment and changing nature of the future investment game to show how the return drag from capitalization weighting and, consequently, the excess returns from the Fundamental Index strategy are likely to persist.

What Can We (Rationally) Expect from Our Investments?

Future prospects for the Fundamental Index strategy are dependent on the equity markets themselves. Determining forward-looking returns by extrapolating the past is perhaps the worst way to forecast the future for any asset class or strategy. An investment will look best retrospectively *after* performing brilliantly. That moment, however, is often precisely when it is least likely to offer strong *prospective* returns.

We need only look at the past quarter century for a stark example. U.S. long-term government bonds since 1982 have provided annual returns of almost 10 percent. Do bond investors look to this past to set expectations? Do they say, "We have earned 10 percent for a quarter century, which is a long time, so we will expect to make 10 percent in the future"? Of course not! Bond investors look to the yield to set expectations. They say, "Thanks for the double-digit returns, but now that yields have tumbled, I'll expect 4 percent or 5 percent because that's the current yield."

The peril of shaping expectations by extrapolating the past is acute in volatile asset classes such as equities. For example, U.S. stocks as measured by the S&P 500 Index have averaged 10.4 percent since 1926, but the index finished within 1 percent of this figure in only three years—1968, 1993, and 2004. Even bonds, where coupons predominantly determine returns, are difficult to predict. The Lehman Brothers Aggregate Bond Index has compounded at an annualized 8.6 percent since its 1976 inception, but only 5 of the 32 calendar years finished within 100 basis points of this average. For this reason, Clive W. J. Granger, the 2003 Nobel Laureate in economics, summed up the art of projecting markets as follows: "The trick on staying alive as a forecaster is to give 'em a number or give 'em a date, but never give 'em both at the same time" (Grinold and Kroner, 2002).

As the time horizon extends to longer periods, however, we *can* forecast with ever more confidence. Figure 13.1 displays the ranges of returns for stocks and bonds over various holding periods. Note how the return band narrows as one moves from 1-year to 20-year horizons. For this reason, we are constantly advised to set longer-term

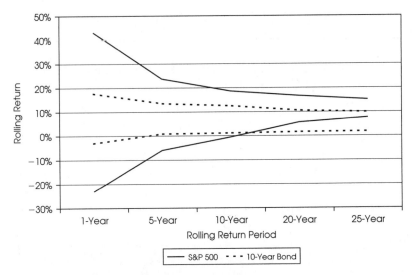

Figure 13.1   Range of Stock and Bond Returns over Various Investment Horizons, 1928 through June 2007

Note: Includes 90 percent of observations.
Source: Research Affiliates, LLC.

expectations. We can then have a greater likelihood of meeting our goals as the natural ups and downs of the markets tend to even out over time. The exhibit also illustrates the difficulty of making short-term predictions.

Forecasting Bond Returns

Ignoring Granger's advice, we will proceed to forecast market returns for the next 10 to 20 years. An investment produces return in three forms: income, growth of income, and change in valuation multiples. Of the three, the first two are the easiest to forecast. We know the near-term yields and the historical income growth rates for the major asset classes. The final component, changes in the price assigned to each dollar of income, is the most tenuous. But even in this case, if yields are low by historical standards, we find that valuation multiples tend to falter, whereas if yields are high, they often presage falling yields and rising valuation multiples.

Although long-run equity returns are our primary focus, a short discussion of prospective bond returns will be helpful so that we can estimate the equity risk premium—the incremental return expected from stocks over government bonds. Bonds compete with equities for investor capital. When fixed-income yields are high, or stock return prospects are low, the market is less likely to accept equity volatility because the safer bonds may provide higher returns.

Fortunately, the projection of long-term bond returns is simple. If an investor buys a bond at par and holds it to maturity, the return is the yield, or the coupon rate, on the bond. Because the buy-and-hold bond investor expects to receive the par value of the bond at maturity, no price appreciation is involved. Therefore, the current yield to maturity on a bond is an excellent predictor of future total returns from the investment. Figure 13.2 shows the starting bond yield on the 10-year government bond series and the subsequent 10-year annualized return. Note how closely future performance tracks the starting yield. With a yield to maturity as of this writing of just over 4 percent, for a diversified portfolio of government, mortgage, and corporate notes, a rational expectation of U.S. bond performance for the next 10 years would be between 3 percent and 5 percent.

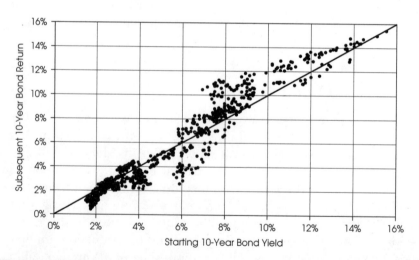

Figure 13.2 Projecting Bond Returns from Starting Yield, 1926 through 2007

Source: Research Affiliates, LLC.

Forecasting Stock Returns

Stock returns are trickier to forecast than bond returns because none of the component parts are "fixed." Two critical components of stock returns, historically, are growth in income, which is somewhat variable, and changes in valuation multiples, which can be large and difficult to predict. Even the income component, which may arguably include both dividends and share buybacks, is less predictable than bond income because companies can change the payout—they can increase or decrease dividends, declare large one-time dividends, buy back large chunks of stock, or skip a dividend payment entirely.

Over the past 25 years, the U.S. stock market, as proxied by the S&P 500, posted a 13.9 percent annualized return. Decomposing this number into its component parts shows that dividends account for 2.7 percent of the annual return, inflation accounts for 3.1 percent per year, followed by real dividend growth at 2.5 percent per year. Repricing the market to a higher price per dollar of dividends, at 5.1 percent per year compounded for 25 years, accounts for the largest part of the impressive 25-year annualized return.[1] Too few people back that immense repricing return out of their future return expectations. No, Virginia, the tripling of valuation multiples in 25 years was a Santa Claus that we cannot expect to visit again any time soon! We *must* temper our future return expectations. And we must *not* look to the past to shape our expectations for the future.

Income

Income is defined as all cash distributed to shareholders. As Figure 13.3 shows, over longer time spans, dividends form the largest component of equity returns. At this writing, the dividend yield of the S&P 500 is 1.8 percent, which is 2.4 percentage points *below* the long-term average.

Historically, dividends have accounted for essentially 100 percent of equity income, but recently share buybacks have become a major factor. The growing role of stock options in management compensation gives added impetus to stock buybacks, which ostensibly boost option values by boosting share prices rather than dividends, which clip the share price when they are paid. While we're sympathetic to those who want to include buybacks in the yield,

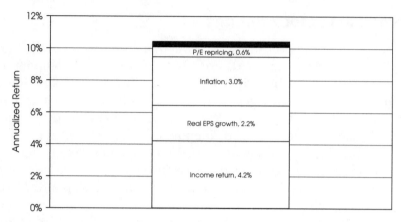

Figure 13.3   Composition of Average Return of S&P 500, 1926 through 2006
Source: Chen (2007).

we note that buybacks are unreliable. They lack the long-term performance of dividends and are far easier to eliminate in hard times. For example, in the early 1990s, net share buybacks turned negative for three years. Dividend yields don't ever go negative. We prefer to wait for their influence to be seen—hopefully—in more rapid future earnings and dividend growth.

An optimistic view is for long-term net repurchases to bolster the income return from stocks by 1.0 percentage point annually. The reality could be far lower but is almost certainly no higher. The result still leaves a deficit versus the long-term income experience of 1.4 percentage points below the long-term average yield of 4.2 percent. Using a forward-looking estimate equivalent to the current dividend yield, and setting aside the uncertain "income" from buybacks, slashes 2.4 percentage points off the 10.4 percent historical base return. Now we're down to an 8 percent long-term return; unfortunately, that's not our only adjustment!

Real Earnings (or Dividend) Growth

Although individual years may show substantial real growth—or drops—in earnings or dividends, the long-term record reflects strong mean reversion and interdependence, as can be seen in Figure 13.4. Over long spans, exceptional growth or decline never persists for

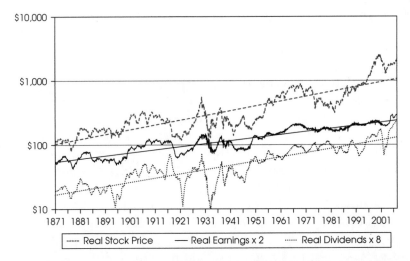

Figure 13.4   Long-Term Real Earnings and Dividends, 1871 through 2007
Source: Research Affiliates, LLC.

very long. In the past century, long-term real earnings and dividend growth have averaged, respectively, 1.3 percent and 1.1 percent per year. Figure 13.3 is somewhat higher at 2.2 percent annually for real earnings growth because of the different time horizon (1926 through 2006) covered. Rising inflation generally hurts stock returns, whereas disinflation (falling rates of inflation) helps. But, eventually, companies can usually pass through the costs of inflation to their customers. So, unlike bonds, company earnings and dividends tend to grow *relative to* inflation. Historically, both have kept pace with inflation with a bit of room to spare. It is worthwhile, however, to look at real income growth separately from inflation.

As Figure 13.4 shows, real earnings and dividend growth have been relatively stable over long periods of time. Twenty-year real earnings growth never exceeds 5.4 percent (3.8 percent for dividends) per year over and above inflation. Even that modest real growth started in the depths of the Great Depression. Nor did earnings growth ever fall short of inflation by more than –2.5 percent (–0.8 percent for dividends) per year. Not surprisingly, this occurred for the span ending in the depths of the Depression. Furthermore, over any 20-year span in the past century, real earnings growth has never exceeded 2.6 percent (1.6 percent for dividends) when the market was coming off of peak earnings. These all-time record growth rates are far lower than most people think is *normal!* From peak earnings or dividends, the historical norm for future real growth is very close to *zero!*

Note that if we want to obtain double-digit equity returns—or about 7 percent real returns—with current dividend yields and valuations, the S&P 500 has to experience real earnings growth in the neighborhood of *6 percent per year,* which is more than four times its 1.3 percent historical rate over the past century and more than twice the all-time fastest long-term growth achieved when the market was coming off of peak earnings. At first glance, the 1.3 percent real earnings growth of the past century appears to be implausibly anemic, especially considering that Wall Street analysts expect long-term earnings growth of 12 percent (which is presumably equivalent to 9 percent to 10 percent real growth *above* inflation) for the Russell 1000 Index.[2] But let's not forget that Wall Street's ultimate products are hope and optimism.

In the past century, only the 1920s and the current (partial!) decade witnessed real earnings growth above 5 percent. As evidenced in Figure 13.5, after the Great Depression, the remaining decades experienced real earnings growth between zero percent and 4 percent.

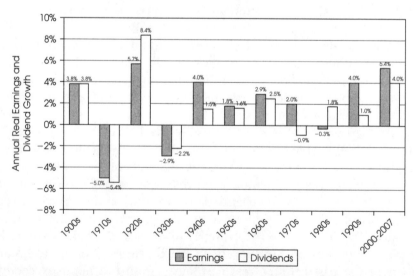

Figure 13.5   Annual Real Earnings Growth and Dividend by Decade
Source: Research Affiliates, based on data from S&P, Shiller, and Cowles Commission.

Of course, given the seesaw effect, with alternating bad and good decades self-evident in this chart, investors will wonder how long the recent rapid growth can continue.

We should also not expect large retained earnings (as a consequence of the low dividend payout ratio) to spur future earnings growth. Our own research found that expected future earnings growth is fastest when current payout ratios are *high* and slowest when payout ratios are low (Arnott and Asness, 2003). We see no compelling reason to expect much more or less real earnings growth than the 1926 through 2006 historical figure of 2.2 percent. Therefore, we don't see any reason here to change our 8 percent long-term return estimate.

Valuation Repricing

The final component of long-term equity returns comes from changes in the price that investors are willing to pay for each dollar of dividends or earnings. This figure is typically measured by a changing price-earnings ratio (P/E) or dividend yield. In the past quarter century, the dividend yield for stocks has plunged from 6.3 percent to 1.9 percent. In other words, investors paid $16 for each dollar of dividend income in 1982 and paid $52 for each dollar of income in 2007. A simplistic way to view this is that we're paying the next 52 years of dividends (ignoring growth) to buy stocks today, while we were only willing to pay 16 years of dividends to buy stocks 25 years ago.

Although P/E repricing has been the smallest contributor to long-term returns historically over the very long run, the size of this contribution depends on how close the current average P/E is to the long-term average. Because earnings are both cyclical and volatile, a sensible approach is to compare the current price of the S&P 500 with the trailing 10 years of earnings, which smooths out the shorter-term swings. On this measure, as evidenced in Figure 13.6, equity prices are trading considerably higher than the long-term P/E average. Perhaps equities historically were priced too cheaply. But it is dangerous to assume that they will trade at higher multiples in the future than today.

The P/E jumped from 8 to 18 over the past quarter century. And if earnings are smoothed over a 10-year span to take out the effects of economic peaks (2007!) and troughs (1982!), this ratio has jumped nearly fourfold, from 6.5 times to 27 times the 10-year average earnings over that same span. With this impressive jump in

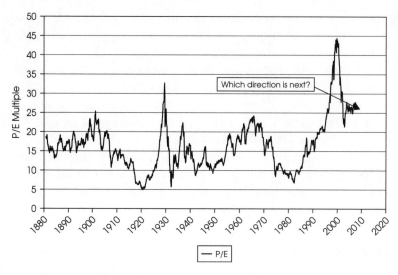

Figure 13.6   S&P 500 P/E Multiples, 1881 through 2007

Source: Research Affiliates, based on updated data by Robert J. Shiller
(www.irrationalexuberance.com/) originally published in *Irrational Exuberance.*

valuation multiples, equity market returns have, of course, been brilliant. Dare we assume another tripling or quadrupling of valuation multiples in the next 25 years?

Because 0.6 percent of the long-term historical returns from 1926 came from rising valuation multiples, which we dare not rely upon in the future, we cut an additional 0.6 percentage points off the historical total return.

The market tells us the consensus expectations for inflation. It is evident in the yield difference between the yield on Treasury inflation-protected securities (TIPS) and the corresponding government bond. The breakeven inflation rate for the 10-year TIPS-bond comparison is 2.4 percent. This is 0.6 percent less than inflation contributed to stock market returns over the past 81 years. So, we're now down to about 6.5 percent—not a whole lot better than we can lock in with long bonds.

Forward-Looking Equity Returns

Taken together, these adjustments lead to an estimate of future nominal equity returns—before fees and expenses—in the range of

5 percent to 7 percent, which is well below the long-term average of 10.4 percent. We might not like this simple arithmetic, but it is predicated on some very sensible assumptions: far less from dividends because the stock market yield has tumbled as share prices soared, no more growth in P/E ratios because they're already high, a slight haircut on the inflation rate (perhaps our weakest assumption, but it's certainly not going to help stock market returns if we're wrong on this!), and real earnings growth similar to historical rates, as illustrated in Figure 13.7.

The 5 percent to 7 percent range for equity returns should be viewed as a *starting point for gauging equity return prospects.* Some might argue with our assumptions and, hence, the conclusions. But the arithmetic is compelling. Arguing with the assumptions will allow us to change these long-term return numbers only modestly. Indeed, our figures may just as easily prove to be too optimistic as too pessimistic. Only time will tell, but one must use aggressive assumptions to paint a scenario as optimistic as most investors' expectations.

Although somewhat sobering compared with recent stock market returns, the view that we are entering an era of lower equity returns is gradually becoming the consensus. Ennis Knupp, a Chicago-based consultant, found in a 2007 survey that leading

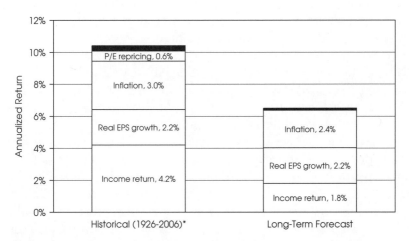

Figure 13.7   Composition of Historical and Expected Return of S&P 500

*Data from Chen (2007). © 2008 Morningstar. All rights reserved. Used with permission.
Source: Research Affiliates, LLC.

institutional investment managers and pension consultants had a median expected long-term U.S. equity return of 7.7 percent per year.[3] With the exception of a couple of outliers, the range of the estimates was rather narrow—throwing out the highest and lowest estimates left all of the forecasts between 5.0 percent and 9.3 percent. The discarded highest projection was for annual returns of 10.0 percent. Thus, even the most optimistic of survey participants couldn't justify stocks providing a return even matching their long-term average since 1926. Our own 5 percent to 7 percent range is below the median but spans most of the bottom half of the consensus range! Bond assumptions were also somewhat meager, with a median long-term assumption of 5.4 percent annualized. Given current yields, even this may prove overly optimistic.

Investing in a Low-Return Environment

Investors should take the low-return scenario very seriously for two reasons (at least). First, if future returns are in the mid-single-digit range, most investors, with their slender savings, will be unprepared for retirement. People really do need to save more for their future *and* find ways to improve the investment performance of those savings. Second, there are strategies that work particularly well when returns are low. For instance, the Fundamental Index concept is powerful in a low-return environment. Figure 13.8 displays how the various developed-country Fundamental Index applications have performed in various market environments.

Aggregating across all 23 countries in the Morgan Stanley Capital International (MSCI) or Financial Times and London Stock Exchange (FTSE) Developed World indexes, Fundamental Index portfolios perform just as they do in the United States: best when markets are weak while holding their own in stronger markets. In "monster" bull markets for the capitalization-weighted market indexes, of 30 percent or more per year for five years, the Fundamental Index portfolios nearly hold their own, winning 41 percent of the time. In these exceptional markets, on average, they fall 3.6 percentage points short of capitalization weighting return. Not bad for a "value" strategy in an immense bull market. The comparison turns notably positive for the Fundamental Index portfolios just one step down, in the powerful 20 percent to 30 percent bull markets. At the other end of the spectrum, when five-year returns are negative, the Fundamental Index portfolios win 97 percent of the time, by an average of 5.2 percentage points per year.

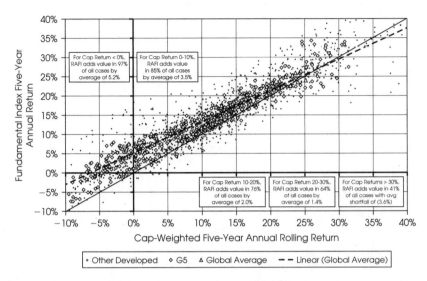

For Cap Return < 0%, RAFI adds value in 97% of all cases by average of 5.2%

For Cap Return 0-10%, RAFI adds value in 85% of all cases by average of 3.5%

For Cap Return 10-20%, RAFI adds value in 76% of all cases by average of 2.0%

For Cap Return 20-30%, RAFI adds value in 64% of all cases by average of 1.4%

For Cap Returns > 30%, RAFI adds value in 41% of all cases with avg shortfall of (3.6%)

Cap-Weighted Five-Year Annual Rolling Return

• Other Developed   ◇ G5   ▲ Global Average   – – Linear (Global Average)

Figure 13.8   Fundamental Index versus MSCI Five-Year Annualized Returns in 23 Developed Countries, through June 2007

Source: Research Affiliates, LLC.

The different results at the extremes are sensible. Fundamental Index portfolios have a value tilt relative to capitalization weighting. Value tends to do better in weak markets and worse in strong markets. We think the reason for this is simple and dovetails with human nature. As markets soar to ever-higher peaks, investors pay more and more attention to growth expectations and less and less attention to objective metrics of *current* business scale or success. In bleak markets, we are less and less willing to pay up for expectations of future growth and are more and more focused on the objective measures of *current* success that can cushion us from further losses. This pattern of returns is consonant with natural human behavior. Of course, capitalization weighting will face a headwind in the weaker markets, while Fundamental Index portfolios will face a headwind in the strongest markets!

As its critics have suggested, the Fundamental Index portfolio benefited from the bursting of the tech bubble of the late 1990s. The cap-weighted indexes held large exposure to growth stocks priced at unprecedented valuation multiples, which subsequent growth failed to justify. These bubble stocks suffered accordingly. But, for the first two years after the top of the bubble, *most stocks did fine!* The Fundamental Index portfolio—and, to a lesser extent, the cap-weighted value indexes—sidestepped much of the carnage, thereby earning sizable excess returns. Those days are over. But if single-digit returns are likely in the years ahead, these data suggest that Fundamental Index applications add an average of 350 basis points, winning 85 percent of the time in such markets. Past is not prologue, but these are dangerous odds to bet against!

The Outlook for Pricing Errors

Some critics suggest that these data are history and that the future markets—aware of these pricing errors in the past—will be different. There is no reply that can satisfy these critics because this argument can be made forever, no matter how much data we assemble and no matter how strong our live asset results may be. Still, just as a plant needs water and sunlight, the Fundamental Index approach requires two conditions to thrive: the existence of pricing errors and their eventual correction. As Jack Treynor (2005) has demonstrated, the latter condition is not necessary, but it sure helps!

We have already discussed the return outlook for the entire equity market. We think single-digit returns will be far more prevalent in the years ahead than double-digit returns, and we recognize that Fundamental Index portfolios tend to perform far better than capitalization weighting in the single-digit environment, while more than holding their own in the double-digit environment. *But, if we are to expect continued success, we need to also address the prospects for continued pricing errors within the market.* If the market more closely matches a security's price with its intrinsic value (i.e., becomes more efficient), excess return prospects for the Fundamental Index portfolio diminish.

Some critics maintain that the future markets will be different because investors are now aware of the pricing errors of the past. Some point to the growth of hedge fund managers as a force that will eliminate, or at least reduce, the existence of mispricing. After all, these wily "alpha hunters" are largely free to seek profit opportunities in multiple markets without the encumbrances borne by the traditional active manager, such as institutional guidelines or regulatory oversight.

Hedge fund managers use powerful tools, including "short selling" and leverage that can rise to multiples of portfolio value, to exploit pricing errors. Their ability to take "short" positions (which allow us to profit from the price declines) allows hedge funds to seek absolute returns regardless of market direction. Descriptors such as "market neutral" and "absolute return" imply that such hedge funds have zero beta (hence, no sensitivity to market direction, with similar return prospects in rising or falling markets). As Cliff Asness (2001) demonstrated, this is not necessarily the reality. Still, eliminating equity risk to obtain an uncorrelated and meaningful absolute return is a huge selling point for these funds, particularly in selling to the large pension plans and endowments, many of which were so badly burned in the aftermath of the bubble.

Short selling not only allows the portfolios to be hedged, but it can also be a valuable source of "alpha." Much has been written about the "long-only constraint" faced by traditional investment managers. An investment manager who is bearish on a particular stock but is constrained to be long only can underweight that stock only by the size of the position in the manager's benchmark index. For example, a manager can easily hold 10 times the market weight of eBay (which is currently 0.3 percent of the cap-weighted index) if he likes the stock. But he can underweight it by only a scant 0.3 percentage point if he thinks it's overvalued. The traditional long-only investor can make more meaningful underweights only in the larger-cap stocks. For instance, we can underweight Exxon Mobil by 3 percentage points because it is 3 percent of the index.

Because few companies make up more than 1 percent to 2 percent of the index, our opportunities to make profits are largely limited to selecting undervalued companies that we wish to overweight, with few opportunities to add value by identifying overvalued stocks that we wish to materially underweight. But if we are allowed to sell stocks short, particularly the smaller ones, our opportunities to add value improve markedly. Most hedge funds can sell short. So, most hedge funds can, with their trading, help to rein in the most overvalued stocks in the market.

Leverage magnifies the hedge fund advantage by allowing a skillful practitioner to make large profits from a small opportunity. Even a small hedge fund manager can quickly exploit a mispricing opportunity by borrowing hundreds of millions of dollars to leverage his or her position. Short-selling roughly doubles an investment manager's potential to add value, and leverage multiplies this potential still further.

Finally, hedge fund managers operate under a compensation system in which a significant portion of overall fees is tied to profits.

This naturally leads the hedge funds to a more aggressive pursuit of pricing errors than traditional managers, who may be more motivated to gather and retain assets than to make large allocations to undervalued assets.

The hedge fund community trumpets these implements in their toolkit as powerful ways to create ever-larger alpha. Of course, the investor must be careful. If a manager has the skill to add 100 basis points to returns, it is wonderful to see that skill multiplied 10-fold by leverage. If a manager has the ineptitude to erode returns by 100 basis points, then the investor will regret allowing the manager to multiply that result 10-fold!

For most of the time span we used to analyze the Fundamental Index strategy, hedge funds were but a blip on the screen in terms of their assets and influence on relative pricings. That is not the case today. As Figure 13.9 shows, hedge funds currently manage nearly $2 trillion, and this exponential growth is showing no signs of slowing. Institutional investors alone are expected to contribute an additional $500 billion to hedge funds through 2010 (Casey, Quirk & Associates, 2006).

Hedge funds are here to stay. Furthermore, the line between traditional managers and hedge fund managers is increasingly blurred. With the proliferation of so-called 130/30 strategies, traditional

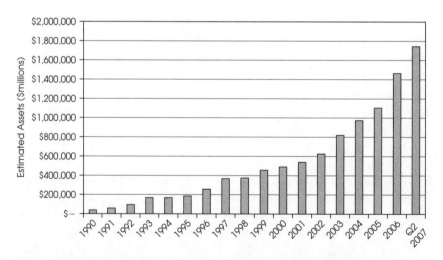

Figure 13.9 Hedge Fund Growth in Assets under Management
Source: HFR Industry Reports, ©HFR, Inc. 2007, www.hedgefundresearch.com.

firms are offering their own versions of long-short products.[4] In short, *the active management game is fast changing.*

So, do hedge funds help dissipate pricing errors in the market, moving us toward a more efficient market? This considerable asset base with the addition of short-selling and leverage theoretically allows the market to price securities more efficiently and, therefore, reduce the premium rewarded to Fundamental Index strategies. We don't think this is an accurate prognosis.

First, hedge funds that used momentum trading may have exacerbated, not moderated, the tremendous run-up in stock prices during the late 1990s/early 2000s—a period that experienced what may have been the largest relative stock mispricing in history. Hedge funds controlled an estimated $450 billion of assets in 2000. Many observers have cited a "Greenspan put" at the time, referring to those who expected Alan Greenspan and his team at the Federal Reserve Board to intervene and mitigate any market unrest.

Second, evidence is building that the vast majority of hedge fund returns are not directly attributable to alpha—the identification and exploitation of mispriced securities. Several recent studies have identified methods to replicate hedge fund returns through existing common risk factors, such as equity indexes, commodities, currency indexes, and credit spreads between corporate and U.S. Treasury bonds (Hasanhodzic and Lo, 2007). Such replication suggests that absolute return strategies, although perceived as alpha sources, are collecting an array of exotic risks, each with a reward that can be captured in the liquid markets at far lower costs. In fact, a study by the EDHEC Risk and Asset Management Research Centre found that only 4 percent of excess performance of hedge funds can be explained by pure alpha (from security selection) (Géhin and Vaissié, 2005). Recent evidence—mediocre returns in 2007 and bleak returns in early 2008—suggest that most hedge funds *neither* hedge *nor* provide reliable "alpha."

We are skeptical about the likelihood that the rise of hedge funds spells the end of mispricing. Remember our $100 bill on the sidewalk? There are those who acknowledge that the Fundamental Index concept worked in the past, worked in almost all markets in which it was tested, and has been largely successful on live assets. But they go on to say that investors have no way of knowing that it will work in the future. They are obviously correct. No one can know the future. This logic dictates we must not even try to pick up the $100 bill lying on the sidewalk.

Could Pricing Errors Actually Increase?

Another factor influencing the outlook for pricing accuracy is the dramatic shift of retirement savings from defined-benefit (DB) plans to defined-contribution (DC) plans, of which the 401(k) plan is the most prominent. According to consultant Watson Wyatt, only 37 percent of Fortune 100 companies had a traditional DB pension plan in 2005, as compared with 89 percent of such companies 20 years ago (Block, 2006). In the DC construct, retirement plan sponsors place the burden of investment decisions on the plan participants. Total savings in participant-directed DC investment vehicles totaled $2.9 trillion as of year-end 2005 versus $1.9 trillion in DB plans. (Again, keep in mind that the vast majority of the historical results of the Fundamental Index strategy occurred before this changing dynamic in retirement savings.)

Intuition leads us to believe that this transformation, unlike the case of hedge fund proliferation, may lead to *greater* pricing errors. These trillions of dollars are being invested by individuals who are often ill equipped to make efficient investment decisions. In a presentation on the shortcomings of the S&P 500, George Keane (2003) commented as follows on the impact of this development:

> The result was that millions of individuals began investing in equity mutual funds for the first time. While 401(k) plans had been around for a number of years, their growth in the 1990s was phenomenal. Between 1990 and 1996 the number of active participants in 401(k) plans grew by more than 10 million people. In the early 90's these investors tended to be cautious, investing in bond funds, money market finds and Guaranteed Investment Contracts issued by insurance companies. As the public became more aware of the attractive returns being generated by the stock market, however, large numbers of 401(k) investors began to allocate money to equity mutual funds. The growth in equity mutual funds was phenomenal. From 1995 through 2000 more than $1 trillion of net new cash flow was directed to equity mutual funds. The total assets held in equity mutual fiends increased tenfold, from $400 billion in 1990 to $4.4 trillion in 2000.
>
> The individuals who were directing this massive cash flow into stocks via equity mutual funds were relatively unsophisticated

investors. In choosing mutual funds they predictably gravitated toward those funds which were reporting good investment results. Unfortunately, there were other major developments underway which led them to chase performance that was not based on sound principles of investing, and which ultimately led to devastating losses of retirement savings for millions of small investors.

DB pension executives retain sophisticated actuaries to calculate how much is needed to meet liabilities, experienced investment consultants to decide the most appropriate asset allocations, and managers to meet the plan's risk and return objectives. In contrast, 401(k) investors tend to "wing it," chasing hot past strategies, funds, and asset classes. The professional DB investors also fall prey to these pitfalls, but not nearly as much as retail investors. Before the great bull market of the 1990s, 401(k) investors held hardly any stocks. By the late 1990s, lured by the tremendous past gains in the stock market, they had shifted to a predominant allocation to equities—just in time to be crushed by the bear market of 2000 through 2002. A study by the Center for Retirement Research at Boston College found that DB plans outperformed 401(k) plans by approximately 1 percentage point *per year* in the 1988 through 2004 period (Munnell, Soto, Libby, and Prinzivalli, 2006).

We can point to several possible causes of this underperformance. For one, 401(k) participants are more likely to pursue recent winners, thereby bidding up securities that have done well. Making informed decisions is often complicated by the increasing number of funds offered in DC plans' mutual fund lineups, which allows participants to chase ever-narrower subsets of the market. Today, the average number of funds offered in a DC plan is 18 versus 7 in 1996 (Economic Systems, Inc., 1998, and Huxley, 2006). The new funds are usually those that have experienced strong recent performance, often in "niche" areas of the market. For example, as the bubble blossomed, many plans added emerging growth or technology-related mutual funds. Brokerage "windows," offering participants more and more fund choices and access to direct investments in individual stocks, also increase opportunities for return-chasing behavior. Cumulatively, such behavior, applied from a nearly $3 trillion asset base, may well *increase* the pricing errors on the performance drag of the cap-weighted indexes.

Conclusion

The future for stock market returns isn't glowing. No matter how we fiddle with the numbers, the forward-looking return of 8 percent to 10 percent (or more) that most investors are depending on is almost impossible to justify. History suggests that Fundamental Index strategies are quite compelling in a lower return environment.

The *nature* of the capital markets of tomorrow are not likely to be materially different from the past, though the returns will be. The one thing we can say with great confidence is that the capital markets will never become clairvoyant; they will never price all assets exactly right. To improve returns in a low-return world, prudent investors can turn to the Fundamental Index concept, which adds rebalancing to equity portfolios and eliminates the return-chasing behavior of a cap-weighted index.

CHAPTER

14

Using the Fundamental
Index Strategy

*Innovation is the ability to see change as an opportunity—not
a threat.*

—Anonymous

Fundamental Index strategies arrive at an opportune time, in a
world of lower returns. The challenge with any new idea is sorting
out how we can use it to maximum advantage. Investment ideas don't
come with an owner's manual. It's up to us to figure out whether,
when, and how to use them.

Many new investment concepts are first made available to the
institutional marketplace and, only after years of success, are made
available to the broader investment community. Emerging market
stocks and bonds, market-neutral products, futures and option strategies, and many other innovations were used in the institutional
marketplace for many years before they were made available to the
retail markets. Venture capital, private equity, arbitrage strategies,
mezzanine financing deals, and many other alternatives are still not
available to the broad investment community, even after many years
of use in the institutional and hedge fund worlds.

Fundamental Index strategies stand in stark contrast. Our work
on the idea, first published in the spring of 2005 (Arnott, Hsu, and
Moore), is already being applied to tens of billions in assets, all over the

world, for many types of investors and in many different applications and markets. We've never seen a new idea in investing gain so much traction in such a short time. We surmise that the rapid pace of adoption is motivated by a combination of overwhelming historical evidence, intuitive appeal, and investors' concerns about the way that capitalization-weighted indexes have drawn them into one bubble after another.

In this chapter, we outline investment management solutions that can draw on the strengths of the Fundamental Index concept. We examine how the strategy can affect our asset allocation and risk management choices, and we explore the question of performance measurement, or benchmarking. We then outline unique considerations in applying the Fundamental Index concept for various categories of investors.

Asset Allocation and the Fundamental Index Strategy

Fundamental Index strategies have a bearing on asset allocation decisions along several dimensions. As we have shown throughout this book, substituting a Fundamental Index portfolio for a cap-weighted portfolio has delivered higher returns with less risk in the past by eliminating the return drag associated with capitalization weighting. As a result, a Fundamental Index portfolio allows investors to increase diversification and reduce the "equity bet."

History suggests that a Fundamental Index portfolio can improve our equity market expectations in any market environment except a strong growth-driven bull market. If we have a more neutral view on the outlook for the equity markets, we can modestly improve performance and reduce risk by replacing a cap-weighted portfolio with a Fundamental Index portfolio. The asset mix doesn't change, but the risk and return improve. We illustrate this principle in Figure 14.1, where the use of the Fundamental Index portfolio to fulfill the equity allocation moves us from "Point X" to "Point 1."

Suppose we are skeptical of the arguments in Chapter 13 and believe that stock market returns in the years ahead will remain strong. Then, a Fundamental Index approach allows us to put more into stocks for the same level of risk, moving us to "Point 2." Because the Fundamental Index concept tends to add the most value in disappointing markets, we will suffer less damage if we are

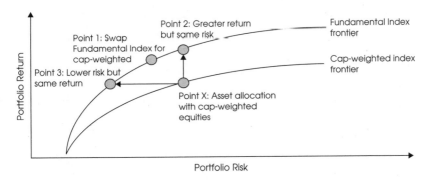

Figure 14.1 Asset Allocation and the Fundamental Index Strategy
Source: Research Affiliates, LLC.

wrong than we would with a cap-weighted portfolio, but we more or less fully participate if we're right and markets march ever higher. Our asset mix becomes more aggressive, investing more in stocks, but our annual volatility does not go up.

Finally, if we fear that equity market returns in the years ahead will be disappointing, a Fundamental Index approach allows us to trim our equity market exposure while earning the same return we would have earned with a more aggressive allocation to cap-weighted stock market indexes. Our allocation to stocks becomes more cautious, but our return does not drop, moving us to "Point 3" on the graph.

Figure 14.1 is hypothetical. Let's consider a real-world example. Whether we use the Fundamental Index concept to lower risk, to boost return, or to do a bit of both, it gives us a sizable advantage. Figure 14.2 illustrates the impact of these three methods on actual market results over the past 20 years. These results compound mightily over time. After 20 years, the bond investor (as measured by the Lehman Brothers Aggregate Bond Index) has achieved 7.7 percent per year (enough for a cumulative return of 342 percent). The S&P 500 Index investor has enjoyed 10.5 percent per year (641 percent cumulatively), and the Fundamental Index investor has garnered 13.0 percent (1,046 percent cumulatively).

The typical investor with a portfolio invested 60 percent in the S&P 500 and 40 percent in bonds (using the Lehman Brothers Aggregate Bond Index) enjoyed a return of 9.7 percent (a cumulative gain of 537 percent), surprisingly close to the S&P 500 investor. The 60/40 investor benefited from systematic rebalancing,

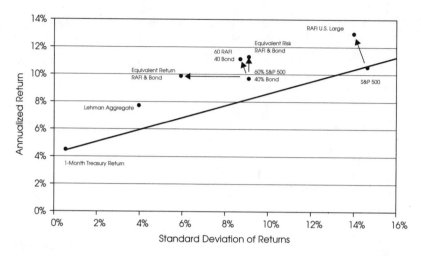

Figure 14.2   Risk and Return of Various Portfolio Strategies, October 1987 through September 2007
Source: Research Affiliates, LLC.

buying stocks after the 1987 crash, selling on the way up to the peak in 2000, and buying again as the 2000–2002 bear market ground downward. This rebalancing added 50 basis points to the 60/40 investor's annual returns.[1] It doesn't sound like a lot, but it compounds nicely over time.

Suppose we want to cut our risks without lowering our 20-year gains. If we put 39 percent in a Fundamental Index portfolio and the rest in bonds, we would have achieved the same ending wealth as the 60/40 investor but with one-third less risk. Alternatively, suppose we want to take advantage of the lower risk profile of a Fundamental Index portfolio by ramping up our equity exposure, but only to the point where our risk is the same as the more conventional 60/40 investor. By putting 63 percent in a Fundamental Index portfolio, we would have achieved the same risk as the 60/40 diversified investor but would have earned a 747 percent return on our portfolio—nearly 40 percent more end-point wealth than conventional 60/40 investors. In this example, we wind up with even more end-point wealth after 20 years than the stock market investor with 100 percent invested in the S&P 500—and with 40 percent less risk. Indeed, if our goal is to match the average *downside* risk for the bad months in the conventional 60/40 portfolio (recall that the

Fundamental Index portfolio earns most of its incremental returns in these months), we could take our exposure to almost 80/20 without exceeding the downside risk of the conventional 60/40 investor in the average bear market.

The Fundamental Index concept allows us to reshape return expectations and achieve our goals with a better spectrum of choices. So long as we believe that the future success for the Fundamental Index strategy will not differ radically from the extensive historical record, these portfolios will allow investors to (1) take less risk in the quest for the same return, (2) take the same risk while expecting more return, or even (3) take *more* risk, and put *more* into stocks, without increasing our downside risk!

Should We Change Our Benchmark?

As the superiority of the index fund over most active managers has become more apparent, many investors have opted for ever larger allocations to passive investments, either as core holdings or to complement their active strategies. Those wishing to begin using a Fundamental Index portfolio naturally question whether such a portfolio falls in a passive or active class. We have suggested that the answer may be a mere matter of semantics. It might, in fact, be a bit of both.

People have embraced the idea in various ways—as a new passive core portfolio, as a new approach to enhanced indexing, or as an active management technique. Those who define an index fund strictly as a strategy that tracks a cap-weighted index will not consider a Fundamental Index portfolio to be an index strategy. For them, Fundamental Index portfolios will fall into the active category, perhaps as an "enhanced index." But for those who define an index as formulaic, objective, and historically replicable, Fundamental Index products qualify as indexes. Fundamental Index portfolios have other attributes consistent with passive strategies, such as low turnover and low costs.

Our definition of *passive index* has a bearing on how one might use the Fundamental Index concept. After all, "indexes" are used not only as investment vehicles, but also as benchmarks against which to measure our (and our managers') investment results. For decades, many investors have asked, "If our active managers can't beat the market, what good are they?" Now, the question is, "If our active managers can't beat a Fundamental Index portfolio, which costs us only a little more than a conventional index fund, are they worth their fees?" Should investors compare their active managers' results with—benchmark them to—a Fundamental Index portfolio? There's no "right answer" to the question. Suffice it to say that some investors will choose to do so and others will view Fundamental Index portfolios as active strategies, not as suitable benchmarks for other managers.

Active managers have had a somewhat schizophrenic reaction to the new Fundamental Index products. Some find the idea distressing because it may create a tougher hurdle for them to beat in order to justify their fees. Others find the idea fascinating because they can use the new indexes as a starting point for making their active bets. Many of those skilled enough to beat an index will naturally shift their frame of reference to make their active bets relative to a Fundamental Index benchmark rather than a cap-weighted benchmark. They may prefer, then, to be measured against conventional cap-weighted indexes in order to get credit for *both* their own skill *and* the value that is added by their Fundamental Index portfolio starting point—as if it's all from their own skill! In any event, we find that the best active managers seem to be the least threatened by the advent of this new indexing approach.

Although benchmarking managers against the Fundamental Index methodology may eventually happen, we expect the Fundamental Index approach to be adopted as an investment strategy rather than a new benchmark—at least for the near term. Choosing a tougher hurdle will probably be the minority reaction. Not only investment managers but also advisers, consultants, and plan sponsors face this dilemma. Life is difficult enough without subjecting ourselves to ever-tougher benchmarks for success. These intermediaries would prefer excess returns to a Fundamental Index strategy to show up as value added, above cap-weighted index returns, instead of a higher starting point for performance attribution.

Diversifying the Passive Allocation

Regardless of where the Fundamental Index portfolio falls in the active-passive spectrum, it is a portfolio designed to excel in markets where prices deviate materially from fair value. As long as we believe that *some* prices in the market may be materially wrong and that those errors will have little to do with whether the underlying company is large or small, it makes sense to at least complement our cap-weighted index investment with a price-indifferent index. This hedges our bets. We do not have to believe pricing errors are permanent to see value in the Fundamental Index idea.

Bubbles are a recurring theme in the history of investments—from the South Sea bubble of 1720 to the technology bubble in 1999 and 2000. Although these big bubbles are rare, mini-bubbles (think Krispy Kreme donuts at 150 times earnings in late 2001—for donuts!) happen *all the time*. Why not contra-trade against them? Most investors would agree that the issue is not "if" another bubble will occur but "when" and "how large." Of course, no one sees a bubble coming until it is upon us. Even then, one often can't be certain until long after the fact. But we do know that when the next bubble hits, the cap-weighted index will take indexed investors along for the ride. Providing some protection by diversifying a portion of funds into a price-indifferent approach is sensible. And, as we've demonstrated, the damage done by embracing the Fundamental Index concept in an efficient market is negligible.

Active managers face a tougher challenge avoiding pricing bubbles than Fundamental Index followers. While believing that they should bypass the latest craze, many will nevertheless succumb to the view that "things are different this time." They are pressured to please their clients (and keep their jobs) by giving in to the latest "bubble logic."[2] The best portfolio managers, who are more concerned with their clients' well-being than with collecting fees from them, still cannot be certain they're right until after the fact. If they are not sure, it is very hard for people to risk a potential career-ending choice, even if it has above-average *odds* of success. In this environment in which managers and advisers act as agents on behalf of others, there can be an immense asymmetry between the upside for being right and the downside for being wrong. This is often referred to as *agency risk*.[3]

Revisiting the two most pronounced U.S. equity bubbles of the past 50 years—the Nifty Fifty era of the early 1970s and the tech bubble of the late 1990s—it is instructive to explore the benefits of diversifying a portfolio's indexed equity exposure. Figure 14.3 compares the tracking error of the RAFI U.S. Large Company Index (RAFI U.S. Large) against the S&P 500 on a rolling three-year basis for the past 45 years. As bubbles develop, capitalization weighting pays an

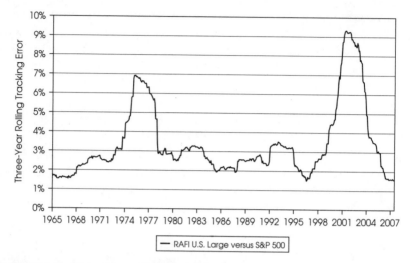

Figure 14.3   Three-Year Rolling Tracking Error: RAFI U.S. Large with Respect to the S&P 500, 1962 through June 2007
Source: Research Affiliates, LLC.

ever larger premium for expectations of future growth. By contra-trading against that ever larger growth premium, a Fundamental Index portfolio will deviate more and more from that of the comparable cap-weighted index. Why? Because at these times, the cap-weighted market is making huge bets on a few growth companies relative to their economic scale. The RAFI strategy reduces these holdings back to their economic weight and, therefore, seems to be making a big bet against the cap-weighted markets.

The RAFI U.S. Large tracking error—which is a modest 2 percent to 3 percent in "normal" market conditions—rose dramatically during the Nifty Fifty and tech bubbles because the RAFI index rebalanced the hot stocks back to their fundamental sizes whereas the cap-weighted index kept magnifying its bets. In each case, the RAFI portfolio went on to produce sizable relative gains as the oft-heard "it's different this time" failed to materialize. Figure 14.4 shows that a diversified passive approach composed of equal parts capitalization weighting and fundamental weighting provided a smoother ride during the last bubble than did a cap-weighted portfolio alone. The steady-as-we-go performance of the RAFI strategy during this bubble—while capitalization weighting, with its growth bias, soared—would have made it tough to stay the course during

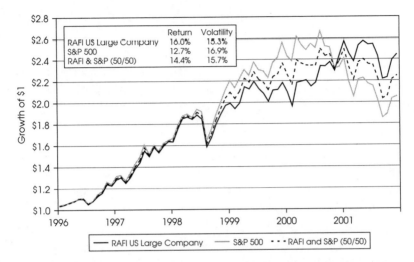

Figure 14.4   Bubble Summary: S&P 500 and RAFI U.S. Large, 1996 through 2001
Source: Research Affiliates, LLC.

the closing months of the bubble. But the eventual rewards were tremendous when the bubble burst.

Outside these bubble episodes, the RAFI U.S. Large behaved much like the cap-weighted market portfolio, with a tracking error consistently in the 2 percent to 3 percent range while reliably adding value in a like range most of the time. The Fundamental Index approach isn't a huge departure from a traditional cap-weighted passive core portfolio—except when the market is making huge bets, at which time performance really matters! When the cap-weighted market portfolio is favoring a few stocks (or sectors or styles) over the rest of the market, a Fundamental Index portfolio will trade against those huge bets and will *seem* to be making a large and opposite bet relative to the market, even though it's just returning these assets back to their economic scale.

We previously discussed how a Fundamental Index portfolio keeps pace in most bull markets while outperforming significantly in most bear markets. We found this same pattern in the U.S. large-company market, the U.S. small-company market, and the developed and emerging international markets. Even more interesting is the tracking error against cap-weighted indexes in bull and bear markets. We found that in all these markets, the tracking error of the Fundamental Index portfolio is rather low in the up markets and widens when stock prices turn south. Isn't that when we want to perform differently from the cap-weighted indexes?

Another advantage of blending the cap-weighted index with a Fundamental Index strategy is that the resulting portfolio hedges some of the growth bias of the cap-weighted portfolio with the value bias of the Fundamental Index portfolio. As we have shown, the cap-weighted portfolio has a structural tilt toward growth stocks; that is, it gives twice the weight to each security with twice the market price-earnings ratio (P/E) and halves the weight to stocks selling at half the market P/E. So, relative to the market, capitalization weighting is utterly neutral and Fundamental Index portfolios seem value tilted. And, relative to the economy, the Fundamental Index portfolios are neutral, while capitalization weighting has a stark growth tilt.

The cap-weighted portfolio's growth bias expands in bubbles because it allows these projected stars of tomorrow to grow to a larger and larger share of the market. The Fundamental Index approach ignores P/E and assigns the same weight to two companies with identical fundamental measures of size. If one company is growing faster, it will be underrepresented—relative to its scale in the market and in the *future* economy (assuming its expected future growth materializes). On the other hand, the slow grower will be overweighted vis-à-vis its prospects, thus ensuring a structural value orientation in a Fundamental Index portfolio. The combination of the two is reassuring and sensible.

Different Markets, Different Investors, Different Needs

We've seen in previous chapters how powerful the Fundamental Index concept is in many different asset classes. Figure 14.5 offers a compelling affirmation of the efficacy of the concept. In each of the "floating bubble" diagrams, the returns of the simple, mechanistic, "passive" RAFI indexes are compared with cap-weighted indexes over the past 10 years for U.S. large-company, U.S. small-company, international large-company, and emerging-markets. These results are compared with the Lipper universe of available mutual funds. The four stacked rectangular "boxes" within each chart represents a quartile of managers, from the top 25 percent of all active managers to the bottom 25 percent. The top and bottom boxes leave out the very best 5 percent and the very worst 5 percent because those outlier managers would stretch the scale of the graph considerably.

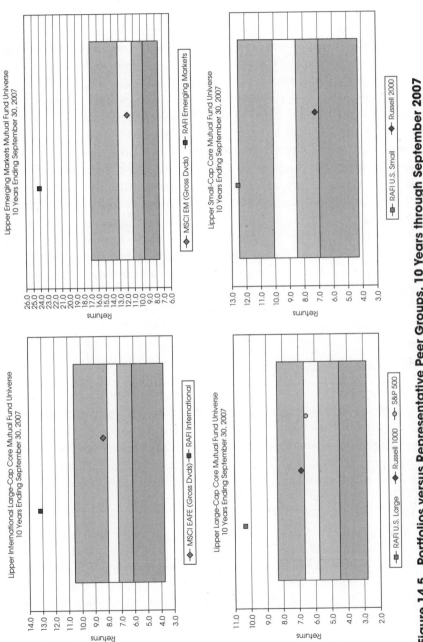

Figure 14.5 Portfolios versus Representative Peer Groups, 10 Years through September 2007

Source: eVestment Alliance.

In each of these graphs, the RAFI portfolio is "off the charts" on the high end, ranking well in the top 5 percent of all active managers in all four market segments. It bears repeating that *the small-company, international, and emerging-market results are all out-of-sample tests, applying the same methodology that we developed and tested in the U.S. large-company domain into three other broad domains.* And yet, in each of these domains, the RAFI strategy outpaces both the median active manager *and* the cap-weighted benchmarks by an even wider margin than in the U.S. large-company domain.

It makes sense, therefore, to explore how this idea can affect different classes of investors in different ways. Differing time horizons, risk metrics, and investor preferences influence investment priorities. Individual investors in 401(k) plans or individual retirement accounts (IRAs) want to accumulate a large enough nest egg to support their so-called golden years. Endowments and foundations are concerned with sustaining their real long-term spending power. Pensions must pay careful attention to the plan's promised benefits in forming an investment strategy. How can the Fundamental Index advantage be maximized for these diverse portfolio needs?

Financial Advisers and Financial Planners

A naive, but defensible, way to use the Fundamental Index concept would be to move all of our existing active manager and passive index money into the corresponding Fundamental Index vehicles. This suggestion is not entirely facetious. The concept raises returns and reduces risk in almost every market we've tested, and typically beats the average active manager by an even wider margin. Commercial products are already available, or are on their way, in each of these domains.

But this naive strategy isn't practical for most investors for a very simple reason. Consider the risk of "regret": What if the idea is embraced just before it has a couple of disappointing years? In the historical record, as reassuring as it may be, there are many years in which the Fundamental Index concept fails to outpace the cap-weighted markets. A common denominator in these years of disappointment is that they almost always happen when growth (hence capitalization weighting with its stark growth tilt) beats value (the tilt of the Fundamental Index portfolios).

A wholesale shift of assets to the Fundamental Index idea will create unacceptable business risk for financial advisers and financial planners. Imagine moving all of a client's assets into Fundamental Index portfolios just before growth takes off so strongly that our newly selected portfolios lag by 5 percent or more. Client second-guessing, and some lost revenues, would be very likely. But this risk cuts both ways. A *failure* to invest at least *some* money into the Fundamental Index when we know that the early adopters may garner outsized benefits as the idea gains traction could carry the opposite risk!

In helping their clients achieve their long-term goals, financial advisers often use sector rotation strategies—shifting money from one economic sector to another. In addition to adding value through dynamic sector allocations in a core RAFI portfolio, the advisers can also obtain excess returns by using sector-based Fundamental Index products, thereby providing a source of alpha in industry segments that may not be the adviser's core competency. As with the broader market measures, the historical record suggests that Fundamental Index sector funds add their best value when the sector performance is weak—which means that if the adviser's choices don't work, the damage is lessened. And, if the manager is correct, the rewards are typically largely or fully captured.

Alternatively, a narrowly focused manager may have stock-picking expertise in financial firms and utilities but have a broader mandate—for example, the value stock universe such as would be benchmarked to the Russell 1000 Value Index. After applying her expertise in individual financial and utility shares, the adviser can use Fundamental Index sector exchange-trade funds (ETFs) to fill in the "holes" outside her designated area, such as consumer and energy value stocks, without giving up projected alpha.

Individual Investors

The Fundamental Index approach has many attractive features for the individual investor. As with conventional indexes, this approach simplifies the investment process by removing the need to pick individual stocks. But, unlike conventional indexes, it reduces our potential need for active managers. Investors can implement a portfolio of Fundamental Index strategies spanning multiple markets that will address their specific investment needs.

No two individuals are alike, and neither are their investment requirements. Realizing this diversity, we encourage individuals and their advisers to determine the Fundamental Index applications that have the most merit for their specific circumstances. For example, the discussion may prove instructive for individuals who are seeking to trim their risk exposure at the margin. The overview of implementation ideas for the asset classes (RAFI U.S. Large, RAFI U.S. Small Company Index, etc.) illustrates that the concept is a reasonable substitute for core equity or for active managers in each of these asset classes.

Detailing how Fundamental Index strategies can be used to address the many varieties of individual investors is an immense task. Instead of trying to cover the field, we will focus on the biggest investment challenge of the coming quarter century: The prospective dissavings of the Baby Boomers as they enter their retirement years.[4] Over the next three decades, between four million and five million of this huge demographic group will begin retirement each and every year. Most have inadequate savings to comfortably retire at a reasonable age. Unfortunately, prospects for a rising equity tide floating all Boomer boats, as in the 1990s, are slim from current valuation levels. Even if we think lofty returns may continue into the future, we dare not *depend* on them. Furthermore, Boomers can be expected to live longer in retirement and incur higher health care costs than previous generations, which places great strain on their portfolios if they hope to keep pace with inflation. Dare we count on the government to fix this problem when the government can do little beyond reallocating resources from those who work to the soaring legions of those who no longer work?

The Fundamental Index strategy can be part of the solution. We have already explored the fact that RAFI U.S. Large produces meaningful gains in most five-year periods when the stock market advances less than 10 percent annually. Because most observers foresee single-digit returns in the years ahead, value added from RAFI indexes may give Boomers a useful boost in their game of catch-up.

The case is even stronger for continuing Fundamental Index exposure in retirement. First, Boomers' substantial remaining life span, rising health care costs, and long-term care costs require the long-term inflation protection that equities can provide. For this reason, bearing equity risk to earn the long-term reward of inflation protection is more palatable if the investor uses the Fundamental Index strategy. A slightly higher dividend yield that can be applied to periodic living expense withdrawals adds a bit of icing to our retirement cake. At the start of 2008, the RAFI U.S. Large had a dividend yield of 2.2 percent, 15 percent higher than the yield on the S&P 500.

Endowments and Foundations

An endowment is a powerful vehicle for funding the long-term needs of an organization serving not-for-profit ends, such as universities, hospitals, and churches. Tax-exempt foundations are required by law to spend 5 percent of the principal annually. Typically, endowments have an annual spending policy (often 4–5 percent of the market value of the portfolio) averaged over several years, so this amount must be withdrawn and distributed annually. The remainder of the portfolio continues to accrue interest and gains until next year's distribution.

Of course, unless we are prepared to spend the corpus of the fund to meet our expenses, the endowment's annual return must exceed the spending policy amount plus—this is the tough part—inflation. If these goals are met, the endowment can meet its intended obligations in perpetuity. For example, a $10 million endowment created in 1946 and invested in a 65 percent equity and 35 percent bond portfolio with a spending policy of 5 percent annually would have distributed approximately $31 million by 2002 and would still have a principal balance of roughly $14 million, with both of these figures netted for inflation (West and Serna, 2003).

The expected low-return environment has endowments scrambling to develop portfolios that can still achieve a long-term annual real return of 4 to 6 percent over inflation. Moreover, tremendous pressure exists to ensure somewhat stable returns because the beneficiaries rely on obtaining smooth distributions. The long-term successes of such leading endowments as those at Yale University and Harvard University have drilled home the message that the way to obtain high returns with predictability is to diversify significantly into alternative asset classes. As a result, endowments and foundations have taken the lead in forays into hedge funds, private equity, venture capital, oil and gas, timberland, and other "outside the box" categories. This effort has been facilitated for many endowments and foundations because the investment committee members come from sophisticated investment and business backgrounds.

Increased diversification has been a tasty free lunch, compared with a more restricted investment diet limited to stocks and bonds. But, embracing these strategies requires considerable attention from endowment and foundation staff, investment committees, and consultants. Many hedge funds have blown up as a result of their leveraged bets. Private equity, timberland, and energy limited partnerships have illiquid securities, typically priced by the managers themselves, which creates a dangerous conflict of interest that must be carefully monitored. Intricate fee schedules with incentive carries, high-water marks, and acquisition charges also need continuous auditing. The fiduciary needs to be vigilant in scrutinizing business issues and the potential for fraud.

Speaking of hedge funds, it's worth noting that hedge funds are collectively very heavy users of ETFs. They use these funds to take on active bets quickly and inexpensively, and they particularly value the fact that one can short-sell an ETF (betting that it will go down and profiting if it does so). It will not be surprising if we see hedge funds begin to use the Fundamental Index ETFs as a tool to arbitrage against the conventional cap-weighted ETFs (typically buying the Fundamental Index ETFs and selling short the cap-weighted ETFs, though perhaps occasionally the other way around). It will also be exciting when long–short variants of the Fundamental Index concept become available in fund form. Endowments and foundations are already active users of this idea in separate accounts and in hedge fund limited partnerships.

Given the resource-intensive nature of a broad alternative investment program, a simple one-stop approach to public equity applications that allows for returns in excess of the cap-weighted benchmarks should be a welcome way to free up time. Additionally, lower fees from using a Fundamental Index strategy in lieu of traditional active managers could let money be deployed to support the high-fee hedge funds and private equity pools. In this manner, the Fundamental Index approach can add value well beyond its direct impact on portfolio returns and risks.

Pensions

Equities are a critical element of pension investing because most plan participants are many years away from retirement. The fact that equity market returns are correlated with the broad economy means that as economic growth drives up wages and, hence, eventual pension payments, equities can protect the pension sponsor against this form of risk. Moreover, the "average dollar" saved in pensions won't be spent for many years because of the longer life expectancies of retirees.

To determine the amounts needed today for future retiree payments, pensions use a discount rate based largely on current interest rates. For example, say we owe $1,000 in 10 years. Each year, we put aside a little money to satisfy our obligation. The present value of our obligation is smaller if interest rates are 10 percent than if they are 5 percent. Likewise, we owe less if the money we set aside is earning 10 percent rather than 5 percent. So, future liabilities are less burdensome with higher interest rates. A portfolio that rises when interest rates fall (and the present value of liabilities grows), such as a bond portfolio, helps the pension sponsor minimize its risk relative to the liabilities.

No wonder the 2000 through 2002 period was labeled "the perfect storm" for pensions: The value of their equity-dominated portfolios fell materially while their liabilities were skyrocketing in the wake of plunging interest rates. Because of the resulting lower funded ratios and such regulatory changes as the Pension Protection Act of 2006, many sponsors are searching for ways to match their assets more closely to their liabilities. This search has spawned a variety of liability-driven investment (LDI) strategies designed to introduce more interest rate exposure—and thus a better fit between assets and liabilities—into pension plan asset allocations.

Regardless of the popularity of LDI strategies, nothing on the horizon suggests that pension plans are likely to reverse their reliance on equities as the *main* tool in their quest for returns. Therefore, a comprehensive understanding of the role of equities, and, in particular, Fundamental Index portfolios, in the asset/liability puzzle is important. A study by IPM of Sweden (Djehiche and Rinné, 2006) indicates that liability matching is improved by shifting pension equity portfolios from cap-weighted indexes to an approach like the Fundamental Index portfolio. The IPM paper examined the performance of cap-weighted indexes and the RAFI strategies in the United States, Japan, Sweden, and Europe to gauge the interest rate sensitivity and liability-hedging characteristics of these indexed portfolios. In the United States, the RAFI U.S. Large displayed a higher correlation with government bonds (0.32 versus 0.23 for the S&P 500) and a longer empirical duration (3.6 years versus 2.5 years).[5]

The higher correlation means that more of the risk of the Fundamental Index portfolio is explained by bonds than is true for cap-weighted indexes. Because the Fundamental Index portfolio has lower risk than the cap-weighted indexes, the portfolio also has much less liability mismatch—risk unrelated to interest rates and, therefore, unrelated to the liabilities—than accompanies cap-weighted indexes. The empirical duration means that, in addition to having its own participation in the growth of earnings and the broad economy, the RAFI portfolios have interest rate sensitivity rather like that of a bond with a 3.6-year duration. A 5-year U.S. Treasury bond has a similar duration. So, this Fundamental Index portfolio resembles a 5-year T-bond with an equity kicker. But unlike most interest rate–sensitive stock portfolios, with their outsized positions in bank and utility stocks, the Fundamental Index portfolio earned a materially higher historical return than the S&P 500. Similar results were found in other markets, as evidenced in Table 14.1.

Higher returns and better asset/liability matching? The results may be surprising, but they make intuitive sense when the Fundamental Index performance in different economic environments is examined. Recall from Chapter 2 that during economic recessions, the RAFI U.S. Large has produced an average annualized return of 6.8 percent,

Table 14.1   Interest Rate Sensitivity: Fundamental and Cap-Weighted Indexes, 1962 through 2005

Market Equity	Bonds	Correlation with Bonds		Empirical Duration versus Bonds	
		RAFI	Market Cap	RAFI	Market Cap
RAFI U.S. Large vs. S&P 500	U.S. 10-year government bonds	0.32	0.23	3.56	2.45
RAFI Euro 150 vs. MSCI Euro	German 10-year government bonds	0.18	0.16	4.26	3.92
RAFI Sweden 100 vs. MSCI Sweden	Swedish 10-year government bonds	0.22	0.07	4.9	2.02
RAFI World ex Japan vs. MSCI World ex Japan	U.S. 10-year government bonds	0.16	0.05	2.1	0.72
Average		0.22	0.13	3.71	2.28

Source: Djehiche and Rinné (2006).

versus 3.0 percent for the S&P 500, for a premium of 3.8 percentage points. During recessions, weaker pension sponsor's earnings, which are the source for plan contributions, make portfolio contributions more difficult. Meanwhile, interest rates generally fall because of falling demand for debt, and lower rates mean, of course, higher liabilities. So, at a time when liabilities are rising and the ability to fund them is falling, the Fundamental Index approach produces larger excess returns for the plan sponsor. Not only does the Fundamental Index strategy achieve higher returns in most market environments, it is a powerful equity tool for plan sponsors seeking to minimize their asset/liability mismatch without throwing in the towel on stocks.

Socially Responsible Preferences

Many fund sponsors and individual investors screen from their portfolios companies that engage in activities or sell products inconsistent with their beliefs or missions. For example, California's state retirement systems exclude tobacco companies from their eligible stock universe. The argument is that while the state must spend hundreds of millions of dollars annually on tobacco-related health issues, investing in the companies that produce the harmful tobacco products is not logical. The counterargument is that constraints diminish our opportunity set. The state is not funding the activities but just buying someone else's preexisting stock holdings. Similar debates have been going on about owning shares in gambling and alcohol businesses or companies that do business in countries that misbehave (South Africa in the 1980s and Sudan today). Some religious organizations eliminate defense companies, adult entertainment companies, or companies engaged in stem cell research.

These "sin stocks" tend to be stable growth industries. Emerging growth sectors are less likely to appear in the various social screens (with the obvious exception of biotech because of birth control or stem cell issues). Because the cap-weighted index represents the anticipated composition of tomorrow's economy whereas a Fundamental Index portfolio represents today's economy, the cap-weighted index may invest less in "sin stocks" than a Fundamental Index portfolio. Table 14.2 tests this hypothesis. Combined, alcohol, tobacco, and gambling represent 2.3 percent of the RAFI U.S. Large and 2.0 percent of the Russell 1000 Index. Finding the number of companies and percentages to be rather close means

Table 14.2   Socially Responsible Comparison, October 24, 2007

Sector	RAFI U.S. Large	Russell 1000
Brewers	0.17%	0.30%
Distillers and vintners	0.07%	0.07%
Tobacco	1.95%	1.17%
Casinos and gaming	0.10%	0.50%
Total	2.29%	2.04%

Source: Research Affiliates, LLC.

that the performance advantage of the Fundamental Index strategy over capitalization weighting shouldn't be meaningfully affected by social screening.

Conclusion

The biggest surprise we had in exploring the Fundamental Index concept is that it is new. If the concept had predated capitalization weighting, capitalization weighting would never have gained traction outside of academia. Why was the idea not explored decades ago? Did the efficient market hypothesis and the capital asset pricing model, both of which point to capitalization weighting as the "right way" to index, discourage people from exploring alternatives? Whatever the reasons, well over 99 percent of the trillions of dollars that are indexed today are cap-weighted.

Fundamental Index portfolios are an important addition to the investment tool kit of investors and their advisers. Investors can use Fundamental Index portfolios as core equity holdings in any segment of the equity markets and in a multitude of diverse value-added applications. Or they can "diversify their benchmark" by having some of their core assets in the cap-weighted market portfolios and some in the economy-weighted Fundamental Index portfolios.

For those who are reluctant to shift their core holdings to a new framework for stock market indexing, there's always the option of treating the Fundamental Index strategy as a niche, value-tilted approach for a portion of their investments. This option, or a modest 20 percent to 30 percent shift of passive money to the concept, may be appealing to financial advisers because the Fundamental

Index portfolios do not always beat capitalization weighting in all market conditions. Clients may not be forgiving if their advisers make a wholesale shift to a new—and still out-of-mainstream—idea just ahead of a period of underperformance.

In addition to its benefits in investment performance, the Fundamental Index approach has an array of additional advantages. Asset allocation is more flexible because of the prospect for higher returns and lower risk. Depending on the market and investor preferences, it can efficiently replace traditional index funds or can be used to replace one's least successful active managers. Its capacity and value added are useful in inefficient market categories (small companies, emerging markets). Its simplicity and transparency free committee time for other necessary pursuits such as goal setting, asset allocation, investment policy, and alternative manager due diligence.

In the years ahead, we believe that Fundamental Index strategies will take hold in many flavors (sectors, both domestic and global, growth and value styles, size categories, countries, regions, asset classes outside equities, and niche markets). Many of these strategies are already being used, although they collectively are as yet too small to be a significant force in the capital markets. The early evidence is that they will become an important part of the indexing community and an important addition to the investor's tool kit. It's been a privilege to work on a new idea with so many applications and to observe the many ways that investors are using the concept.

Appendix

In the pages that follow, the performance characteristics of eight widely utilized Fundamental Index applications are summarized:

- RAFI U.S. Large
- RAFI U.S. Small
- RAFI International
- RAFI International Small
- RAFI Pan-Europe
- RAFI Japan
- RAFI Asia Pacific ex Japan
- RAFI Emerging Markets

The Appendix is designed to provide a standard summary presentation of the research results presented throughout the book. Each application includes the following:

- A Standardized Performance table (Tables A.1), which illustrates trailing annualized results of the Fundamental Index strategy versus representative cap-weighted benchmarks. Periods longer than one year are annualized.
- A Calendar Year Performance table (Tables A.2), which displays individual calendar year returns for the Fundamental Index strategy versus a cap-weighted index. These tables can be read by selecting the decade column first, then finding the individual calendar year row. For instance, the column labeled "2000s" and row labeled "1" are for the year "2001." Annualized return and standard deviation for each decade are also summarized at the bottom of each decade row.

- A Five-Year Rolling Return scatterplot (Figures A.1), which illustrates rolling five-year annualized returns for the Fundamental Index strategy (on the vertical axis) versus the cap-weighted index (on the horizontal axis). Observations above the 45-degree solid line indicate the Fundamental Index outperformed in that five-year period.

Readers should note that the material contained in this Appendix relates only to application of the four-metric Fundamental Index methodology to various markets, though many other variations of the Fundamental Index concept could just as easily be applied. Returns represent back-tested performance based on rules used in the creation of the index and are not indicative of any specific investment. As with other indexes, these research results presented do not adjust for trading costs or management fees, which would reduce investment performance.

RAFI U.S. Large

Table A.1 Standardized Performance as of December 31, 2007

	12-Mo	3-Yr (ann.)	5-Yr (ann.)	10-Yr (ann.)	1962–2007 (ann.)	Bull Markets	Bear Markets
RAFI U.S. Large	3.2%	9.4%	15.3%	9.5%	12.3%	20.3%	−18.1%
S&P 500 Index	5.5%	8.6%	12.8%	5.9%	10.3%	19.6%	−23.9%
Russell 1000 Index	5.8%	9.1%	13.4%	6.2%	N/A	N/A	N/A
U.S. 3-Month T-Bill	5.1%	4.5%	3.2%	3.6%	5.7%	5.4%	7.2%
RAFI U.S. Large Volatility	9.7%	8.0%	9.4%	14.0%	14.4%	13.2%	16.3%
S&P 500 Volatility	9.7%	7.8%	8.6%	14.7%	14.6%	13.2%	16.4%
Russell 1000 Volatility	9.7%	7.9%	8.7%	14.9%	N/A	N/A	N/A
RAFI U.S. Large Sharpe Ratio	−0.2	0.6	1.3	0.4	0.5	1.1	−1.5
S&P 500 Sharpe Ratio	0.0	0.5	1.1	0.2	0.3	1.1	−1.9
Russell 1000 Sharpe Ratio	0.1	0.6	1.2	0.2	N/A	N/A	N/A
RAFI U.S. Large Excess Return over S&P 500	−2.3%	0.8%	2.5%	3.6%	2.0%	0.7%	5.8%
RAFI U.S. Large Tracking Error with respect to S&P 500	1.8%	1.7%	2.1%	5.6%	3.8%	3.2%	5.7%
RAFI Information Ratio	−1.3	0.5	1.2	0.6	0.5	0.2	1.0

Source: Research Affiliates, LLC.

Table A.2 Calendar Year Performance

	1960s		1970s		1980s		1990s		2000s	
	RAFI	S&P 500	RAFI	S&P 500	RAFI	S&P 500	RAFI	S&P 500	RAFI	S&P 500
0			6.9%	3.9%	26.8%	32.5%	−8.6%	−3.1%	11.7%	−9.1%
1			13.3%	14.3%	1.9%	−4.9%	31.3%	30.5%	0.3%	−11.9%
2	−7.5%	−8.8%	13.9%	19.0%	26.0%	21.5%	14.9%	7.6%	−18.3%	−22.1%
3	22.1%	22.7%	−13.9%	−14.7%	27.0%	22.6%	16.2%	10.1%	34.7%	28.7%
4	18.3%	16.4%	−21.6%	−26.5%	9.5%	6.3%	0.1%	1.3%	15.5%	10.9%
5	15.2%	12.4%	47.2%	37.2%	32.8%	31.7%	37.1%	37.6%	6.4%	4.9%
6	−11.5%	−10.1%	34.9%	23.9%	19.0%	18.7%	22.1%	23.0%	19.4%	15.8%
7	26.7%	23.9%	−3.3%	−7.2%	2.3%	5.3%	33.6%	33.4%	3.2%	5.5%
8	16.4%	11.0%	6.2%	6.6%	23.2%	16.6%	20.7%	28.6%		
9	−14.2%	−8.5%	22.7%	18.6%	28.2%	31.7%	10.6%	21.0%		
Average	7.1%	6.5%	8.8%	5.9%	19.2%	17.6%	17.0%	18.2%	8.1%	1.7%
Volatility	12.5%	12.3%	16.5%	16.0%	15.6%	16.4%	13.0%	13.4%	13.4%	13.8%

Source: Research Affiliates, LLC.

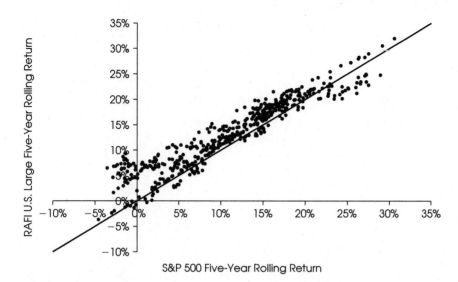

FIGURE A.1   Five-Year Rolling Return Scatterplot, 1962 through 2007
Source: Research Affiliates, LLC.

RAFI U.S. Small

Table A.1 Standardized Performance as of December 31, 2007

	12-Mo	3-Yr (ann.)	5-Yr (ann.)	10-Yr (ann.)	1979–2007 (ann.)	Bull Markets	Bear Markets
RAFI U.S. Small	−1.5%	8.6%	20.8%	12.7%	16.4%	33.1%	−26.7%
Russell 2000	−1.6%	6.8%	16.2%	7.1%	12.9%	30.8%	−31.9%
U.S. 3-Month T-Bill	5.1%	4.5%	3.2%	3.6%	6.1%	5.5%	7.6%
RAFI U.S. Small Volatility	10.7%	12.2%	14.4%	19.3%	18.6%	15.1%	23.3%
Russell 2000 Volatility	12.4%	13.3%	14.4%	19.8%	19.0%	15.5%	23.0%
RAFI U.S. Small Sharpe Ratio	−0.6	0.3	1.2	0.5	0.6	1.8	−1.5
Russell 2000 Sharpe Ratio	−0.5	0.2	0.9	0.2	0.4	1.6	−1.7
RAFI U.S. Small Excess Return over Russell 2000	0.1%	1.8%	4.6%	5.6%	3.5%	2.3%	5.2%
RAFI U.S. Small Tracking Error with respect to Russell 2000	3.3%	2.6%	2.9%	6.1%	4.1%	3.4%	5.7%
RAFI Information Ratio	0.0	0.7	1.6	0.9	0.8	0.7	0.9

Source: Research Affiliates, LLC.

Table A.2 Calendar Year Performance

	1970s		1980s		1990s		2000s	
	RAFI	Russell 2000	RAFI	Russell 2000	RAFI	Russell 2000	RAFI	Russell 2000
0			33.4%	38.6%	−17.9%	−19.5%	5.3%	−3.0%
1			7.4%	2.0%	48.4%	46.0%	20.4%	2.5%
2			32.2%	24.9%	21.9%	18.4%	−15.2%	−20.5%
3			37.5%	29.1%	21.3%	18.9%	61.6%	47.3%
4			−5.7%	−7.3%	0.2%	−1.8%	24.4%	18.3%
5			29.0%	31.0%	27.0%	28.5%	8.7%	4.6%
6			8.9%	5.7%	21.3%	16.5%	19.5%	18.4%
7			−7.1%	−8.8%	24.5%	22.4%	−1.5%	−1.6%
8			28.2%	25.0%	−1.7%	−2.5%		
9	42.4%	43.1%	17.0%	16.3%	21.3%	21.3%		
Average	42.4%	43.1%	17.0%	14.5%	15.2%	13.4%	13.6%	6.7%
Volatility	21.0%	21.7%	19.9%	20.5%	17.2%	17.3%	18.6%	19.1%

Source: Research Affiliates, LLC.

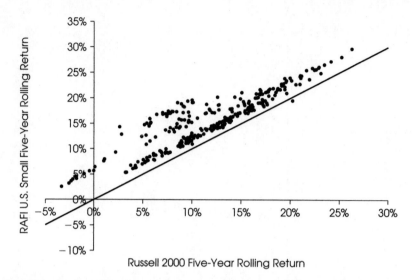

FIGURE A.1   Five-Year Rolling Return Scatterplot, 1979 through 2007
Source: Research Affiliates

RAFI International

Table A.1   Standardized Performance as of December 31, 2007

	12-Mo	3-Yr (ann.)	5-Yr (ann.)	10-Yr (ann.)	1984–2007 (ann.)	Bull Markets	Bear Markets
RAFI International	15.0%	20.6%	25.9%	14.0%	15.6%	26.2%	−12.9%
MSCI EAFE Index	11.6%	17.3%	22.1%	9.0%	12.3%	24.0%	−18.6%
U.S. 3-Month T-Bill	5.1%	4.5%	3.2%	3.6%	4.9%	5.1%	4.3%
RAFI International Volatility	9.9%	9.6%	10.8%	14.4%	15.7%	14.7%	16.2%
MSCI EAFE Volatility	9.7%	9.5%	10.7%	14.5%	16.7%	15.4%	17.5%
RAFI International Sharpe Ratio	1.0	1.7	2.1	0.7	0.7	1.4	−1.1
MSCI EAFE Sharpe Ratio	0.7	1.3	1.8	0.4	0.4	1.2	−1.3
RAFI International Excess Return over MSCI EAFE	3.3%	3.2%	3.8%	5.0%	3.3%	2.2%	5.7%
RAFI International Tracking Error with respect to MSCI EAFE	1.9%	1.6%	1.9%	4.3%	4.4%	4.0%	5.5%
RAFI Information Ratio	1.8	2.1	2.0	1.2	0.8	0.5	1.0

Source: Research Affiliates, LLC.

Table A.2   Calendar Year Performance

	1980s		1990s		2000s	
	RAFI	MSCI EAFE	RAFI	MSCI EAFE	RAFI	MSCI EAFE
0			−16.9%	−23.2%	−3.2%	−14.0%
1			12.1%	12.5%	−15.2%	−21.2%
2			−11.8%	−11.8%	−9.4%	−15.7%
3			36.4%	32.9%	46.9%	39.2%
4	4.6%	7.9%	12.9%	8.1%	22.6%	20.7%
5	63.0%	56.7%	12.6%	11.6%	16.4%	14.0%
6	58.0%	69.9%	12.1%	6.4%	30.9%	26.9%
7	26.6%	24.9%	3.1%	2.1%	15.0%	11.6%
8	30.5%	28.6%	18.2%	20.3%		
9	19.5%	10.8%	33.7%	27.3%		
Average	32.1%	31.3%	10.0%	7.3%	11.3%	5.6%
Volatility	17.1%	18.4%	16.0%	17.1%	13.8%	14.0%

Source: Research Affiliates, LLC.

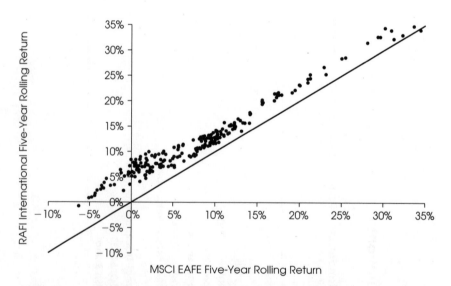

FIGURE A.1   Five-Year Rolling Return Scatterplot, 1984 through 2007
Source: Research Affiliates

RAFI International Small

Table A.1   Standardized Performance as of December 31, 2007

	12-Mo	3-Yr (ann.)	5-Yr (ann.)	10-Yr (ann.)	1999–2007 (ann.)	Bull Markets	Bear Markets
RAFI International Small	7.2%	18.7%	29.7%	N/A	17.1%	31.4%	−10.8%
MSCI EAFE Small Company Index	1.8%	15.5%	26.8%	N/A	12.9%	29.7%	−21.4%
U.S. 3-Month T-Bill	5.1%	4.5%	3.2%	N/A	3.5%	3.4%	3.8%
RAFI International Small Volatility	10.0%	10.1%	11.3%	N/A	13.3%	11.1%	14.7%
MSCI EAFE Small Company Volatility	13.3%	12.5%	13.3%	N/A	15.2%	11.9%	17.3%
RAFI International Small Sharpe Ratio	0.2	1.4	2.3	N/A	1.0	2.5	−1.0
MSCI EAFE Small Company Sharpe Ratio	−0.2	0.9	1.8	N/A	0.6	2.2	−1.5
RAFI International Small Excess Return over MSCI EAFE Small Company	5.5%	3.1%	2.9%	N/A	4.2%	1.7%	10.6%
RAFI International Small Tracking Error with respect to MSCI EAFE Small Company	4.7%	3.5%	3.6%	N/A	4.4%	4.4%	5.8%
RAFI Information Ratio	1.2	0.9	0.8	N/A	0.9	0.4	2.8

Source: Research Affiliates, LLC.

Table A.2   Calendar Year Performance

| | 1990s | | 2000s | |
	RAFI	MSCI EAFE Small Company	RAFI	MSCI EAFE Small Company
0			−3.5%	−7.2%
1			−9.0%	−12.1%
2			4.2%	−7.4%
3			64.2%	62.1%
4			33.9%	31.3%
5			24.0%	26.6%
6			25.7%	19.7%
7			7.2%	1.8%
8				
9	22.9%	20.2%		
Average	22.9%	20.2%	16.4%	12.0%
Volatility	12.9%	11.9%	13.3%	15.6%

Source: Research Affiliates, LLC.

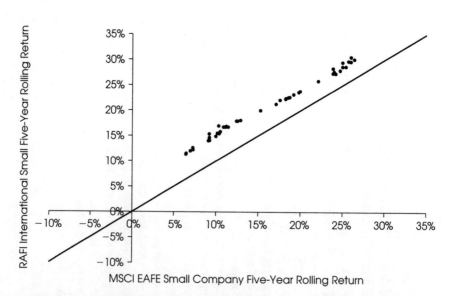

FIGURE A.1   Five-Year Rolling Return Scatterplot, 1999 through 2007
Source: Research Affiliates

RAFI Pan-Europe

Table A.1   Standardized Performance as of December 31, 2007

	12-Mo	3-Yr (ann.)	5-Yr (ann.)	10-Yr (ann.)	1984–2007 (ann.)	Bull Markets	Bear Markets
RAFI Pan-Europe	16.6%	22.2%	27.0%	14.2%	17.8%	25.7%	−24.3%
MSCI Europe Index	14.4%	19.1%	23.3%	10.0%	14.8%	23.4%	−29.8%
U.S. 3-Month T-Bill	5.1%	4.5%	3.2%	3.6%	4.9%	5.1%	4.2%
RAFI Pan-Europe Volatility	11.3%	10.1%	12.7%	15.8%	16.2%	14.4%	21.6%
MSCI Europe Volatility	11.0%	9.8%	12.0%	15.7%	16.1%	14.4%	20.5%
RAFI Pan-Europe Sharpe Ratio	1.0	1.7	1.9	0.7	0.8	1.4	−1.3
MSCI Europe Sharpe Ratio	0.8	1.5	1.7	0.4	0.6	1.3	−1.7
RAFI Pan-Europe Excess Return over MSCI Europe	2.2%	3.1%	3.6%	4.2%	3.0%	2.3%	5.4%
RAFI Pan-Europe Tracking Error with respect to MSCI Europe	2.0%	1.7%	2.2%	4.2%	3.5%	2.9%	6.0%
RAFI Information Ratio	1.1	1.8	1.7	1.0	0.8	0.8	0.9

Source: Research Affiliates, LLC.

Table A.2   Calendar Year Performance

	1980s		1990s		2000s	
	RAFI	MSCI Europe	RAFI	MSCI Europe	RAFI	MSCI Europe
0			-3.6%	-3.4%	-0.6%	-8.2%
1			12.4%	13.7%	-13.0%	-19.6%
2			-5.1%	-4.2%	-12.4%	-18.1%
3			40.7%	29.8%	46.3%	39.1%
4	2.1%	1.3%	5.9%	2.7%	23.6%	21.4%
5	84.4%	79.8%	20.4%	22.1%	12.8%	9.9%
6	41.5%	44.5%	25.4%	21.6%	38.7%	34.4%
7	14.7%	4.1%	24.7%	24.2%	16.6%	14.4%
8	17.3%	16.4%	26.9%	28.9%		
9	30.1%	29.1%	18.6%	16.2%		
Average	29.2%	26.2%	15.8%	14.5%	12.1%	7.1%
Volatility	19.1%	19.0%	14.4%	14.6%	15.8%	15.5%

Source: Research Affiliates, LLC.

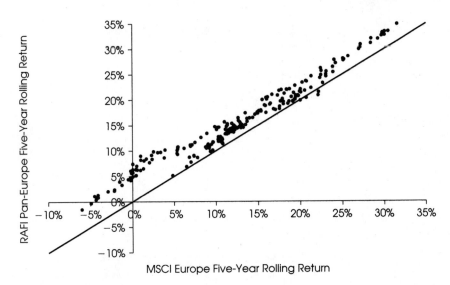

FIGURE A.1 **Five-Year Rolling Return Scatterplot, 1984 through 2007**
Source: Research Affiliates

RAFI Japan

Table A.1   Standardized Performance as of December 31, 2007

	12-Mo	3-Yr (ann.)	5-Yr (ann.)	10-Yr (ann.)	1984–2007 (ann.)	Bull Markets	Bear Markets
RAFI Japan	–8.7%	12.7%	16.3%	8.2%	7.2%	31.5%	–19.0%
MSCI Japan Index	–10.1%	11.8%	13.7%	3.1%	4.3%	31.2%	–23.6%
U.S. 3-Month T-Bill	0.6%	0.3%	0.4%	0.3%	2.5%	2.8%	2.2%
RAFI Japan Volatility	10.3%	12.7%	12.9%	16.1%	19.1%	17.3%	18.5%
MSCI Japan Volatility	10.8%	14.1%	13.6%	16.1%	19.4%	17.4%	18.5%
RAFI Japan Sharpe Ratio	–0.9	1.0	1.2	0.5	0.2	1.7	–1.1
MSCI Japan Sharpe Ratio	–1.0	0.8	1.0	0.2	0.1	1.6	–1.4
RAFI Japan Excess Return over MSCI Japan	1.4%	1.0%	2.6%	5.2%	2.8%	0.4%	4.7%
RAFI Japan Tracking Error with respect to MSCI Japan	3.0%	2.9%	3.0%	5.9%	5.2%	5.1%	5.3%
RAFI Information Ratio	0.5	0.3	0.9	0.9	0.5	0.1	0.9

Source: Research Affiliates, LLC.

Table A.2 Calendar Year Performance

	1980s		1990s		2000s	
	RAFI	MSCI Japan	RAFI	MSCI Japan	RAFI	MSCI Japan
0			−38.8%	−39.5%	−0.8%	−19.8%
1			−0.7%	0.3%	−12.6%	−18.8%
2			−21.1%	−21.4%	−12.7%	−18.6%
3			16.0%	12.4%	31.8%	23.0%
4	22.5%	27.0%	12.9%	8.7%	12.9%	10.9%
5	18.3%	14.6%	2.9%	4.3%	42.2%	44.7%
6	56.2%	59.0%	−2.8%	−4.8%	10.4%	7.3%
7	12.9%	8.8%	−19.2%	−14.4%	−8.7%	−10.1%
8	50.8%	39.7%	−3.0%	−8.7%		
9	21.9%	17.1%	40.9%	46.8%		
Average	29.4%	26.6%	−3.6%	−4.0%	6.2%	0.1%
Volatility	17.5%	18.6%	22.4%	22.4%	14.5%	14.9%

Source: Research Affiliates, LLC.

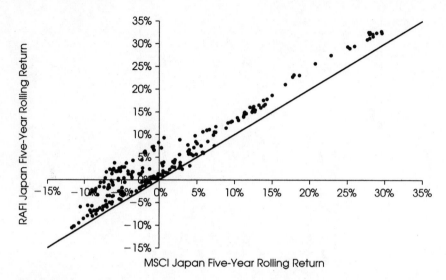

FIGURE A.1   Five-Year Rolling Return Scatterplot, 1984 through 2007
Source: Research Affiliates

RAFI Asia Pacific ex Japan

Table A.1 Standardized Performance as of December 31, 2007

	12-Mo	3-Yr (ann.)	5-Yr (ann.)	10-Yr (ann.)	1988–2007 (ann.)	Bull Markets	Bear Markets
RAFI AP ex Japan	46.2%	35.6%	39.9%	24.3%	17.2%	35.2%	−24.0%
MSCI Pacific ex Japan Index	31.7%	26.3%	30.9%	14.1%	12.7%	30.5%	−27.5%
U.S. 3-Month T-Bill	5.1%	4.5%	3.2%	3.6%	4.5%	4.3%	5.1%
RAFI AP ex Japan Volatility	20.5%	16.6%	16.1%	24.1%	21.1%	18.6%	23.5%
MSCI Pacific ex Japan Volatility	14.3%	13.7%	12.5%	20.8%	19.3%	16.4%	22.2%
RAFI AP ex Japan Sharpe Ratio	2.0	1.9	2.3	0.9	0.6	1.7	−1.2
MSCI Pacific ex Japan Sharpe Ratio	1.9	1.6	2.2	0.5	0.4	1.6	−1.5
RAFI AP ex Japan Excess Return Over							
MSCI Pacific ex Japan	14.5%	9.3%	9.0%	10.3%	4.5%	4.7%	3.5%
RAFI AP ex Japan Tracking Error wrt							
MSCI Pacific ex Japan	8.6%	6.9%	7.3%	12.0%	10.2%	9.0%	13.4%
RAFI Information Ratio	1.7	1.4	1.2	0.9	0.4	0.5	0.3

Source: Research Affiliates, LLC.

Table A.2   Calendar Year Performance

	1980s		1990s		2000s	
	RAFI	MSCI Pacific ex Japan	RAFI	MSCI Pacific ex Japan	RAFI	MSCI Pacific ex Japan
0			−13.7%	−10.1%	−23.7%	−15.1%
1			27.2%	36.6%	6.2%	−9.4%
2			3.1%	7.0%	6.7%	−5.8%
3			67.2%	80.4%	68.4%	47.0%
4			4.2%	−14.0%	27.4%	29.6%
5			5.4%	13.4%	25.2%	14.8%
6			8.9%	21.0%	36.3%	33.2%
7			−33.3%	−30.8%	46.2%	31.7%
8	52.3%	30.6%	21.5%	−6.2%		
9	17.0%	16.0%	56.7%	43.0%		
Average	33.5%	23.1%	11.1%	10.0%	21.1%	13.6%
Volatility	17.2%	17.6%	23.3%	21.7%	19.0%	16.6%

Source: Research Affiliates, LLC.

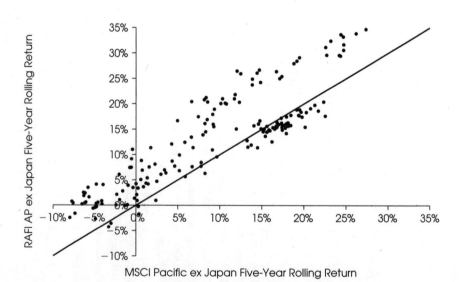

FIGURE A.1   Five-Year Rolling Return Scatterplot, 1988 through 2007
Source: Research Affiliates

RAFI Emerging Markets

Table A.1   Standardized Performance as of December 31, 2007

	12-Mo	3-Yr (ANN.)	5-Yr (ANN.)	10-Yr (ANN.)	1994–2007 (ANN.)	Bull Markets	Bear Markets
RAFI EM	49.0%	46.7%	52.0%	28.0%	19.4%	47.7%	−36.8%
MSCI EM Index	39.8%	35.6%	37.5%	14.5%	8.7%	36.6%	−44.8%
U.S. 3-Month T-Bill	5.1%	4.5%	3.2%	3.6%	4.0%	3.8%	4.6%
RAFI EM Volatility	18.4%	16.9%	16.9%	24.8%	23.3%	19.1%	26.2%
MSCI EM Volatility	18.4%	18.4%	17.1%	23.7%	22.4%	17.0%	26.9%
RAFI EM Sharpe Ratio	2.4	2.5	2.9	1.0	0.7	2.3	−1.6
MSCI EM Sharpe Ratio	1.9	1.7	2.0	0.5	0.2	1.9	−1.8
RAFI EM Excess Return over MSCI EM	9.2%	11.1%	14.5%	13.5%	10.7%	11.2%	8.0%
RAFI EM Tracking Error with respect to MSCI EM	2.1%	5.8%	6.1%	8.9%	9.3%	9.0%	10.1%
RAFI Information Ratio	4.3	1.9	2.4	1.5	1.2	1.2	0.8

Source: Research Affiliates, LLC.

Table A.2   Calendar Year Performance

	1990s		2000s	
	RAFI	MSCI EM	RAFI	MSCI EM
0			−22.1%	−30.7%
1			8.9%	−2.4%
2			2.1%	−6.0%
3			89.9%	56.3%
4	10.9%	−7.3%	35.1%	26.0%
5	−20.0%	−5.2%	51.0%	34.5%
6	16.6%	6.0%	40.4%	32.6%
7	−2.8%	−11.6%	49.0%	39.8%
8	−1.8%	−25.3%		
9	72.1%	66.6%		
Average	9.2%	0.4%	27.6%	15.3%
Volatility	27.0%	24.7%	20.1%	20.6%

Source: Research Affiliates, LLC.

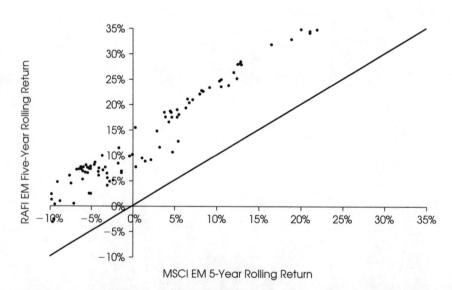

FIGURE A.1   Five-Year Rolling Return Scatterplot, 1994 through 2007
Source: Research Affiliates

Notes

Preface

1. This is often paraphrased as "Success has many fathers, but failure is an orphan."
2. The Fundamental Index is a registered trademark of Research Affiliates.

Chapter 1

1. Russell Investment Group is the source and owner of the Russell Index data contained or reflected in this book and all trademarks and copyrights related thereto. Russell Investment Group is not responsible for the formatting or configuration of this material or for any inaccuracy in Research Affiliates' presentation thereof.
2. A stock's market capitalization is the total dollar value of the outstanding stock—that is, price × shares outstanding. So, weighting on the basis of market capitalization, or "cap weighting" for short, is holding stocks in direct proportion to the total value of the stock of each company. This approach is the dominant form of index fund investing and drives more than 99 percent of all index fund assets worldwide.
3. One of the authors—we decline to say which—owned all three at the time!

Chapter 2

1. We use the term *valuation multiple* to refer generically to price-earnings, price-sales, price-book, price-dividend, or other similar valuation ratios that many investors use to gauge an investment's value.
2. When we first did this research, some of our clients said, "Hey, why don't you introduce an 'S&P 490' strategy?" It's a blunt-instrument approach and it's not elegant, but, surprisingly, it would work. When we test the idea, we find that we would have added some 80 basis points

per year for 80 years just by leaving out the top 10 names. That's a lot of damage from 10 names.

3. Of course, equal weighting is equivalent to random weighting if one has enough darts to fill the whole list!

4. George F. Keane is the founding president of Commonfund, which manages some $40 billion in commingled university endowment assets. At the time of these discussions, he also served on the boards of several large funds, including the New York State Common Retirement Fund, which had very large commitments to S&P 500 indexed funds.

5. At the time, Martin L. Leibowitz was at the Teachers Insurance and Annuity Association–College Retirement Equity Fund (TIAA-CREF), which manages the pension assets for most university professors in the United States and has a long history as one of the largest and most sophisticated pension management organizations in the world. Brett Hammond is still at TIAA-CREF.

6. Peter L. Bernstein is a founding editor of the *Journal of Portfolio Management* and one of the most prolific authors in the finance community. His book *Against the Gods* is a study of the history of risk that became a best-seller. A history book on probability and risk in finance as a long-running *New York Times* best seller? Only Peter could do that!

7. Jack L. Treynor is often credited as the co-originator of the capital asset pricing model (CAPM). His model was developed independently of, but concurrent with, the CAPM of William F. Sharpe and John V. Lintner.

8. Harry M. Markowitz invented mean-variance optimization—also known as quadratic programming—in 1952. He is generally considered the father of Modern Portfolio Theory.

9. For Table 2.3 and subsequent discussions of our long-term research, we list the "Cap 1000." The Cap 1000 is an annually rebalanced portfolio of the top 1,000 U.S. stocks by capitalization dating back to 1962. The historical results of the Russell 1000 Index, which is widely used as the standard large-cap index by investors today, extend back to 1979.

10. This result assumes, of course, that the "price-indifferent" methods are comprehensively applied to a large universe of stocks.

11. Reweighting of relatively narrow pre-existing indexes like the S&P 500 long predates our work. Bob Jones, of Goldman Sachs Asset Management, launched a profit-weighted S&P 500 strategy in 1990. David Morris, then of John Morrell Associates, launched a profit-and-book-value-weighted S&P 500 strategy in 1997 and experimented with reweighting the countries in

the MSCI EAFE index based on profits, revenues, and book values about that same time. In each of these cases, these were positioned as active strategies or enhanced indexes rather than as better indexes. Paul Wood and Richard Evans (2003) were the first to see this as a better index in their article examining a profits-weighted S&P 500, which Paul has managed live from 2001. Still, even here, there was no effort to reconstitute the index by selecting and weighting companies based on the fundamental scale of the underlying enterprises.

12. RAFI is an abbreviation for Research Affiliates Fundamental Index, our own four-metric Fundamental Index approach.

13. The Fundamental Index Composite of the original research became the RAFI U.S. Large composite.

14. The Sharpe ratio is a measure of the mean return per unit of risk, typically calculated as the return in excess of the risk-free rate divided by the standard deviation of return. Sharpe ratios listed were related by monthly excess return of the portfolio multiplied by 12 divided by the annualized monthly standard deviation of the portfolio.

15. The information ratio measures excess return per unit of risk relative to a benchmark, where the ratio is defined as the excess return divided by the tracking error (or return in excess of the benchmark).

16. Tracking error is a measure of how closely a portfolio follows its index and is measured as the standard deviation of the difference between the portfolio and index returns.

Chapter 3

1. Within the United States, in mainstream stocks and bonds, historical evidence suggests rebalancing adds 25 to 50 basis points. For global rebalancing of risk-adjusted returns, historical gains from rebalancing are about twice as large, ranging from roughly 50 to 100 basis points. These are gains on risk-adjusted returns. A drifting mix, in the very long run, appears to perform as well as, or even better than, rebalancing, because of steadily drifting into more and more exposure to the riskiest—and highest-return—markets. But, this comes at a cost of higher risk, which rises more than proportional to the performance.

Chapter 4

1. Any adviser or investor who uses active management is making the implicit assumption that prices do not always equal intrinsic value.

2. We've never fully understood why the float adjustment is consistent with an "efficient market." Do we really want to penalize companies with concentrated ownership by people who care deeply about—and depend on—the companies' success? Do we really want to favor companies with no closely held shares, companies with management teams that often have less "skin in the game" than the owner/operators of closely held companies?

3. Index funds must adjust for corporate actions that affect the equity securities issued by the company, including mergers, spin-offs, stock buybacks, and secondary equity offerings (the sale of additional stock to raise capital for the company).

4. The fact that active management on average does not add value is a testament to the importance of the active management industry. Active managers serve a critical purpose by establishing prices and correcting mispricings. The fierce competition in this space has made prices fairly efficient; analysts with average resources and skill cannot gain any further advantage over the average market participant.

5. The 2000 Arnott, Berkin, and Ye study covered only those equity funds that maintained at least $100 million in assets over the 20-year evaluation period.

6. By no means are we attempting to trivialize the job of the index portfolio manager. They must vote proxies, manage taxable gains, lend securities, and continually update the portfolio (mergers, delistings, rebalancings, etc.) in a cost-effective manner. Successful implementation of these activities often covers a few basis points of expense.

7. The world of cap-weighted indexes may be the one area in all of investment management where bigger (as defined by assets under management) is most definitely better.

8. The key here is that style definitions are linked to the cap-weighted indexes. A case can be made, however, that narrowly led, extreme bull markets (recall the Nifty Fifty era or technology bubble) cause style drift within indexes. Traditional value managers in the late 1990s protested the composition of the Russell 1000 Value Index; they claimed it held a large proportion of stocks that failed to meet traditional value criteria.

9. This comment isn't meant to be an indictment of the financial media. They are in the business of selling magazines or newspapers or ads, and readers tend to buy stories that are interesting and encourage investors to *do* something.

Chapter 5

1. For many years the British cartoonist W. E. Hill was thought to be the creator of this famous figure. According to experts, Hill almost certainly adapted the figure from an original concept in the late nineteenth century.

2. Here, we are referring to a company being undervalued relative to its unknown and unknowable future, its eventual intrinsic value. This definition is distinct from the finance theory definition of *fair value*, which is that in an efficient market, fair value is the value based on everything that could have been known about the company at the time. Nevertheless, even by this strict definition of *fair value*, we question the rationale of the pricing of Cisco or of Pets.com at the peak of the bubble.

3. This example is exclusive of management costs, brokerage transactions, taxes, and other real-world impediments to "paper portfolios."

4. The upside capture of a portfolio measures the average relative performance of a portfolio in positive-return markets. Thus, a figure of 104 percent would indicate that the SP EWI "captures" all of the market's gains in rising markets and then some. By contrast, the downside capture measures how much of the negative returns of falling markets are captured in the portfolio. Based on data from eVestment Alliance.

Chapter 6

1. See Treynor (2005).

2. Treynor (2005) suggested that a fundamentals-based index could be built by using a "number of corporate jets or corporate limousines." Treynor had his tongue firmly in his cheek, but with the serious lapses in corporate governance in the 2000–2002 period on the part of Enron Corporation, Adelphia Communications Corporation, Tyco, and so on, metrics that directly link the weight in the portfolio to corporate excesses and disregard of shareholder interests might be the first valuation-indifferent metrics to show serious underperformance relative to cap-weighted indexes!

3. A fifth valid measure of size is number of employees, which we considered but decided to exclude, as discussed later.

4. We can't think of a better "poster child" for the law of unintended consequences!

5. Interestingly, this process punishes growth companies as they shift from no yield to low yield. History suggests, however, that such punishment

is not a bad thing: Long-term historical return data imply that no-yield companies generally have higher returns than low-yield companies. Microsoft Corporation chose an interesting way to make this transition; it returned substantial corporate cash reserves to the shareholders in one massive distribution, followed by ongoing dividend distributions. Because of our five-year-averaging approach, Microsoft's introduction of dividends barely altered its RAFI weight.

6. These figures refer to the *names* that are zero-yield companies. By *market value,* the percentages are somewhat less but still significant— 12 percent of the S&P 500 and 53 percent of the Russell 2000 as of December 2006.

7. This exchange-traded fund was the first dividend-weighted fund and remains the largest fundamentally reweighted strategy in the world as of this writing. Introduced in 2003, the S&P 900 is a broad market portfolio combining the S&P 500 and the S&P 400 representing selected (and ostensibly "representative") large-cap and mid-cap companies of the U.S. equity market.

8. Among measures of profits, we favor cash flow, which has fewer accrual items, ignores goodwill, and generally includes fewer subjective components than other profit measures.

9. The index based on dividends was at the bottom of the performance list, so the inclusion of the employment metric at the expense of dividends might have led to better RAFI U.S. Large historical results. The representation and comparability flaws of using number of employees, however, were serious enough that the metric was dropped from consideration. Is Kelly Services really one of the 10 largest U.S. companies?

10. It's worth noting that, even for capitalization weighting, the increasing reliance on float adjustments, and different rules for defining float, makes the size of a company in an index more ambiguous—and more subjective—than the indexing community would like us to believe.

11. It is not uncommon for companies to misreport their financials or for data providers to record incorrect numbers. Even employing dozens of analysts to scrutinize every number won't completely eliminate this risk.

12. As mentioned, the S&P 500 is constructed in a committee approach that can lead to varying levels of turnover, largely as a result of capital market and merger activity. Accordingly, direct turnover comparisons of the S&P 500 and a rules-based, formulaic approach such as the Fundamental Index strategy or Russell approach is difficult.

13. We tested more frequent rebalancing periods—monthly, quarterly, and semiannually. They were found to have little effect on performance and led only to higher trading activity. Additionally, in the first years of our studies, financial data were available only annually.

14. Book value tends to be a more stable measure and less susceptible to cyclical swings than sales or cash flow and less susceptible to sudden management decisions than dividends. For companies with fewer than five years of available data, we used whatever span of data was available.

Chapter 7

1. In the 1960s, Bill Sharpe proposed this simple ratio for comparing the risk-adjusted performance of two distinct investments.

2. A proprietary method, similar to the Russell Growth/Value methodology, was used by Research Affiliates to create the growth/value split.

3. See www.investinreits.com/learn/reitstory.cfm.

4. This work has survivorship bias; the 100 companies were, by definition, survivors of World War II and its aftermath. But that bias affects all of the results more or less equally, so we're not troubled by that vulnerability in the Davis (2007) study.

Chapter 8

1. Not all of these results span the full 24 years. For some of the countries, historical data in the 1980s are spotty. For Greece, Finland, Ireland, New Zealand, Portugal, Singapore, and Spain, results are available for 18 to 20 years, not quite the full 23 years.

2. Drawn from the S&P mutual funds database from Ibbotson Associates.

Chapter 9

1. The title was chosen by *Institutional Investor* magazine, but we think it's a *wonderful* title.

2. The story may be apocryphal.

3. As of year-end 2007, the S&P 500 represents approximately 75 percent of the total capitalization of the U.S. equity market.

4. In measuring the central tendency of a sample, the median often provides the better measure. It is calculated by figuring which value

lands in the middle of the range of observations. Salaries are one variable that is typically quoted in median terms. A few, successful individuals in a company or industry can skew the simple average considerably higher than what the average person typically takes home. These select, big earners are considered outliers—observations well out of the normal range—and can significantly bias the average.

5. The CAPM, introduced in the mid-1960s, is largely attributed to Bill Sharpe (1964), although John Lintner (1965), Jack Treynor (1962), and Jan Mossin (1966) independently derived their own versions.

6. In the parlance of the finance community, this portfolio is a mean-variance-efficient portfolio on the efficient frontier in Markowitz's framework.

7. In fact, the higher the payout ratio, the faster the subsequent earnings growth (Arnott and Asness, 2003).

8. The authenticated quote is considerably longer, and less elegant. But, this succinct variant is often attributed to Einstein. The "KISS" principle is reminiscent of another famous quote frequently attributed to Einstein: "Two things are infinite: the universe and human stupidity. And I'm not sure about the former."

Chapter 10

1. Da Vinci used the word *enemies*. We prefer *critics*, because many of the critics of the Fundamental Index concept are our friends and even mentors. Over dinner in 2001, Jack Bogle encouraged Rob Arnott to launch Research Affiliates; after all, Bogle had launched Vanguard at a similar age. Indeed, Arnott views Bogle as one of his heroes in the business and sees the Fundamental Index concept as a natural and important extension of Bogle's impressive legacy. Cliff Asness and Rob Arnott coauthored a *Financial Analysts Journal* Graham & Dodd Award-winning paper (2003) cited in Chapter 13. Burt Malkiel serves on Research Affiliates' Advisory Panel and was instrumental in our initial conversations concerning portfolio turnover and Fundamental Index construction methodology.

2. Sharpe (1988) used a technique called quadratic optimization that compares the returns of the portfolio in question with those of predetermined indexes that define the style and size spectrums. If the returns closely track the Russell 2000 Value Index and bear little resemblance to

the returns of the Russell 1000 Growth Index, the portfolio is classified as a small-cap value index.

Chapter 11

1. The Compustat database was used for tabulating company financials. Although Compustat's data begin earlier in the 1950s, the number of companies that have five-year data in the early years for all the fundamental metrics is far less than 1,000.

2. The most incorrigible critics argue that, regardless of historical returns *or* live returns, an idea might not work in the future. There is no answer to that criticism.

3. The FTSE Group, the world's largest index provider, signed on in December 2005 to be the global index provider for the RAFI suite of indexes. The live results shown are those published by FTSE (Financial Times and London Stock Exchange).

Chapter 12

1. SEC required language for every document with performance information.

2. The classic reference for this idea is Ian M. D. Little's 1962 masterpiece, "Higgledy-Piggledy Growth," which appeared in the *Bulletin of Oxford Institute of Statistics*. As with so many of the pioneers of modern finance, Little is still with us, although he's fast approaching 90 years of age!

3. See Barberis, Shleifer, and Vishny, 1998; Benartzi and Thaler, 1995; Camerer, Loewenstein, and Rabin, 2003; Daniel, Hirshleifer, and Subrahmanyam, 1998; Kahneman and Tversky, 1979; Rabin, 1998; Shefrin, 2002; and Shleifer, 1999.

4. Those who know better are not immune. Our marketing team has a tradition of buying lottery tickets for everyone in the company for our annual party. This year, with $175 in tickets, we had $10 in winners. Thank goodness our strategies for clients have not matched this return on invested capital!

5. If you have two assets, both of which are worth $50, but one is priced $10 too high and the other is priced $10 too low, as the market price eventually nears fair value, capitalization weighting has a performance

drag of 4 percent compared with equal weighting. But if the errors are only $1 either way, the drag falls to 0.04 percent, which is too small to be of much interest.

Chapter 13

1. Note that these gains are not quite additive. They compound. Just as earning 10 percent on top of a 10 percent gain leads to an overall gain of 21 percent, not 20 percent, these four numbers compound to match the total return of stocks.

2. IBES long-term growth estimate from September 30, 2007, Russell 1000 Index Fact Sheet, www.russell.com/indexes/PDF/Fact_Sheets/1000.pdf.

3. See www.ennisknupp.com/Portals/57ad7180-c5e7-49f5-b282-c6475 cdb7ee7/Survey%20Results%20with%20EnnisKnupp.pdf.

4. Short extension strategies give the manager the ability to short some allocation of the portfolio. In the case of 130/30 implementation, the portfolio would have 130 percent invested in long positions and 30 percent placed in short sales, keeping the aggregate exposure to the equity market at 100 percent, as in a traditional stock fund.

Chapter 14

1. If we earned 10.7 percent on stocks and 7.4 percent on bonds, that 60/40 blend would be expected to have delivered 9.4 percent, as against the 9.9 percent that the rebalanced 60/40 portfolio actually produced over these years. Surprisingly, even on a raw-returns basis, not risk adjusted, the buy-and-hold strategy doesn't match rebalancing, even though its mix leaps past 75 percent stocks by the end of the 20 years, with commensurately higher risk.

2. We're indebted to Cliff Asness (2000) who used this marvelous expression as part of the title for a working paper.

3. Agency risk is a particularly large factor for investment firms owned by publicly traded parent organizations because these managers are expected to keep revenues growing to meet shareholder demands. Bogle (2005) examined the equal-weighted relative returns of mutual fund complexes versus their organizational structures over a 10-year period (1994 through 2003). He found that 8 of the 10 top-performing fund families were privately owned. Of the remaining two, Pacific Investment Management Company was the sole manager owned by a parent company.

4. Net savings occur when people are saving some of their income. Dissavings occur when people spend from past savings and so spend more than they earn. Collective dissavings of the Baby Boomers will be the biggest spending challenge for the United States (and world) economy and government since World War II.

5. Duration is a measure of interest rate sensitivity in which a higher figure indicates a greater degree of price change in the wake of changing rates. A duration of three years indicates a portfolio would incur a price gain of 3 percent if instantaneously rates fell by 1 percent and, conversely, a 3 percent price loss if rates rose by 1 percent.

References

Arnott, Robert D. (2006). "An Overwrought Orthodoxy." *Institutional Investor,* December: 36–41.

———. (2004). "Can We Keep Our Promises?" *Financial Analysts Journal,* vol. 60, no. 6, November/December: 6–10.

Arnott, Robert D., and Clifford S. Asness. (2003). "Surprise! Higher Dividends = Higher Earnings Growth." *Financial Analysts Journal,* vol. 59, no. 1, January/February: 70–87.

Arnott, Robert D., and Jason C. Hsu. (2008). "Noise, CAPM and the Size and Value Effects." *Journal of Investment Management,* vol. 6, no. 1, First Quarter: 1–11.

Arnott, Robert D., and Feifei Li. (2008). "Clairvoyant Value." Working Paper, Research Affiliates, January.

Arnott, Robert D., Andrew L. Berkin, and Jia Ye. (2000). "How Well Have Taxable Investors Been Served in the 1980s and 1990s?" *Journal of Portfolio Management,* Summer: 84–93.

Arnott, Robert D., Jason C. Hsu, Jun Liu, and Harry Markowitz. (2007). "Does Noise Create Size and Value Effects?" Working Paper, Research Affiliates, March.

Arnott, Robert D., Jason Hsu, and Philip Moore. (2005). "Fundamental Indexation." *Financial Analysts Journal,* vol. 61, no. 2, March/April: 83–99.

Asness, Clifford S. (2000). "Bubble Logic: Or, How to Learn to Stop Worrying and Love the Bull." Working Paper, AQR Capital Management, LLC.

Asness, Clifford S., Robert Krail, and John M. Liew. (2001). "Do Hedge Funds Hedge?" *Journal of Portfolio Management,* Fall: 16–19.

Barberis, Nicholas, Andrei Shleifer, and Robert Vishny. (1998). "A Model of Investor Sentiment." *Journal of Financial Economics,* vol. 49: 307–343.

Bary, Andrew. (2006). "Still Too Stingy—Part II." *Barron's,* May 21.

Benartzi, Shlomo, and Richard H. Thaler. (1995). "Myopic Loss Aversion and the Equity Premium Puzzle." *Quarterly Journal of Economics,* vol. 110, no. 1, February: 73–92.

Benford, Gregory. (1980). *Timescape.* New York: Simon & Schuster.

Bernstein, Peter L. (2005a). "Capital Ideas: From the Past to the Future." *Financial Analysts Journal,* vol. 61, no. 6, November/December: 55–59.

———. (2005b). "Dividends and the Frozen Orange Juice Syndrome." *Financial Analysts Journal,* vol. 61, no. 2, March/April: 25–30.

Block, Sandra. (2006). "DuPont to Cut Traditional Pension Benefits, Push 401(k)." *USA Today,* August 28: www.usatoday.com/money/perfi/retirement/2006-08-28-dupont-pension_x.htm.

Blume, Marshall E., and Roger M. Edelen. (2003). "S&P Indexers, Delegation Costs and Liquidity Mechanisms." The Wharton School, The Rodney L. White Center for Financial Research, University of Pennsylvania, April: http://knowledge. wharton.upenn.edu/papers/1230.pdf.

Bogle, John C. (2007). *The Little Book of Common Sense Investing.* Hoboken, NJ: John Wiley & Sons, pp. 156–157.

———. (2005). "The Relentless Rules of Humble Arithmetic." *Financial Analysts Journal,* vol. 61, no. 6, November/December: 22–35.

Brinson, Gary P. (2005). "The Future of Investment Management." *Financial Analysts Journal,* vol. 61, no. 4, July/August: 24–28.

Buffett, Warren (1996). "Chairman's Letter." *Berkshire Hathaway Inc. 1996 Annual Report.* www.berkshirehathaway.com/letters/1996.html.

———(1985). "Chairman's Letter." *Berkshire Hathaway Inc. 1985 Annual Report.* www.berkshirehathaway.com/letters/1985.html.

Business Week. (1979). "The Death of Equities: How Inflation Is Destroying the Stock Market." August 13: 54.

Camerer, C. F., G. Loewenstein, and R. Rabin, eds. (2003). *Advances in Behavioral Economics.* Princeton, NJ: Princeton University Press.

Carey, Benedict. (2007). "Lotto Makes Sense, Even for Losers." *New York Times,* March 11.

Casey, Quirk, & Associates and The Bank of New York. (2006). "Institutional Demand for Hedge Funds 2: A Global Perspective." *Thought Leadership Series,* October: 1–26.

Chen, Peng. (2007). "Managing Asset Allocation Portfolios." Ibbotson Associates Presentation, October.

Daniel, Kent, David Hirshleifer, and Avanidhar Subrahmanyam. (1998). "Investor Psychology and Security Market Over- and Underreactions." *Journal of Finance,* vol. 53, no. 6, December: 1839–1885.

Davis, James L. (2007). "Fundamental Variables and Portfolio Weights: Some Pre-Compustat Evidence." *Dimensional Fund Advisors,* February.

Djehiche, Boualem, and Jonas Rinné. (2006). "Can Stocks Help Mend the Asset and Liability Mismatch?" IPM Informed Portfolio Management AB Stockholm Draft Paper, August 13.

Economic Systems, Inc. (1998). "Study of 401(k) Plan Fees and Expenses," April 13.

Edelen, Roger M., Richard B. Evans, and Gregory B. Kadlec. (2007). "Scale Effects in Mutual Fund Performance: The Role of Trading Costs," March 17: 1–41.

Ennis, Richard M. (2005). "Are Active Management Fees Too High?" *Financial Analysts Journal,* vol. 61, no. 5, September/October: 44–51.

Fama, Eugene. (1965). "The Behavior of Stock-Market Prices." *Journal of Business,* vol. 38, no. 1, January: 34–105.

Fama, Eugene F., and Kenneth R. French. (2004). "The Capital Asset Pricing Model: Theory and Evidence." *Journal of Economic Perspectives,* vol. 18, no. 3: 25–46.

———(1992). "The Cross-Section of Expected Stock Returns," *Journal of Finance,* vol. 47, no. 2, June: 427–465.

Géhin, Walter, and Mathieu Vaissié. (2005). The Right Place for Alternative Betas in Hedge Fund Performance: An Answer to the Capacity Effect Fantasy." Edhec-Risk Asset Management Research, June: 1–21.

Goyal, Amit, and Sunil Wahal. (2005). "The Selection and Termination of Investment Management Firms by Plan Sponsors." Paper presented at annual AFA meeting, Boston, Massachusetts, May: 1–47.

Graham, Benjamin. (1976). "A Conversation with Benjamin Graham." *Financial Analysts Journal*, vol. 32, no. 5, September/October: 20–23.

Graham, Benjamin, and David Dodd. (1934). *Security Analysis.* New York: McGraw-Hill.

Grinold, Richard, and Kenneth Kroner. (2002). "The Equity Risk Premium." *Investment Insights,* Barclays Global Investors, vol. 5, no. 3, July: 1–24.

Hasanhodzic, Jasmina, and Andrew W. Lo. (2007). "Can Hedge-Fund Returns Be Replicated?: The Linear Case." *Journal of Investment Management,* vol. 5, no. 2, Second Quarter: 5–45.

Hume, David. (1777). *An Enquiry Concerning Human Understanding.* London:Oxford University Press Selby-Bigge.

Huxley, Aldous. (2006). "2006 Plansponsor DC Survey: Brave New World." *PlanSponsor. com Magazine,* November.

Kahneman, Daniel, and Amos Tversky. (1979). "Prospect Theory: An Analysis of Decision under Risk." *Econometrica,* vol 47, no. 2, March: 263–292.

Keane, George. (2003). "Yes to Stocks, Yes to (some) Indexing, No to Indexing the S&P 500—A Viewpoint on the U.S. Market." Paper presented at the annual First Quadrant Advisory Panel, Scottsdale, Arizona, April.

Keynes, John Maynard. (1936). *The General Theory of Employment, Interest and Money.* London: Macmillan Cambridge University Press, pp. 157–158.

Kinnel, Russel. (2005). "Mind the Gap: How Good Funds Can Yield Bad Results." *Morningstar FundInvestor,* vol. 13, no. 11, July: 1–3.

Kittsley, Dodd. (2006). "Dividend-Weighted Indexes: Tactical Plays, Not Broad Market Investments." *SSgA ViewPoints,* October.

Lintner, John. (1965). "The Valuation of Risk Assets and the Selection of Risky Investments in Stock Portfolios and Capital Budgets." *Review of Economics and Statistics,* vol. 47, no. 1, February: 13–37.

Malkiel, Burton G. (2007). *A Random Walk Down Wall Street.* New York: W. W. Norton & Company, Inc., pp. 271–272.

Markowitz, Harry. (2005). "Market Efficiency: A Theoretical Distinction and So What?" *Financial Analysts Journal,* vol. 61, no. 5, September/October: 17–30.

———. (1952). "Portfolio Selection." *Journal of Finance,* vol. 7, no. 1, March: 77–91.

McVey, Henry H., David R. McNellis, and Frances Lim. (2007). "US Portfolio Strategy—Capital Management: The Roof Is on Fire." Research Report, Morgan Stanley Research North America, May 3.

Mossin, Jan. (1966). "Equilibrium in a Capital Asset Market." *Econometrica,* vol. 34, no. 4, October: 768–783.

Munnell, Alicia H., Mauricio Soto, Jerilyn Libby, and John Prinzivalli. (2006). "Investment Returns: Defined Benefit vs. 401(k) Plans." *An Issue in Brief— Center for Retirement Research at Boston College,* no. 52, September: 1–11.

Rabin, Matthew. (1998). "Psychology and Economics." *Journal of Economic Literature,* vol. 36, no. 1, March: 11–46.

Samuelson, Paul. (1965). "Proof that Properly Anticipated Prices Fluctuate Randomly." *Industrial Management Review,* vol. 6, no. 2, Spring: 41–49.

Sharpe, William F. (1988). "Determining a Fund's Effective Asset Mix" (Corrected Version). *Investment Management Review,* vol. *2,* no. 6, November/December: 59–69.

————. (1970). *Portfolio Theory and Capital Markets.* New York: McGraw-Hill.

————. (1964). "Capital Asset Prices: A Theory of Market Equilibrium under Conditions of Risk." *Journal of Finance,* vol. 19, no. 3, September: 425–442.

Shefrin, Hersh. (2007). "Behavioral Finance: Biases, Mean-Variance Returns, and Risk Premiums." *CFA Institute Conference Proceedings Quarterly,* June: 4–12.

Shefrin, Hersh. (2002). *Beyond Greed and Fear: Understanding Behavioral Finance and the Psychology of Investing.* Oxford:Oxford University Press.

Shiller, Robert J. (2005). *Irrational Exuberance.* Princeton, N.J.: Princeton University Press.

————. (1981). "Do Stock Prices Move Too Much to Be Justified by Subsequent Changes in Dividends?" *American Economic Review,* vol. 71, no. 3, June: 421–436.

Shleifer, Andrei. (1999). *Inefficient Markets: An Introduction to Behavioral Finance.* Oxford: Oxford University Press.

Siegel, Jeremy. (2006). "The Noisy Market Hypothesis." *Wall Street Journal,* June 14: A14.

Standard & Poor's. (2007). "S&P U.S. Indices Index Methodology," January: 1–20.

State Street Global Advisors. (2007). "US ETF Snapshot," July: http://statestreetspdrs. com/snapshots/books/print_view/11.

Statman, Meir. (2005). "Normal Investors, Then and Now." *Financial Analysts Journal,* vol. 61, no. 2, March/April: 31–37.

Steinbeck, John. (1977). "On Critics." *Writers at Work,* George Plimpton, ed. New York: Penguin.

Swensen, David. (2000). *Pioneering Portfolio Management: An Unconventional Approach to Institutional Investment.* New York: The Free Press, p. 293.

Tamura, H., and Y. Shimizu. (2005). "Global Fundamental Indices—Do They Outperform Market-Cap Weighted Indices on a Global Basis?" *Nomura Securities Co. Ltd Tokyo, Global Quantitative Research,* October 28.

The Economist. (2006). "Weights and Measures." Buttonwood Column, December 13.

Treynor, Jack. (2005). "Why Market-Valuation-Indifferent Indexing Works." *Financial Analysts Journal,* vol. 61, no. 5, September/October: 65–69.

————. (1962). "Toward a Theory of Market Value of Risky Assets." Unpublished manuscript. A final version was published in 1999 in Robert A. Korajczyk, ed. *Asset Pricing and Portfolio Performance: Models, Strategy and Performance Metrics.* London: Risk Books, pp. 15–22.

West, John M., and Magdalia Serna. (2003). "Spending Dilemma." *Wurts & Associates— Topics of Interest,* March.

Wood, Paul, and Richard Evans. (2003). "Fundamental Profit Based Equity Indexation: A Better Way to Hold the Market." *Journal of Indexes,* Second Quarter: 1–8.

Index